FREE Test Taking Tips DVD Offer

To help us better serve you, we have developed a Test Taking Tips DVD that we would like to give you for FREE. **This DVD covers world-class test taking tips that you can use to be even more successful when you are taking your test.**

All that we ask is that you email us your feedback about your study guide. Please let us know what you thought about it – whether that is good, bad or indifferent.

To get your **FREE Test Taking Tips DVD**, email freedvd@studyguideteam.com with "FREE DVD" in the subject line and the following information in the body of the email:

a. The title of your study guide.

b. Your product rating on a scale of 1-5, with 5 being the highest rating.

c. Your feedback about the study guide. What did you think of it?

d. Your full name and shipping address to send your free DVD.

If you have any questions or concerns, please don't hesitate to contact us at freedvd@studyguideteam.com.

Thanks again!

Complete Guide to English Language Arts (ELA)

High School and College English Book with 3 Practice Tests Covering Reading Comprehension, Grammar, and Composition [Includes Detailed Answer Explanations]

Joshua Rueda

Written and edited by TPB Publishing.

ISBN 13: 9781637755921
ISBN 10: 1637755929

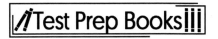

Table of Contents

Quick Overview

As you draw closer to taking your exam, effective preparation becomes more and more important. Thankfully, you have this study guide to help you get ready. Use this guide to help keep your studying on track and refer to it often.

This study guide contains several key sections that will help you be successful on your exam. The guide contains tips for what you should do the night before and the day of the test. Also included are test-taking tips. Knowing the right information is not always enough. Many well-prepared test takers struggle with exams. These tips will help equip you to accurately read, assess, and answer test questions.

A large part of the guide is devoted to showing you what content to expect on the exam and to helping you better understand that content. In this guide are practice test questions so that you can see how well you have grasped the content. Then, answer explanations are provided so that you can understand why you missed certain questions.

Don't try to cram the night before you take your exam. This is not a wise strategy for a few reasons. First, your retention of the information will be low. Your time would be better used by reviewing information you already know rather than trying to learn a lot of new information. Second, you will likely become stressed as you try to gain a large amount of knowledge in a short amount of time. Third, you will be depriving yourself of sleep. So be sure to go to bed at a reasonable time the night before. Being well-rested helps you focus and remain calm.

Be sure to eat a substantial breakfast the morning of the exam. If you are taking the exam in the afternoon, be sure to have a good lunch as well. Being hungry is distracting and can make it difficult to focus. You have hopefully spent lots of time preparing for the exam. Don't let an empty stomach get in the way of success!

When travelling to the testing center, leave earlier than needed. That way, you have a buffer in case you experience any delays. This will help you remain calm and will keep you from missing your appointment time at the testing center.

Be sure to pace yourself during the exam. Don't try to rush through the exam. There is no need to risk performing poorly on the exam just so you can leave the testing center early. Allow yourself to use all of the allotted time if needed.

Remain positive while taking the exam even if you feel like you are performing poorly. Thinking about the content you should have mastered will not help you perform better on the exam.

Once the exam is complete, take some time to relax. Even if you feel that you need to take the exam again, you will be well served by some down time before you begin studying again. It's often easier to convince yourself to study if you know that it will come with a reward!

Test-Taking Strategies

1. Predicting the Answer

When you feel confident in your preparation for a multiple-choice test, try predicting the answer before reading the answer choices. This is especially useful on questions that test objective factual knowledge. By predicting the answer before reading the available choices, you eliminate the possibility that you will be distracted or led astray by an incorrect answer choice. You will feel more confident in your selection if you read the question, predict the answer, and then find your prediction among the answer choices. After using this strategy, be sure to still read all of the answer choices carefully and completely. If you feel unprepared, you should not attempt to predict the answers. This would be a waste of time and an opportunity for your mind to wander in the wrong direction.

2. Reading the Whole Question

Too often, test takers scan a multiple-choice question, recognize a few familiar words, and immediately jump to the answer choices. Test authors are aware of this common impatience, and they will sometimes prey upon it. For instance, a test author might subtly turn the question into a negative, or he or she might redirect the focus of the question right at the end. The only way to avoid falling into these traps is to read the entirety of the question carefully before reading the answer choices.

3. Looking for Wrong Answers

Long and complicated multiple-choice questions can be intimidating. One way to simplify a difficult multiple-choice question is to eliminate all of the answer choices that are clearly wrong. In most sets of answers, there will be at least one selection that can be dismissed right away. If the test is administered on paper, the test taker could draw a line through it to indicate that it may be ignored; otherwise, the test taker will have to perform this operation mentally or on scratch paper. In either case, once the obviously incorrect answers have been eliminated, the remaining choices may be considered. Sometimes identifying the clearly wrong answers will give the test taker some information about the correct answer. For instance, if one of the remaining answer choices is a direct opposite of one of the eliminated answer choices, it may well be the correct answer. The opposite of obviously wrong is obviously right! Of course, this is not always the case. Some answers are obviously incorrect simply because they are irrelevant to the question being asked. Still, identifying and eliminating some incorrect answer choices is a good way to simplify a multiple-choice question.

4. Don't Overanalyze

Anxious test takers often overanalyze questions. When you are nervous, your brain will often run wild, causing you to make associations and discover clues that don't actually exist. If you feel that this may be a problem for you, do whatever you can to slow down during the test. Try taking a deep breath or counting to ten. As you read and consider the question, restrict yourself to the particular words used by the author. Avoid thought tangents about what the author *really* meant, or what he or she was *trying* to say. The only things that matter on a multiple-choice test are the words that are actually in the question. You must avoid reading too much into a multiple-choice question, or supposing that the writer meant something other than what he or she wrote.

5. No Need for Panic

It is wise to learn as many strategies as possible before taking a multiple-choice test, but it is likely that you will come across a few questions for which you simply don't know the answer. In this situation, avoid panicking. Because most multiple-choice tests include dozens of questions, the relative value of a single wrong answer is small. As much as possible, you should compartmentalize each question on a multiple-choice test. In other words, you should not allow your feelings about one question to affect your success on the others. When you find a question that you either don't understand or don't know how to answer, just take a deep breath and do your best. Read the entire question slowly and carefully. Try rephrasing the question a couple of different ways. Then, read all of the answer choices carefully. After eliminating obviously wrong answers, make a selection and move on to the next question.

6. Confusing Answer Choices

When working on a difficult multiple-choice question, there may be a tendency to focus on the answer choices that are the easiest to understand. Many people, whether consciously or not, gravitate to the answer choices that require the least concentration, knowledge, and memory. This is a mistake. When you come across an answer choice that is confusing, you should give it extra attention. A question might be confusing because you do not know the subject matter to which it refers. If this is the case, don't eliminate the answer before you have affirmatively settled on another. When you come across an answer choice of this type, set it aside as you look at the remaining choices. If you can confidently assert that one of the other choices is correct, you can leave the confusing answer aside. Otherwise, you will need to take a moment to try to better understand the confusing answer choice. Rephrasing is one way to tease out the sense of a confusing answer choice.

7. Your First Instinct

Many people struggle with multiple-choice tests because they overthink the questions. If you have studied sufficiently for the test, you should be prepared to trust your first instinct once you have carefully and completely read the question and all of the answer choices. There is a great deal of research suggesting that the mind can come to the correct conclusion very quickly once it has obtained all of the relevant information. At times, it may seem to you as if your intuition is working faster even than your reasoning mind. This may in fact be true. The knowledge you obtain while studying may be retrieved from your subconscious before you have a chance to work out the associations that support it. Verify your instinct by working out the reasons that it should be trusted.

8. Key Words

Many test takers struggle with multiple-choice questions because they have poor reading comprehension skills. Quickly reading and understanding a multiple-choice question requires a mixture of skill and experience. To help with this, try jotting down a few key words and phrases on a piece of scrap paper. Doing this concentrates the process of reading and forces the mind to weigh the relative importance of the question's parts. In selecting words and phrases to write down, the test taker thinks about the question more deeply and carefully. This is especially true for multiple-choice questions that are preceded by a long prompt.

9. Subtle Negatives

One of the oldest tricks in the multiple-choice test writer's book is to subtly reverse the meaning of a question with a word like *not* or *except*. If you are not paying attention to each word in the question, you can easily be led astray by this trick. For instance, a common question format is, "Which of the following is...?" Obviously, if the question instead is, "Which of the following is not...?," then the answer will be quite different. Even worse, the test makers are aware of the potential for this mistake and will include one answer choice that would be correct if the question were not negated or reversed. A test taker who misses the reversal will find what he or she believes to be a correct answer and will be so confident that he or she will fail to reread the question and discover the original error. The only way to avoid this is to practice a wide variety of multiple-choice questions and to pay close attention to each and every word.

10. Reading Every Answer Choice

It may seem obvious, but you should always read every one of the answer choices! Too many test takers fall into the habit of scanning the question and assuming that they understand the question because they recognize a few key words. From there, they pick the first answer choice that answers the question they believe they have read. Test takers who read all of the answer choices might discover that one of the latter answer choices is actually *more* correct. Moreover, reading all of the answer choices can remind you of facts related to the question that can help you arrive at the correct answer. Sometimes, a misstatement or incorrect detail in one of the latter answer choices will trigger your memory of the subject and will enable you to find the right answer. Failing to read all of the answer choices is like not reading all of the items on a restaurant menu: you might miss out on the perfect choice.

11. Spot the Hedges

One of the keys to success on multiple-choice tests is paying close attention to every word. This is never truer than with words like almost, most, some, and sometimes. These words are called "hedges" because they indicate that a statement is not totally true or not true in every place and time. An absolute statement will contain no hedges, but in many subjects, the answers are not always straightforward or absolute. There are always exceptions to the rules in these subjects. For this reason, you should favor those multiple-choice questions that contain hedging language. The presence of qualifying words indicates that the author is taking special care with his or her words, which is certainly important when composing the right answer. After all, there are many ways to be wrong, but there is only one way to be right! For this reason, it is wise to avoid answers that are absolute when taking a multiple-choice test. An absolute answer is one that says things are either all one way or all another. They often include words like *every*, *always*, *best*, and *never*. If you are taking a multiple-choice test in a subject that doesn't lend itself to absolute answers, be on your guard if you see any of these words.

12. Long Answers

In many subject areas, the answers are not simple. As already mentioned, the right answer often requires hedges. Another common feature of the answers to a complex or subjective question are qualifying clauses, which are groups of words that subtly modify the meaning of the sentence. If the question or answer choice describes a rule to which there are exceptions or the subject matter is complicated, ambiguous, or confusing, the correct answer will require many words in order to be expressed clearly and accurately. In essence, you should not be deterred by answer choices that seem excessively long. Oftentimes, the author of the text will not be able to write the correct answer without offering some qualifications and modifications. Your job is to read the answer choices thoroughly and completely and to select the one that most accurately and precisely answers the question.

13. Restating to Understand

Sometimes, a question on a multiple-choice test is difficult not because of what it asks but because of how it is written. If this is the case, restate the question or answer choice in different words. This process serves a couple of important purposes. First, it forces you to concentrate on the core of the question. In order to rephrase the question accurately, you have to understand it well. Rephrasing the question will concentrate your mind on the key words and ideas. Second, it will present the information to your mind in a fresh way. This process may trigger your memory and render some useful scrap of information picked up while studying.

14. True Statements

Sometimes an answer choice will be true in itself, but it does not answer the question. This is one of the main reasons why it is essential to read the question carefully and completely before proceeding to the answer choices. Too often, test takers skip ahead to the answer choices and look for true statements. Having found one of these, they are content to select it without reference to the question above. Obviously, this provides an easy way for test makers to play tricks. The savvy test taker will always read the entire question before turning to the answer choices. Then, having settled on a correct answer choice, he or she will refer to the original question and ensure that the selected answer is relevant. The mistake of choosing a correct-but-irrelevant answer choice is especially common on questions related to specific pieces of objective knowledge. A prepared test taker will have a wealth of factual knowledge at his or her disposal, and should not be careless in its application.

15. No Patterns

One of the more dangerous ideas that circulates about multiple-choice tests is that the correct answers tend to fall into patterns. These erroneous ideas range from a belief that B and C are the most common right answers, to the idea that an unprepared test-taker should answer "A-B-A-C-A-D-A-B-A." It cannot be emphasized enough that pattern-seeking of this type is exactly the WRONG way to approach a multiple-choice test. To begin with, it is highly unlikely that the test maker will plot the correct answers according to some predetermined pattern. The questions are scrambled and delivered in a random order. Furthermore, even if the test maker was following a pattern in the assignation of correct answers, there is no reason why the test taker would know which pattern he or she was using. Any attempt to discern a pattern in the answer choices is a waste of time and a distraction from the real work of taking the test. A test taker would be much better served by extra preparation before the test than by reliance on a pattern in the answers.

FREE DVD OFFER

Don't forget that doing well on your exam includes both understanding the test content and understanding how to use what you know to do well on the test. We offer a completely FREE Test Taking Tips DVD that covers world class test taking tips that you can use to be even more successful when you are taking your test.

All that we ask is that you email us your feedback about your study guide. To get your **FREE Test Taking Tips DVD**, email freedvd@studyguideteam.com with "FREE DVD" in the subject line and the following information in the body of the email:

- The title of your study guide.
- Your product rating on a scale of 1-5, with 5 being the highest rating.
- Your feedback about the study guide. What did you think of it?
- Your full name and shipping address to send your free DVD.

Introduction

Purpose

The purpose of this High School English Language Arts (ELA) guide is for students in high school or entering high school to brush up on their ELA skills. This guide features topics that are critical to a general high-school education and three practice tests at the end that compare to other standardized end-of-year high school exams. Reviewing the topics in this guide and reviewing the practice tests will help your student become familiar with the classroom as well as exams given to ELA students across the nation.

Topics

The topics in this guide include the following:

- Reading Comprehension
    - Literature: The literature section in this guide includes key ideas and details, craft and structure, and integration of knowledge and ideas specifically for literary texts. Literary texts include genres such as fiction, poetry, and drama. Students will become familiar with how to read these texts, their characteristics, and how authors and readers engage with these texts. Your student will learn vocabulary pertaining to literature in high school.
    - Informational Text: This section focuses on informational text, which is text used to relay information such as in business, marketing, or personal and professional communication. Similar to the literature section, information text focuses on key ideas and details, craft and structure, and integration of knowledge and ideas, but through the lens of information sharing. Students will learn why informational text is important to their lives and the guidelines for reading and writing this text.
- English Language
    - Speaking and Listening: This section is comprised of comprehension and collaboration, and presentation of knowledge and ideas. Groupwork is an essential component of high school. Many times, students will gather in groups and then present their findings to the classroom. Other times, students will be expected to do their own research at home and then return with a presentation for their classmates. This section teaches students how to work with others and speak to an audience.
    - Grammar and Usage: This section goes over the basics of English grammar: conventions of standard English, knowledge of language, and vocabulary acquisition and use. Students will brush up on how words are made through affixes, review vocabulary, and determine the context clues in passages they will read.

- Writing
    - Throughout high school, students will be expected to write essays, journals, or reading responses in many of their classes. They will also be asked to write arguments or persuasive papers for exams. The writing section in this guide teaches students the basic of writing. Depending on the genre and setting, students will learn the appropriate way to plan, structure, and write an essay in academia. This section features text types and purposes, production and distribution of writing, and research to build and present knowledge.

End-of-Guide Exams

Finally, three practice tests are presented at the end of the guide for students to practice. These tests include three sections each:

- Reading Comprehension: The reading comprehension practice test models many exams students will be expected to take throughout their high-school career. Students will read a high-school level passage and then answer multiple-choice questions about that passage to determine their comprehension level. Students should read passages slowly and carefully before they answer the questions.

- English Language: The English language test draws on the information in the language section. Students will be asked questions about grammar and sentence structure to review how much they know about the English language. Students will read the passage and then review the corresponding practice question to see if the sentence contains any mistakes.

- Writing Test: The writing test asks students to formulate and execute an essay. They will be given a prompt and then asked to analyze the prompt, state their perspective, and then explain the difference between their perspective and the one given in the prompt. This prompt encourages students to write in argument form, where they will offer a similar argument to the one given or counter against it.

Study Prep Plan

1 **Schedule -** Use one of our study schedules below or come up with one of your own.

2 **Relax -** Test anxiety can hurt even the best students. There are many ways to reduce stress. Find the one that works best for you.

3 **Execute -** Once you have a good plan in place, be sure to stick to it.

One Week Study Schedule

Day	Topic
Day 1	Reading Comprehension
Day 2	English Language
Day 3	Writing
Day 4	Practice Test #1
Day 5	Practice Test #2
Day 6	Practice Test #3
Day 7	Take Your Exam!

Two Week Study Schedule

Day	Topic	Day	Topic
Day 1	Literature	Day 8	Practice Test #1
Day 2	Informational Text	Day 9	Review Answer Explanations
Day 3	Speaking and Listening	Day 10	Practice Test #2
Day 4	Grammar and Usage	Day 11	Review Answer Explanations
Day 5	Text Types	Day 12	Practice Test #3
Day 6	Effective Language Use	Day 13	Review Answer Explanations
Day 7	Practice Questions & Writing Prompt	Day 14	Take Your Exam!

One Month Study Schedule

Day	Topic	Day	Topic	Day	Topic
Day 1	Central Ideas and Themes	Day 11	Organizational Structure within Informational Texts	Day 21	Effective Language Use
Day 2	Drawing Logical Inferences and Conclusions	Day 12	Practice Questions	Day 22	Quantitative Information
Day 3	Understanding the Characteristics of LIterary Genres	Day 13	Understanding Effective Delivery of a Speech or Presentation	Day 23	Writing Prompt
Day 4	Identifying Characteristics of Major Forms Within Each Genre	Day 14	Understanding the Conventions of Standard English	Day 24	Practice Test #1
Day 5	Identifying Literary Elements	Day 15	Analyzing Nuances of Word Meaning and Figures of Speech	Day 25	Review Answer Explanations
Day 6	Recognizing the Structure of Texts in Various Formats	Day 16	Identifying Dialect and Diction	Day 26	Practice Test #2
Day 7	Analyzing an Author's Rhetorical Choices	Day 17	Understanding the Use of Affixes, Context, and Syntax	Day 27	Review Answer Explanations
Day 8	Interpreting Authorial Decisions Rhetorically	Day 18	Practice Questions	Day 28	Practice Test #3
Day 9	Identifying Literary Contexts	Day 19	Test Types	Day 29	Review Answer Explanations
Day 10	Understanding Development of a Written Argument	Day 20	Introductions and Conclusions	Day 30	Take Your Exam!

Reading Comprehension

Literature

Central Ideas and Themes

Topic, Main Idea, Supporting Details, and Themes

The **topic** of a text is the overall subject, and the **main idea** more specifically builds on that subject. Consider a paragraph that begins with the following: "The United States government is made of up three branches: executive, judicial, and legislative." If this sentence is divided into its essential components, there is the topic (United States Government) and the main idea (the three branches of government).

A main idea must be supported with details, which usually appear in the form of quotations, paraphrasing, or analysis. Authors should connect details and analysis to the main point. Readers should always be cautious when accepting the validity of an argument and look for logical fallacies, such as slippery slope, straw man, and begging the question. It's okay for a reader to disagree with an author, because arguments may seem sound, but further analysis often reveals they are flawed.

It is important to remember that when most authors write, they want to make a point or send a message. This point, or the message of a text, is known as the theme. Authors may state themes explicitly, like in *Aesop's Fables*. More often, especially in modern literature, readers must infer the theme based on textual details. Usually, after carefully reading and analyzing an entire text, the theme emerges. Typically, the longer the piece, the more numerous its themes, though often one theme dominates the rest, as evidenced by the author's purposeful revisiting of it throughout the passage.

Identifying Theme or Central Message

The **theme** is the central message of a fictional work, whether that work is structured as prose, drama, or poetry. It is the heart of what an author is trying to say to readers through the writing, and theme is largely conveyed through literary elements and techniques.

In literature, a theme can often be determined by considering the over-arching narrative conflict within the work. Though there are several types of conflicts and several potential themes within them, the following are the most common:

- **Individual against the self**—relevant to themes of self-awareness, internal struggles, pride, coming of age, facing reality, fate, free will, vanity, loss of innocence, loneliness, isolation, fulfillment, failure, and disillusionment
- **Individual against nature**— relevant to themes of knowledge vs. ignorance, nature as beauty, quest for discovery, self-preservation, chaos and order, circle of life, death, and destruction of beauty
- **Individual against society**— relevant to themes of power, beauty, good, evil, war, class struggle, totalitarianism, role of men/women, wealth, corruption, change vs. tradition, capitalism, destruction, heroism, injustice, and racism
- **Individual against another individual**— relevant to themes of hope, loss of love or hope, sacrifice, power, revenge, betrayal, and honor

For example, in Hawthorne's *The Scarlet Letter*, one possible narrative conflict could be the individual against the self, with a relevant theme of internal struggles. This theme is alluded to through characterization—Dimmesdale's moral struggle with his love for Hester and Hester's internal struggles with the truth and her daughter, Pearl. It's also alluded to through plot—Dimmesdale's suicide and Hester helping the very townspeople who initially condemned her.

Sometimes, a text can convey a **message** or **universal lesson**—a truth or insight that the reader infers from the text, based on analysis of the literary and/or poetic elements. This message is often presented as a statement. For example, a potential message in Shakespeare's *Hamlet* could be "Revenge is what ultimately drives the human soul." This message can be immediately determined through plot and characterization in numerous ways, but it can also be determined through the setting of Norway, which is bordering on war.

How Authors Develop Theme

Authors employ a variety of techniques to present a theme. They may compare or contrast characters, events, places, ideas, or historical or invented settings to speak thematically. They may use analogies, metaphors, similes, allusions, or other literary devices to convey the theme. An author's use of diction, syntax, and tone can also help convey the theme. Authors will often develop themes through the development of characters, use of the setting, repetition of ideas, use of symbols, and through contrasting value systems. Authors of both fiction and nonfiction genres will use a variety of these techniques to develop one or more themes.

Regardless of the literary genre, there are commonalities in how authors, playwrights, and poets develop themes or central ideas.

Authors often do research, the results of which contributes to theme. In prose fiction and drama, this research may include real historical information about the setting the author has chosen or include elements that make fictional characters, settings, and plots seem realistic to the reader. In nonfiction, research is critical since the information contained within this literature must be accurate and, moreover, accurately represented.

In fiction, authors present a narrative conflict that will contribute to the overall theme. In fiction, this conflict may involve the storyline itself and some trouble within characters that needs resolution. In nonfiction, this conflict may be an explanation or commentary on factual people and events.

Authors will sometimes use character motivation to convey theme, such as in the example from *Hamlet* regarding revenge. In fiction, the characters an author creates will think, speak, and act in ways that effectively convey the theme to readers. In nonfiction, the characters are factual, as in a biography, but authors pay particular attention to presenting those motivations to make them clear to readers.

Authors also use literary devices as a means of conveying theme. For example, the use of moon symbolism in Shelley's *Frankenstein* is significant as its phases can be compared to the phases that the Creature undergoes as he struggles with his identity.

The selected point of view can also contribute to a work's theme. The use of first-person point of view in a fiction or non-fiction work engages the reader's response differently than third person point of view. The central idea or theme from a first-person narrative may differ from a third-person limited text.

In literary nonfiction, authors usually identify the purpose of their writing, which differs from fiction, where the general purpose is to entertain. The purpose of nonfiction is usually to inform, persuade, or entertain the audience. The stated purpose of a non-fiction text will drive how the central message or theme, if applicable, is presented.

Authors identify an audience for their writing, which is critical in shaping the theme of the work. For example, the audience for J.K. Rowling's *Harry Potter* series would be different than the audience for a biography of George Washington. The audience an author chooses to address is closely tied to the purpose of the work. The choice of an audience also drives the choice of language and level of diction an author uses. Ultimately, the intended audience determines the level to which that subject matter is presented and the complexity of the theme.

Recognizing Universal Themes

Regardless of culture, place, or time, certain themes are universal to the human condition. Because all humans experience certain feelings and engage in similar experiences—birth, death, marriage, friendship, finding meaning, etc.—certain themes span cultures. However, different cultures have different norms and general beliefs concerning these themes. For example, the theme of maturing and crossing from childhood to adulthood is a global theme; however, the literature from one culture might imply that this happens in someone's twenties, while another culture's literature might imply that it happens in the early teenage years.

Summarizing Information Accurately

Summarizing is an effective way to draw a conclusion from a passage. A **summary** is a shortened version of the original text, written by the reader in his or her own words. Focusing on the main points of the original text and including only the relevant details can help readers reach a conclusion. It's important to retain the original meaning of the passage.

Like summarizing, **paraphrasing** can also help a reader fully understand different parts of a text. Paraphrasing calls for the reader to take a small part of the passage and list or describe its main points. However, paraphrasing is more than rewording the original passage; it should be written in the reader's own words, while still retaining the meaning of the original source. This will indicate an understanding of the original source, yet still help the reader expand on his or her interpretation.

Understanding Relationships

Inferences are useful in gaining a deeper understanding of how people, events, and ideas are connected in a passage. Readers can use the same strategies used with general inferences and analyzing texts—paying attention to details and using them to make reasonable guesses about the text—to read between the lines and get a more complete picture of how (and why) characters are thinking, feeling, and acting. Read the following passage from O. Henry's story "The Gift of the Magi":

> One dollar and eighty-seven cents. That was all. And sixty cents of it was in pennies. Pennies saved one and two at a time by bulldozing the grocer and the vegetable man and the butcher until one's cheeks burned with the silent imputation of parsimony that such close dealing implied. Three times Della counted it. One dollar and eighty-seven cents. And the next day would be Christmas.
>
> There was clearly nothing to do but flop down on the shabby little couch and howl. So Della did it.

These paragraphs introduce the reader to the character Della. Even though the author doesn't include a direct description of Della, the reader can already form a general impression of her personality and emotions. One detail that should stick out to the reader is repetition: "one dollar and eighty-seven cents." This amount is repeated twice in the first paragraph, along with other descriptions of money: "sixty cents of it was in pennies," "pennies saved one and two at a time." The story's preoccupation with money parallels how Della herself is constantly thinking about her finances—"three times Della counted" her meager savings. Already the reader can guess that Della is having money problems. Next, think about her emotions.

The first paragraph describes haggling over groceries "until one's cheeks burned"—another way to describe blushing. People tend to blush when they are embarrassed or ashamed, so readers can infer that Della is ashamed by her financial situation. This inference is also supported by the second paragraph, when she flops down and howls on her "shabby little couch." Clearly, she's in distress. Without saying, "Della has no money and is embarrassed to be poor," O. Henry is able to communicate the same impression to readers through his careful inclusion of details.

A character's **motive** is their reason for acting a certain way. Usually, characters are motivated by something that they want. In the passage above, why is Della upset about not having enough money? There's an important detail at the end of the first paragraph: "the next day would be Christmas." Why is money especially important around Christmas? Christmas is a holiday when people exchange gifts. If Della is struggling with money, she's probably also struggling to buy gifts. So a shrewd reader should be able to guess that Della's motivation is wanting to buy a gift for someone—but she's currently unable to afford it, leading to feelings of shame and frustration.

In order to understand characters in a text, readers should keep the following questions in mind:

- What words does the author use to describe the character? Are these words related to any specific emotions or personality traits (for example, characteristics like rude, friendly, unapproachable, or innocent)?
- What does the character say? Does their dialogue seem to be straightforward, or are they hiding some thoughts or emotions?
- What actions can be observed from this character? How do their actions reflect their feelings?
- What does the character want? What do they do to get it?

Drawing Logical Inferences and Conclusions

Predictions

Some texts use suspense and foreshadowing to captivate readers. For example, an intriguing aspect of murder mysteries is that the reader is never sure of the culprit until the author reveals the individual's identity. Authors often build suspense and add depth and meaning to a work by leaving clues to provide hints or predict future events in the story; this is called foreshadowing. While some instances of foreshadowing are subtle, others are quite obvious.

Inferences

Another way to read actively is to identify examples of inference within text. Making an inference requires the reader to read between the lines and look for what is implied rather than what is directly stated. That is, using information that is known from the text, the reader is able to make a logical assumption about information that is *not* directly stated but is probably true.

Authors employ literary devices such as tone, characterization, and theme to engage the audience by showing details of the story instead of merely telling them. For example, if an author said *Bob is selfish*, there's little left to infer. If the author said, *Bob cheated on his test, ignored his mom's calls, and parked illegally*, the reader can infer Bob is selfish. Authors also make implications through character dialogue, thoughts, effects on others, actions, and looks. Like in life, readers must assemble all the clues to form a complete picture.

Read the following passage:

> "Hey, do you wanna meet my new puppy?" Jonathan asked.
>
> "Oh, I'm sorry but please don't—" Jacinta began to protest, but before she could finish, Jonathan had already opened the passenger side door of his car and a perfect white ball of fur came bouncing towards Jacinta.
>
> "Isn't he the cutest?" beamed Jonathan.
>
> "Yes—achoo!—he's pretty—aaaachooo!!—adora—aaa—aaaachoo!" Jacinta managed to say in between sneezes. "But if you don't mind, I—I—achoo!—need to go inside."

Which of the following can be inferred from Jacinta's reaction to the puppy?

a. she hates animals
b. she is allergic to dogs
c. she prefers cats to dogs
d. she is angry at Jonathan

An inference requires the reader to consider the information presented and then form their own idea about what is probably true. Based on the details in the passage, what is the best answer to the question? Important details to pay attention to include the tone of Jacinta's dialogue, which is overall polite and apologetic, as well as her reaction itself, which is a long string of sneezes. Answer choices (a) and (d) both express strong emotions ("hates" and "angry") that are not evident in Jacinta's speech or actions. Answer choice (c) mentions cats, but there is nothing in the passage to indicate Jacinta's feelings about cats. Answer choice (b), "she is allergic to dogs," is the most logical choice—based on the fact that she began sneezing as soon as a fluffy dog approached her, it makes sense to guess that Jacinta might be allergic to dogs. So even though Jacinta never directly states, "Sorry, I'm allergic to dogs!" using the clues in the passage, it is still reasonable to guess that this is true.

Making inferences is crucial for readers of literature, because literary texts often avoid presenting complete and direct information to readers about characters' thoughts or feelings, or they present this information in an unclear way, leaving it up to the reader to interpret clues given in the text. In order to make inferences while reading, readers should ask themselves:

- What details are being presented in the text?
- Is there any important information that seems to be missing?
- Based on the information that the author does include, what else is probably true?
- Is this inference reasonable based on what is already known?

Conclusions

Active readers should also draw **conclusions**. When doing so, the reader should ask the following questions: What is this piece about? What does the author believe? Does this piece have merit? Do I believe the author? Would this piece support my argument? The reader should first determine the author's intent. Identify the author's viewpoint and connect relevant evidence to support it. Readers may then move to the most important step: deciding whether to agree and determining whether they are correct. Always read cautiously and critically. Interact with text, and record reactions in the margins. These active reading skills help determine not only what the author thinks, but what you think as the reader.

Determining conclusions requires being an active reader, as a reader must make a prediction and analyze facts to identify a conclusion. A reader should identify key words in a passage to determine the logical conclusion from the information presented. Consider the passage below:

> Lindsay, covered in flour, moved around the kitchen frantically. Her mom yelled from another room, "Lindsay, we're going to be late!"

Readers can conclude that Lindsay's next steps are to finish baking, clean herself up, and head off somewhere with her baked goods. It's important to note that the conclusion cannot be verified factually. Many conclusions are not spelled out specifically in the text; thus, they have to be inferred and deduced by the reader.

Evaluating a Passage

Readers **draw conclusions** about what an author has presented. This helps them better understand what the writer has intended to communicate and whether or not they agree with what the author has offered. There are a few ways to determine a logical conclusion, but careful reading is the most important. It's helpful to read a passage a few times, noting details that seem important to the piece. Sometimes, readers arrive at a conclusion that is different than what the writer intended or they may come up with more than one conclusion.

Textual evidence within the details helps readers draw a conclusion about a passage. **Textual evidence** refers to information—facts and examples—that support the main point. Textual evidence will likely come from outside sources and can be in the form of quoted or paraphrased material. In order to draw a conclusion from evidence, it's important to examine the credibility and validity of that evidence as well as how (and if) it relates to the main idea.

If an author presents a differing opinion or a **counterargument**, in order to refute it, the reader should consider how and why this information is being presented. It is meant to strengthen the original argument and shouldn't be confused with the author's intended conclusion, but it should also be considered in the reader's final evaluation.

Sometimes, authors explicitly state the conclusion that they want readers to understand. Alternatively, a conclusion may not be directly stated. In that case, readers must rely on the implications to form a logical conclusion:

> On the way to the bus stop, Michael realized his homework wasn't in his backpack. He ran back to the house to get it and made it back to the bus just in time.

In this example, although it's never explicitly stated, it can be inferred that Michael is a student on his way to school in the morning. When forming a conclusion from implied information, it's important to read the text carefully to find several pieces of evidence to support the conclusion.

Understanding the Characteristics of Literary Genres

Classifying literature involves an understanding of the concept of genre. A **genre** is a category of literature that possesses similarities in style and in characteristics. Based on form and structure, there are four basic genres.

Fictional Prose

Fictional prose consists of fictional works written in standard form with a natural flow of speech and without poetic structure. Fictional prose primarily utilizes grammatically complete sentences and a paragraph structure to convey its message.

Drama

Drama is fiction that is written to be performed in a variety of media, intended to be performed for an audience, and structured for that purpose. It might be composed using poetry or prose, often straddling the elements of both in what actors are expected to present. Action and dialogue are the tools used in drama to tell the story.

Poetry

Poetry is fiction in verse that has a unique focus on the rhythm of language and focuses on intensity of feeling. It is not an entire story, though it may tell one; it is compact in form and in function. Poetry can be considered as a poet's brief word picture for a reader. Poetic structure is primarily composed of lines and stanzas. Together, poetic structure and devices are the methods that poets use to lead readers to feeling an effect and, ultimately, to the interpretive message.

Literary Nonfiction

Literary nonfiction is prose writing that is based on current or past real events or real people and includes straightforward accounts as well as those that offer opinions on facts or factual events. Students can distinguish between literary nonfiction—a form of writing that incorporates literary styles and techniques to create factually-based narratives—and informational texts, which will be addressed in the next section.

Identifying Characteristics of Major Forms Within Each Genre

Fictional Prose

Fiction written in prose can be further broken down into **fiction genres**—types of fiction. Some of the more common genres of fiction are as follows:

- **Classical fiction**: A work of fiction considered timeless in its message or theme, remaining noteworthy and meaningful over decades or centuries—e.g., Charlotte Brontë's *Jane Eyre*, Mark Twain's *Adventures of Huckleberry Finn*
- **Fables**: Short fiction that generally features animals, fantastic creatures, or other forces within nature that assume human-like characters and has a moral lesson for the reader—e.g., *Aesop's Fables*

- **Fairy tales**: Children's stories with magical characters in imaginary, enchanted lands, usually depicting a struggle between good and evil, a sub-genre of folklore—e.g., Hans Christian Anderson's *The Little Mermaid*, *Cinderella* by the Brothers Grimm

- **Fantasy**: Fiction with magic or supernatural elements that cannot occur in the real world, sometimes involving medieval elements in language, usually includes some form of sorcery or witchcraft and sometimes set on a different world—e.g., J.R.R. Tolkien's *The Hobbit*, J.K. Rowling's *Harry Potter and the Sorcerer's Stone*, George R.R. Martin's *A Game of Thrones*

- **Folklore**: Types of fiction passed down from oral tradition, stories indigenous to a particular region or culture, with a local flavor in tone, designed to help humans cope with their condition in life and validate cultural traditions, beliefs, and customs—e.g., William Laughead's *Paul Bunyan and The Blue Ox*, the Buddhist story of "The Banyan Deer"

- **Mythology**: Closely related to folklore but more widespread, features mystical, otherworldly characters and addresses the basic question of why and how humans exist, relies heavily on allegory and features gods or heroes captured in some sort of struggle—e.g., Greek myths, Genesis I and II in the Bible, Arthurian legends

- **Science fiction**: Fiction that uses the principle of extrapolation—loosely defined as a form of prediction—to imagine future realities and problems of the human experience—e.g., Robert Heinlein's *Stranger in a Strange Land*, Ayn Rand's *Anthem*, Isaac Asimov's *I, Robot*, Philip K. Dick's *Do Androids Dream of Electric Sheep?*

- **Short stories**: Short works of prose fiction with fully-developed themes and characters, focused on mood, generally developed with a single plot, with a short period of time for settings—e.g., Edgar Allan Poe's "Fall of the House of Usher," Shirley Jackson's "The Lottery," Isaac Bashevis Singer's "Gimpel the Fool"

Drama

Drama refers to a form of literature written for the purpose of performance for an audience. Like prose fiction, drama has several genres. The following are the most common ones:

- **Comedy**: A humorous play designed to amuse and entertain, often with an emphasis on the common person's experience, generally resolved in a positive way—e.g., Richard Sheridan's *School for Scandal*, Shakespeare's *Taming of the Shrew*, Neil Simon's *The Odd Couple*

- **History**: A play based on recorded history where the fate of a nation or kingdom is at the core of the conflict—e.g., Christopher Marlowe's *Edward II*, Shakespeare's *King Richard III*, Arthur Miller's *The Crucible*

- **Tragedy**: A serious play that often involves the downfall of the protagonist. In modern tragedies, the protagonist is not necessarily in a position of power or authority—e.g., Jean Racine's *Phèdre*, Arthur Miller's *Death of a Salesman*, John Steinbeck's *Of Mice and Men*

- **Melodrama**: A play that emphasizes heightened emotion and sensationalism, generally with stereotypical characters in exaggerated or realistic situations and with moral polarization—e.g., Jean-Jacques Rousseau's *Pygmalion*

- **Tragi-comedy**: A play that has elements of both tragedy—a character experiencing a tragic loss—and comedy—the resolution is often positive with no clear distinctive mood for either—e.g., Shakespeare's *The Merchant of Venice*, Anton Chekhov's *The Cherry Orchard*

Poetry

The genre of **poetry** refers to literary works that focus on the expression of feelings and ideas through the use of structure and linguistic rhythm to create a desired effect.

Different poetic structures and devices are used to create the various major forms of poetry. Some of the most common forms are discussed in the following chart.

Type	Poetic Structure	Example
Ballad	A poem or song passed down orally which tells a story and in English tradition usually uses an ABAB or ABCB rhyme scheme	William Butler Yeats' "The Ballad of Father O'Hart"
Epic	A long poem from ancient oral tradition which narrates the story of a legendary or heroic protagonist	Homer's *The Odyssey* Virgil's *The Aeneid*
Haiku	A Japanese poem of three unrhymed lines with five, seven, and five syllables (in English) with nature as a common subject matter	Matsuo Bashō "An old silent pond . . . A frog jumps into the pond, splash! Silence again."
Limerick	A five-line poem written in an AABBA rhyme scheme, with a witty focus	From Edward Lear's *Book of Nonsense*: "There was a Young Person of Smyrna Whose grandmother threatened to burn her . . ."
Ode	A formal lyric poem that addresses and praises a person, place, thing, or idea	Edna St. Vincent Millay's "Ode to Silence"
Sonnet	A fourteen-line poem written in iambic pentameter	Shakespeare's Sonnets 18 and 130

Literary Nonfiction

Nonfiction works are best characterized by their subject matter, which must be factual and real, describing true life experiences. There are several common types of literary non-fiction.

Biography

A **biography** is a work written about a real person (historical or currently living). It involves factual accounts of the person's life, often in a re-telling of those events based on available, researched factual information. The re-telling and dialogue, especially if related within quotes, must be accurate and reflect reliable sources. A biography reflects the time and place in which the person lived, with the goal of creating an understanding of the person and his/her human experience. Examples of well-known biographies include *The Life of Samuel Johnson* by James Boswell and *Steve Jobs* by Walter Isaacson.

Autobiography

An **autobiography** is a factual account of a person's life written by that person. It may contain some or all of the same elements as a biography, but the author is the subject matter. An autobiography will be told in first person narrative. Examples of well-known autobiographies in literature include *Night* by Elie Wiesel and *Margaret Thatcher: The Autobiography* by Margaret Thatcher.

Memoir

A **memoir** is a historical account of a person's life and experiences written by one who has personal, intimate knowledge of the information. The line between memoir, autobiography, and biography is often muddled, but generally speaking, a memoir covers a specific timeline of events as opposed to the other forms of nonfiction. A memoir is less all-encompassing. It is also less formal in tone and tends to focus on the emotional aspect of the presented timeline of events. Some examples of memoirs in literature include *Angela's Ashes* by Frank McCourt and *All Creatures Great and Small* by James Herriot.

Journalism

Some forms of **journalism** can fall into the category of literary nonfiction—e.g., travel writing, nature writing, sports writing, the interview, and sometimes, the essay. Some examples include Elizabeth Kolbert's "The Lost World, in the Annals of Extinction series for *The New Yorker* and Gary Smith's "Ali and His Entourage" for *Sports Illustrated*.

Identifying Literary Elements

There is no one, final definition of what literary elements are. They can be considered features or characteristics of fiction, but they are really more of a way that readers can unpack a text for the purpose of analysis and understanding the meaning. The elements contribute to a reader's literary interpretation of a passage as to how they function to convey the central message of a work. The most common literary elements used for analysis are presented below.

Point of View

The **point of view** is the position the narrator takes when telling the story in prose. If a narrator is incorporated in a drama, the point of view may vary; in poetry, point of view refers to the position the speaker in a poem takes.

First Person

The **first-person point of view** is when the writer uses the word "I" in the text. Poetry often uses first person, e.g., William Wordsworth's "I Wandered Lonely as a Cloud." Two examples of prose written in first person are Suzanne Collins' *The Hunger Games* and Anthony Burgess's *A Clockwork Orange*.

Second Person

The **second-person point of view** is when the writer uses the pronoun "you." It is not widely used in prose fiction, but as a technique, it has been used by writers such as William Faulkner in *Absalom, Absalom!* and Albert Camus in *The Fall*. It is more common in poetry—e.g., Pablo Neruda's "If You Forget Me."

Third Person

Third-person point of view is when the writer utilizes pronouns such as him, her, or them. It may be the most utilized point of view in prose as it provides flexibility to an author and is the one with which readers are most familiar. There are two main types of third person used in fiction. **Third person omniscient** uses a narrator that is all-knowing, relating the story by conveying and interpreting thoughts/feelings of all characters. In **third person limited**, the narrator relates the story through the perspective of one character's thoughts/feelings, usually the main character.

Plot

The **plot** is what happens in the story. Plots may be singular, containing one problem, or they may be very complex, with many sub-plots. All plots have exposition, a conflict, a climax, and a resolution. The **conflict** drives the plot and is something that the reader expects to be resolved. The plot carries those events along until there is a resolution to the conflict.

Tone

The **tone** of a story reflects the author's attitude and opinion about the subject matter of the story or text. Tone can be expressed through word choice, imagery, figurative language, syntax, and other details. The emotion or mood the reader experiences relates back to the tone of the story. Some examples of possible tones are humorous, somber, sentimental, and ironic.

Setting

The **setting** is the time, place, or set of surroundings in which the story occurs. It includes time or time span, place(s), climates, geography—man-made or natural—or cultural environments. Emily Dickinson's poem "Because I could not stop for Death" has a simple setting—the narrator's symbolic ride with Death through town towards the local graveyard. Conversely, Leo Tolstoy's *War and Peace* encompasses numerous settings within settings in the areas affected by the Napoleonic Wars, spanning 1805 to 1812.

Dialogue and Story Events

Dialogue refers to the conversations that occur within a story. Dialogue can help to move the plot along and also to give insight into characters, setting, mood, and other aspects of the story. **Story events** are the different elements of a story that are ordered to create the plot.

Characters

Characters are the story's figures that assume primary, secondary, or minor roles. **Central characters** are those integral to the story—the plot cannot be resolved without them. A central character can be a **protagonist** or hero. There may be more than one protagonist, and he/she doesn't always have to possess good characteristics. A character can also be an **antagonist**—the force against a protagonist.

Dynamic characters change over the course of the plot time. **Static characters** do not change. A **symbolic character** is one that represents an author's idea about society in general—e.g., Napoleon in Orwell's *Animal Farm*. **Stock characters** are those that appear across genres and embrace stereotypes—e.g., the cowboy of the Wild West or the blonde bombshell in a detective novel. A **flat character** is one that does not present a lot of complexity or depth, while a **rounded character** does. Sometimes, the **narrator** of a story or the **speaker** in a poem can be a character—e.g., Nick Carraway in F. Scott Fitzgerald's *The Great Gatsby* or the speaker in Robert Browning's "My Last Duchess." The narrator might also function as a character in prose, though not be part of the story—e.g., Charles Dickens' narrator of *A Christmas Carol*.

Understanding Poetic Devices and Structure

Poetic Devices

Rhyme is the poet's use of corresponding word sounds in order to create an effect. Most rhyme occurs at the ends of a poem's lines, which is how readers arrive at the **rhyme scheme**. Each line that has a corresponding rhyming sound is assigned a letter—A, B, C, and so on. When using a rhyme scheme, poets will often follow lettered patterns. Robert Frost's "The Road Not Taken" uses the ABAAB rhyme scheme:

Two roads diverged in a yellow wood, A

And sorry I could not travel both B

And be one traveler, long I stood A

And looked down one as far as I could A

To where it bent in the undergrowth; B

Another important poetic device is **rhythm**—metered patterns within poetry verses. When a poet develops rhythm through **meter**, he or she is using a combination of stressed and unstressed syllables to create a sound effect for the reader.

Rhythm is created by the use of **poetic feet**—individual rhythmic units made up of the combination of stressed and unstressed syllables. A line of poetry is made up of one or more poetic feet. There are five standard types in English poetry, as depicted in the chart below.

Foot Type	Rhythm	Pattern
Iamb	buh Buh	Unstressed/stressed
Trochee	Buh buh	Stressed/unstressed
Spondee	Buh Buh	Stressed/stressed
Anapest	buh buh Buh	Unstressed/unstressed/stressed
Dactyl	Buh buh buh	Stressed/unstressed/unstressed

Structure

Poetry is most easily recognized by its structure, which varies greatly. For example, a structure may be strict in the number of lines it uses. It may use rhyming patterns or may not rhyme at all. There are three main types of poetic structures:

- **Verse**—poetry with a consistent meter and rhyme scheme
- **Blank verse**—poetry with consistent meter but an inconsistent rhyme scheme
- **Free verse**—poetry with inconsistent meter or rhyme

Verse poetry is most often developed in the form of **stanzas**—groups of word lines. Stanzas can also be considered verses. The structure is usually formulaic and adheres to the protocols for the form. For example, the English **sonnet** form uses a structure of fourteen lines and a variety of different rhyming patterns. The English **ode** typically uses three ten-line stanzas and has a particular rhyming pattern.

Poets choose poetic structure based on the effect they want to create. Some structures—such as the ballad and haiku—developed out of cultural influences and common artistic practice in history, but in more modern poetry, authors choose their structure to best fit their intended effect.

Recognizing the Structure of Texts in Various Formats

Writing can be classified under four passage types: narrative, expository, descriptive (sometimes called technical), and persuasive. Though these types are not mutually exclusive, one form tends to dominate the rest. By recognizing the type of passage you're reading, you gain insight into how you should read. If you're reading a narrative, you can assume the author intends to entertain, which means you may skim the text without losing meaning. A technical document might require a close read, because skimming the passage might cause the reader to miss salient details.

1. **Narrative writing**, at its core, is the art of storytelling. For a narrative to exist, certain elements must be present. It must have characters. While many characters are human, characters could be defined as anything that thinks, acts, and talks like a human. For example, many recent movies, such as *Lord of the Rings* and *The Chronicles of Narnia*, include animals, fantastical creatures, and even trees that behave like humans. It must have a plot or sequence of events.

Typically, those events follow a standard plot diagram, but recent trends start *in medias res* or in the middle (near the climax). In this instance, foreshadowing and flashbacks often fill in plot details. Along with characters and a plot, there must also be conflict. Conflict is usually divided into two types: internal and external. Internal conflict indicates the character is in turmoil. Internal conflicts are presented through the character's thoughts. External conflicts are visible. Types of external conflict include a person versus nature, another person, and society.

2. **Expository writing** is detached and to the point. Since expository writing is designed to instruct or inform, it usually involves directions and steps written in second person ("you" voice) and lacks any persuasive or narrative elements. Sequence words such as *first*, *second*, and *third*, or *in the first place*, *secondly*, and *lastly* are often given to add fluency and cohesion. Common examples of expository writing include instructor's lessons, cookbook recipes, and repair manuals.

3. Due to its empirical nature, **technical writing** is filled with steps, charts, graphs, data, and statistics. The goal of technical writing is to advance understanding in a field through the scientific method. Experts such as teachers, doctors, or mechanics use words unique to the profession in which they operate. These words, which often incorporate acronyms, are called **jargon**. Technical writing is a type of expository writing but is not meant to be understood by the general public. Instead, technical writers assume readers have received a formal education in a particular field of study and need no explanation as to what the jargon means. Imagine a doctor trying to understand a diagnostic reading for a car or a mechanic trying to interpret lab results. Only professionals with proper training will fully comprehend the text.

4. **Persuasive writing** is designed to change opinions and attitudes. The topic, stance, and arguments are found in the thesis, positioned near the end of the introduction. Later supporting paragraphs offer relevant quotations, paraphrases, and summaries from primary or secondary sources, which are then interpreted, analyzed, and evaluated. The goal of persuasive writers is not to stack quotes, but to develop original ideas by using sources as a starting point. Good persuasive writing makes powerful arguments with valid sources and thoughtful analysis. Poor persuasive writing is riddled with bias and

logical fallacies. Sometimes, logical and illogical arguments are sandwiched together in the same piece. Therefore, readers should display skepticism when reading persuasive arguments.

Word and Phrase Meanings

Most experts agree that learning new words is worth the time it takes. It helps readers understand what they are reading, and it expands their vocabulary. An extensive vocabulary improves one's ability to think. When words are added to someone's vocabulary, he or she is better able to make sense of the world.

One of the fastest ways to decode a word is through context. **Context**, or surrounding words, gives clues as to what unknown words mean. Take the following example:

> When the students in the classroom teased Johnny, he was so *discombobulated* that he couldn't finish a simple math problem.

Even though a reader might be unfamiliar with the word *discombobulated,* he or she can use context clues in the sentence to make sense of the word. In this case, it can be deduced that *discombobulated* means confused or distracted.

Although context clues provide a rudimentary understanding of a word, using a dictionary can provide the reader with a more comprehensive meaning of the word. Printed dictionaries list words in alphabetical order, and all versions—including those online—include a word's multiple meanings. Typically, the first definition is the most widely used or known. The second, third, and subsequent entries move toward the more unusual or archaic. Dictionaries also indicate the part(s) of speech of each word, such as noun, verb, adjective, etc.

Dictionaries are not fixed in time. The English language today looks nothing like it did in Shakespeare's time, and Shakespeare's English is vastly different from Chaucer's. The English language is constantly evolving, as evidenced by the deletion of old words and the addition of new ones. *Ginormous* and *bling-bling*, for example, can both be found in *Merriam-Webster's* latest edition, yet they were not found in prior editions.

How Words Affect Tone

Tone refers to the writer's attitude toward the subject matter. For example, the tone conveys how the writer feels about the topic he or she is writing about. A lot of nonfiction writing has a neutral tone, which is an important tone for the writer to take. A neutral tone demonstrates that the writer is presenting a topic impartially and letting the information speak for itself. On the other hand, nonfiction writing can be just as effective and appropriate if the tone isn't neutral. For instance, consider this example:

> Seat belts save more lives than any other automobile safety feature. Many studies show that airbags save lives as well; however, not all cars have airbags. For instance, some older cars don't. Furthermore, air bags aren't entirely reliable. For example, studies show that in 15% of accidents, airbags don't deploy as designed; but, on the other hand, seat belt malfunctions are extremely rare. The number of highway fatalities has plummeted since laws requiring seat belt usage were enacted.

In this passage, the writer mostly chooses to retain a neutral tone when presenting information. If the writer would instead include their own personal experience of losing a friend or family member in a car accident, the tone would change dramatically. The tone would no longer be neutral and would show that the writer has a personal stake in the content, allowing them to interpret the information in a different way. When analyzing tone, consider what the writer is trying to achieve in the text and how they *create* the tone using style.

An author's choice of words—also referred to as **diction**—helps to convey his or her meaning in a particular way. Through diction, an author can convey a particular tone—e.g., a humorous tone, a serious tone—in order to support the thesis in a meaningful way to the reader.

Connotation and Denotation

Connotation is when an author chooses words or phrases that invoke ideas or feelings other than their literal meaning. An example of the use of connotation is the word *cheap*, which suggests something is poor in value or negatively describes a person as reluctant to spend money. When something or someone is described this way, the reader is more inclined to have a particular image or feeling about it or him/her. Thus, connotation can be a very effective language tool in creating emotion and swaying opinion. However, connotations are sometimes hard to pin down because varying emotions can be associated with a word. Generally, though, connotative meanings tend to be fairly consistent within a specific cultural group.

Denotation refers to words or phrases that mean exactly what they say. It is helpful when a writer wants to present hard facts or vocabulary terms with which readers may be unfamiliar. Some examples of denotation are the words *inexpensive* and *frugal*. *Inexpensive* refers to the cost of something, not its value, and *frugal* indicates that a person is conscientiously watching his or her spending. These terms do not elicit the same emotions that *cheap* does.

Authors sometimes choose to use both, but what they choose and when they use it is what critical readers need to differentiate. One method isn't inherently better than the other; however, one may create a better effect, depending upon an author's intent. If, for example, an author's purpose is to inform, to instruct, and to familiarize readers with a difficult subject, his or her use of connotation may be helpful. However, it may also undermine credibility and confuse readers. An author who wants to create a credible, scholarly effect in his or her text would most likely use denotation, which emphasizes literal, factual meaning and examples.

Analyzing an Author's Rhetorical Choices

Authors utilize a wide range of techniques to tell a story or communicate information. Readers should be familiar with the most common of these techniques. Techniques of writing are also known as **rhetorical devices**.

In nonfiction writing, authors employ argumentative techniques to present their opinions to readers in the most convincing way. Persuasive writing usually includes at least one type of appeal: an appeal to logic (logos), emotion (pathos), or credibility and trustworthiness (ethos). When writers appeal to logic, they are asking readers to agree with them based on research, evidence, and an established line of reasoning. An author's argument might also appeal to readers' emotions, perhaps by including personal stories and anecdotes (a short narrative of a specific event). A final type of appeal—appeal to authority—asks the reader to agree with the author's argument on the basis of their expertise or credentials. Three different approaches to arguing the same opinion are exemplified below:

Logic (Logos)

> Our school should abolish its current ban on cell phone use on campus. This rule was adopted last year as an attempt to reduce class disruptions and help students focus more on their lessons. However, since the rule was enacted, there has been no change in the number of disciplinary problems in class. Therefore, the rule is ineffective and should be done away with.

The above is an example of an appeal to logic. The author uses evidence to disprove the logic of the school's rule (the rule was supposed to reduce discipline problems, but the number of problems has not been reduced; therefore, the rule is not working) and to call for its repeal.

Emotion (Pathos)

An author's argument might also appeal to readers' emotions, perhaps by including personal stories and anecdotes.

The next example presents an appeal to emotion. By sharing the personal anecdote of one student and speaking about emotional topics like family relationships, the author invokes the reader's empathy in asking them to reconsider the school rule.

> Our school should abolish its current ban on cell phone use on campus. If they aren't able to use their phones during the school day, many students feel isolated from their loved ones. For example, last semester, one student's grandmother had a heart attack in the morning. However, because he couldn't use his cell phone, the student didn't know about his grandmother's accident until the end of the day—when she had already passed away and it was too late to say goodbye. By preventing students from contacting their friends and family, our school is placing undue stress and anxiety on students.

Credibility (Ethos)

Finally, an appeal to authority includes a statement from a relevant expert. In this case, the author uses a doctor in the field of education to support the argument. All three examples begin from the same opinion—the school's phone ban needs to change—but rely on different argumentative styles to persuade the reader.

> Our school should abolish its current ban on cell phone use on campus. According to Dr. Bartholomew Everett, a leading educational expert, "Research studies show that cell phone usage has no real impact on student attentiveness. Rather, phones provide a valuable technological resource for learning. Schools need to learn how to integrate this new technology into their curriculum." Rather than banning phones altogether, our school should follow the advice of experts and allow students to use phones as part of their learning.

Figurative Language

Similes and **metaphors** are types of figurative language that are used as rhetorical devices. Both are comparisons between two things, but their formats differ slightly. A simile says that two things are similar and makes a comparison using "like" or "as"—*A* is like *B,* or *A* is as [some characteristic] as *B*—whereas a metaphor states that two things are exactly the same—*A* is *B*. In both cases, similes and metaphors invite the reader to think more deeply about the characteristics of the two subjects and consider where they overlap. Sometimes the poet develops a complex metaphor throughout the entire poem; this is known as an extended metaphor. An example of metaphor can be found in the sentence:

"His pillow was a fluffy cloud." An example of simile can be found in the first line of Robert Burns' famous poem:

My love is like a red, red rose

This is comparison using "like," and the two things being compared are love and a rose. Some characteristics of a rose are that it is fragrant, beautiful, blossoming, colorful, vibrant—by comparing his love to a red, red rose, Burns asks the reader to apply these qualities of a rose to his love. In this way, he implies that his love is also fresh, blossoming, and brilliant.

In addition to rhetorical devices that play on the *meanings* of words, there are also rhetorical devices that use the sounds of words. These devices are most often found in poetry, but may also be found in other types of literature and in nonfiction writing like texts for speeches.

Alliteration and **assonance** are both varieties of sound repetition. Other types of sound repetition include: **anaphora**—repetition that occurs at the beginning of the sentences; **epiphora**—repetition occurring at the end of phrases; **antimetabole**—repetition of words in a succession; and **antiphrasis**—a form of denial of an assertion in a text.

Alliteration refers to the repetition of the first sound of each word. Recall Robert Burns' opening line:

My love is like a red, red rose

This line includes two instances of alliteration: "love" and "like" (repeated *L* sound), as well as "red" and "rose" (repeated *R* sound). Next, assonance refers to the repetition of vowel sounds, and can occur anywhere within a word (not just the opening sound). Here is the opening of a poem by John Keats:

When I have fears that I may cease to be

Before my pen has glean'd my teeming brain

Assonance can be found in the words "fears," "cease," "be," "glean'd," and "teeming," all of which stress the long *E* sound. Both alliteration and assonance create a harmony that unifies the writer's language.

Another sound device is **onomatopoeia**—words whose spelling mimics the sound they describe. Words like "crash," "bang," and "sizzle" are all examples of onomatopoeia. Use of onomatopoetic language adds auditory imagery to the text.

Readers are probably most familiar with the technique of using a pun. A **pun** is a play on words, taking advantage of two words that have the same or similar pronunciation. Puns can be found throughout Shakespeare's plays, for instance:

Now is the winter of our discontent

Made glorious summer by this son of York

These lines from *Richard III* contain a play on words. Richard III refers to his brother—the newly crowned King Edward IV—as the "son of York," referencing their family heritage from the house of York. However, while drawing a comparison between the political climate and the weather (times of political trouble were the "winter," but now the new king brings "glorious summer"), Richard's use of the word "son" also implies another word with the same pronunciation, "sun"—so Edward IV is also like the sun, bringing light, warmth, and hope to England. Puns are a clever way for writers to suggest two meanings at once.

Authorial Purpose and Perspective

No matter the genre or format, all authors are writing to persuade, inform, entertain, or express feelings. Often, these purposes are blended, with one dominating the rest. It's useful to learn to recognize the author's intent.

Persuasive writing is used to persuade or convince readers of something. It often contains two elements: the argument and the counterargument. The **argument** takes a stance on an issue, while the **counterargument** pokes holes in the opposition's stance. Authors rely on logic, emotion, and writer credibility to persuade readers to agree with them. If readers are opposed to the stance before reading, they are unlikely to adopt that stance. However, those who are undecided or committed to the same stance are more likely to agree with the author.

Informative writing tries to teach or inform. Workplace manuals, instructor lessons, statistical reports, and cookbooks are examples of informative texts. Informative writing is usually based on facts and is often without emotion and persuasion. Informative texts generally contain statistics, charts, and graphs. Although most informative texts lack a persuasive agenda, readers must examine the text carefully to determine whether one exists within a given passage.

Stories or **narratives** are designed to entertain. When people go to the movies, they often want to escape for a few hours, not necessarily to think critically. **Entertaining writing** is designed to delight and engage the reader. However, sometimes this type of writing can be woven into more serious materials, such as persuasive or informative writing, to hook the reader before transitioning into a more scholarly discussion.

Emotional writing works to evoke the reader's feelings, such as anger, euphoria, or sadness. The connection between reader and author is an attempt to cause the reader to share the author's intended emotion or tone. Sometimes, in order to make a text more poignant, the author simply wants readers to feel the emotions that the author has felt. Other times, the author attempts to persuade or manipulate the reader into adopting their stance. While it's okay to sympathize with the author, readers should be aware of the individual's underlying intent.

Characters' Point of View

Point of view is another important writing device to consider. In fiction writing, point of view refers to who tells the story or from whose perspective readers are observing the story. In nonfiction writing, the point of view refers to whether the author refers to himself or herself, his or her readers, or chooses not to refer to either. Whether fiction or nonfiction, the author carefully considers the impact the perspective will have on the purpose and main point of the writing.

- **First-person point of view**: The story is told from the writer's perspective. In fiction, this would mean that the main character is also the narrator. First-person point of view is easily recognized by the use of personal pronouns such as *I, me, we, us, our, my*, and *myself*.

- **Third-person point of view**: In a more formal essay, this would be an appropriate perspective because the focus should be on the subject matter, not the writer or the reader. Third-person point of view is recognized by the use of the pronouns *he, she, they*, and *it*. In fiction writing, third-person point of view has a few variations.

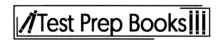

- **Third-person limited point of view** refers to a story told by a narrator who has access to the thoughts and feelings of just one character.
- In **third-person omniscient point of view**, the narrator has access to the thoughts and feelings of all the characters.
- In **third-person objective point of view**, the narrator is like a fly on the wall and can see and hear what the characters do and say but does not have access to their thoughts and feelings.

- **Second-person point of view**: This point of view isn't commonly used in fiction or nonfiction writing because it directly addresses the reader using the pronouns *you, your*, and *yourself*. Second-person perspective is more appropriate in direct communication, such as business letters or emails.

Point of View	**Pronouns used**
First person	I, me, we, us, our, my, myself
Second person	You, your, yourself
Third person	He, she, it, they

Interpreting Authorial Decisions Rhetorically

There are a few ways for readers to engage actively with the text, such as making inferences and predictions. An **inference** refers to a point that is implied (as opposed to directly-stated) by the evidence presented:

> Bradley packed up all of the items from his desk in a box and said goodbye to his coworkers for the last time.

From this sentence, although it is not directly stated, readers can infer that Bradley is leaving his job. It's necessary to use inference in order to draw conclusions about the meaning of a passage. When making an inference about a passage, it's important to rely only on the information that is provided in the text itself. This helps readers ensure that their conclusions are valid.

Readers will also find themselves making predictions when reading a passage or paragraph. **Predictions** are guesses about what's going to happen next. This is a natural tendency, especially when reading a good story or watching a suspenseful movie. It's fun to try to figure out how it will end. Authors intentionally use suspenseful language and situations to keep readers interested:

> A cat darted across the street just as the car came careening around the curve.

One unfortunate prediction might be that the car will hit the cat. Of course, predictions aren't always accurate, so it's important to read carefully to the end of the text to determine the accuracy of one's predictions.

Readers should pay attention to the **sequence**, or the order in which details are laid out in the text, as this can be important to understanding its meaning as a whole. Writers will often use transitional words to help the reader understand the order of events and to stay on track. Words like *next, then, after*, and *finally* show that the order of events is important to the author. In some cases, the author omits these transitional words, and the sequence is implied. Authors may even purposely present the information out of order to make an impact or have an effect on the reader. An example might be when a narrative writer uses **flashback** to reveal information.

Drawing conclusions is also important when actively reading a passage. **Hedge phrases** such as *will, might, probably*, and *appear to be* are used by writers who want to cover their bases and show there are exceptions to their statements. **Absolute phrasing**, such as *always* and *never*, should be carefully considered, as the use of these words and their intended meanings are often incorrect.

Identifying Reading Strategies

A **reading strategy** is the way a reader interacts with text in order to understand its meaning. It is a skill set that a reader brings to the reading. It employs a reader's ability to use prior knowledge when addressing literature and utilizes a set of methods in order to analyze text. A reading strategy is not simply tackling a text passage as it appears. It involves a more complex system of planning and thought during the reading experience. Current research indicates readers who utilize strategies and a variety of critical reading skills are better thinkers who glean more interpretive information from their reading. Consequently, they are more successful in their overall comprehension.

Pre-reading Strategies

Pre-reading strategies are important, yet often overlooked. Non-critical readers will often begin reading without taking the time to review factors that will help them understand the text. Skipping pre-reading strategies may result in a reader having to re-address a text passage more times than is necessary. Some pre-reading strategies include the following:

- Previewing the text for clues
- Skimming the text for content
- Scanning for unfamiliar words in context
- Formulating questions on sight
- Making predictions
- Recognizing needed prior knowledge

Before reading a text passage, a reader can enhance his or her ability to comprehend material by previewing the text for clues. This may mean making careful note of any titles, headings, graphics, notes, introductions, important summaries, and conclusions. It can involve a reader making physical notes regarding these elements or highlighting anything he or she thinks is important before reading. Often, a reader will be able to gain information just from these elements alone. Of course, close reading is required in order to fill in the details. A reader needs to be able to ask what he or she is reading about and what a passage is trying to say. The answers to these general questions can often be answered in previewing the text itself.

It's helpful to use pre-reading clues to determine the main idea and organization. First, any titles, sub-headings, and chapter headings should be read, and the test taker should make note of the author's credentials if any are listed. It's important to deduce what these clues may indicate as it pertains to the focus of the text and how it's organized.

During pre-reading, readers should also take special note of how text features contribute to the central idea or thesis of the passage. Is there an index? Is there a glossary? What headings, footnotes, or other visuals are included and how do they relate to the details within the passage? Again, this is where any pre-reading notes come in handy, since a test taker should be able to relate supporting details to these textual features.

Next, a reader should skim the text for general ideas and content. This technique does not involve close reading; rather, it involves looking for important words within the passage itself. These words may have something to do with the author's theme. They may have to do with structure—for example, words such as *first, next, therefore*, and *last*. Skimming helps a reader understand the overall structure of a passage and, in turn, this helps him or her understand the author's theme or message.

From there, a reader should quickly scan the text for any unfamiliar words. When reading a print text, highlighting these words or making other marginal notation is helpful when going back to read text critically. A reader should look at the words surrounding any unfamiliar ones to see what contextual clues unfamiliar words carry. Being able to define unfamiliar terms through contextual meaning is a critical skill in reading comprehension.

A reader should also formulate any questions he or she might have before conducting close reading. Questions such as "What is the author trying to tell me?" or "Is the author trying to persuade my thinking?" are important to a reader's ability to engage critically with the text. Questions will focus a reader's attention on what is important in terms of the main idea and supporting details.

Along with formulating questions, it is helpful to make predictions of what the answers to these questions and others will be. Making predictions involves using information from the text and personal experiences to make a thoughtful guess as to what will happen in the story and what outcomes can be expected.

Last, a reader should recognize that authors assume readers bring a prior knowledge set to the reading experience. Not all readers have the same experience, but authors seek to communicate with their readers. In turn, readers should strive to interact with the author of a particular passage by asking themselves what the passage demands they know during reading. This is also known as making a text-to-self connection. If a passage is informational in nature, a reader should ask "What do I know about this topic from other experiences I've had or other works I've read?" If a reader can relate to the content, he or she will better understand it.

All of the above pre-reading strategies will help the reader prepare for a closer reading experience. They will engage a reader in active interaction with the text by helping to focus the reader's full attention on the details that he or she will encounter during the next round or two of critical, closer reading.

Strategies During Reading

After pre-reading, a test taker can employ a variety of other reading strategies while conducting one or more closer readings. These strategies include the following:

- Clarifying during a close read
- Questioning during a close read
- Organizing the main ideas and supporting details
- Summarizing the text effectively

A reader needs to be able to clarify what he or she is reading. This strategy demands a reader think about how and what he or she is reading. This thinking should occur during and after the act of reading. For example, a reader may encounter one or more unfamiliar ideas during reading, then be asked to apply thoughts about those unfamiliar concepts after reading when answering test questions.

Questioning during a critical read is closely related to clarifying. A reader must be able to ask questions in general about what he or she is reading and questions regarding the author's supporting ideas. Questioning also involves a reader's ability to self-question. When closely reading a passage, it's not enough to simply try and understand the author. A reader must consider critical thinking questions to ensure he or she is comprehending intent. It's advisable, when conducting a close read, to write out margin notes and questions during the experience. These questions can be addressed later in the thinking process after reading and during the phase where a reader addresses the test questions. A reader who is successful in reading comprehension will iteratively question what he or she reads, search text for clarification, then answer any questions that arise.

A reader should organize main ideas and supporting details cognitively as he or she reads, as it will help the reader understand the larger structure at work. The use of quick annotations or marks to indicate what the main idea is and how the details function to support it can be helpful. Understanding the structure of a text passage is sometimes critical to answering questions about an author's approach, theme, messages, and supporting detail. This strategy is most effective when reading informational or nonfiction text. Texts that try to convince readers of a particular idea, that present a theory, or that try to explain difficult concepts are easier to understand when a reader can identify the overarching structure at work.

Post-Reading Strategies

After completing a text, a reader should be able to summarize the author's theme and supporting details in order to fully understand the passage. Being able to effectively restate the author's message, sub-themes, and pertinent, supporting ideas will help a reader gain an advantage when addressing standardized test questions.

A reader should also evaluate the strength of the predictions that were made in the pre-reading stage. Using textual evidence, predictions should be compared to the actual events in the story to see if the two were similar or not. Employing all of these strategies will lead to fuller, more insightful reading comprehension.

Identifying Literary Contexts

Understanding that works of literature emerged either because of a particular context—or perhaps despite a context—is key to analyzing them effectively.

Historical Context

The **historical context** of a piece of literature can refer to the time period, setting, or conditions of living at the time it was written as well as the context of the work. For example, Hawthorne's *The Scarlet Letter* was published in 1850, though the setting of the story is 1642–1649. Historically, then, when Hawthorne wrote his novel, the United States found itself at odds as the beginnings of a potential Civil War were in view. Thus, the historical context is potentially significant as it pertains to the ideas of traditions and values, which Hawthorne addresses in his story of Hester Prynne in the era of Puritanism.

Cultural Context

The **cultural context** of a piece of literature refers to cultural factors, such as the beliefs, religions, and customs that surround and are in a work of literature. The Puritan's beliefs, religion, and customs in Hawthorne's novel would be significant as they are at the core of the plot—the reason Hester wears the A and why Arthur kills himself. The customs of people in the Antebellum Period, though not quite as restrictive, were still somewhat similar. This would impact how the audience of the time received the novel.

Literary Context

Literary context refers to the consideration of the genre, potentially at the time the work was written. In 1850, Realism and Romanticism were the driving forces in literature in the U.S., with depictions of life as it was at the time in which the work was written or the time it was written *about* as well as some works celebrating the beauty of nature. Thus, an audience in Hawthorne's time would have been well satisfied with the elements of both offered in the text. They would have been looking for details about everyday things and people (Realism), but they also would appreciate his approach to description of nature and the focus on the individual (American Romanticism). The contexts would be significant as they would pertain to evaluating the work against those criteria.

Here are some questions to use when considering context:

- When was the text written?
- What was society like at the time the text was written, or what was it like, given the work's identified time period?
- Who or what influenced the writer?
- What political or social influences might there have been?
- What influences may there have been in the genre that may have affected the writer?

Additionally, students should familiarize themselves with literary periods such as Old and Middle English, American Colonial, American Renaissance, American Naturalistic, and British and American Modernist and Post-Modernist movements. Most students of literature will have had extensive exposure to these literary periods in history, and while it is not necessary to recognize every major literary work on sight and associate that work to its corresponding movement or cultural context, the test taker should be familiar enough with the historical and cultural significance of each test passage in order to be able to address test questions correctly.

The following brief description of some literary contexts and their associated literary examples follows. It is not an all-inclusive list. The test taker should read each description, then follow up with independent study to clarify each movement, its context, its most familiar authors, and their works.

Metaphysical Poetry

Metaphysical poetry is the descriptor applied to 17th century poets whose poetry emphasized the lyrical quality of their work. These works contain highly creative poetic conceits or metaphoric comparisons between two highly dissimilar things or ideas. Metaphysical poetry is characterized by highly prosaic language and complicated, often layered, metaphor.

Poems such as John Donne's "The Flea," Andrew Marvell's "To His Coy Mistress," George Herbert's "The Collar," Henry Vaughan's "The World," and Richard Crashaw's "A Song" are associated with this type of poetry.

British Romanticism

British Romanticism was a cultural and literary movement within Europe that developed at the end of the 18th century and extended into the 19th century. It occurred partly in response to aristocratic, political, and social norms and partly in response to the Industrial Revolution of the day. Characterized by intense emotion, major literary works of British Romanticism embrace the idea of aestheticism and the beauty of nature. Literary works exalted folk customs and historical art and encouraged spontaneity of artistic endeavor. The movement embraced the heroic ideal and the concept that heroes would raise the quality of society.

Authors who are classified as British Romantics include Samuel Taylor Coleridge, John Keats, George Byron, Mary Shelley, Percy Bysshe Shelley, and William Blake. Well-known works include Samuel Taylor Coleridge's "Kubla Khan," John Keats' "Ode on a Grecian Urn," George Byron's "Childe Harold's Pilgrimage," Mary Shelley's *Frankenstein*, Percy Bysshe Shelley's "Ode to the West Wind," and William Blake's "The Tyger."

American Romanticism

American Romanticism occurred within the American literary scene beginning early in the 19th century. While many aspects were similar to British Romanticism, it is further characterized as having gothic aspects and the idea that individualism was to be encouraged. It also embraced the concept of the **noble savage**—the idea that indigenous culture uncorrupted by civilization is better than advanced society.

Well-known authors and works include Nathanial Hawthorne's *The House of the Seven Gables*, Edgar Allan Poe's "The Raven" and "The Cask of Amontillado," Emily Dickinson's "I Felt a Funeral in My Brain" and James Fenimore Cooper's *The Last of the Mohicans.*

Transcendentalism

Transcendentalism was a movement that applied to a way of thinking that developed within the United States, specifically New England, around 1836. While this way of thinking originally employed philosophical aspects, transcendentalism spread to all forms of art, literature, and even to the ways people chose to live. It was born out of a reaction to traditional rationalism and purported concepts such as a higher divinity, feminism, humanitarianism, and communal living. Transcendentalism valued intuition, self-reliance, and the idea that human nature was inherently good.

Well-known authors include Ralph Waldo Emerson, Henry David Thoreau, Louisa May Alcott, and Ellen Sturgis Hooper. Works include Ralph Waldo Emerson's "Self-Reliance" and "Uriel," Henry David Thoreau's *Walden* and *Civil Disobedience*, Louisa May Alcott's *Little Women*, and Ellen Sturgis Hooper's "I Slept, and Dreamed that Life was Beauty."

The Harlem Renaissance

The **Harlem Renaissance** is the descriptor given to the cultural, artistic, and social boom that developed in Harlem, New York, at the beginning of the 20th century, spanning the 1920s and 1930s. Originally termed *The New Negro Movement*, it emphasized African-American urban cultural expression and migration across the United States. It had strong roots in African-American Christianity, discourse, and intellectualism. The Harlem Renaissance heavily influenced the development of music and fashion as well. Its singular characteristic was to embrace Pan-American culturalisms; however, strong themes of the slavery experience and African-American folk traditions also emerged. A hallmark of the Harlem Renaissance was that it laid the foundation for the future Civil Rights Movement in the United States.

Well-known authors and works include Zora Neale Hurston's *Their Eyes Were Watching God*, Richard Wright's *Native Son*, Langston Hughes' "I, Too," and James Weldon Johnson's "God's Trombones: Seven Negro Sermons in Verse" and *The Book of American Negro Poetry.*

Understanding Literary Interpretation

Literary interpretation is an interpretation and analysis of a literary work, based on the textual evidence in the work. It is often subjective as critical readers may discern different meanings in the details. Students need to be prepared for questions that will test how well they can read a passage, make an analysis, and then provide evidence to support that analysis.

Literal and Figurative Meanings

When analyzing and interpreting fiction, readers must be active participants in the experience. Some authors make their messages clearer than others, but the onus is on the reader to add layers to what is read through interpretation. In literary interpretation, the goal is not to offer an opinion as to the inherent value of the work. Rather, the goal is to determine what the text means by analyzing the literal and figurative meanings of the text through critical reading.

Critical reading is close reading that elicits questions as the reader progresses. Many authors of fiction use literary elements and devices to further theme and to speak to their audience. These elements often utilize language that has an alternate or figurative meaning in addition to their actual or literal meaning. Readers should be asking questions about these and other important details as a passage is analyzed. What unfamiliar words are there? What is their contextual definition? How do they contribute to the overall feel of the work? How do they contribute to the mood and general message? Literal and figurative meanings are discussed further in the informational texts and rhetoric section.

Drawing Inferences

An **inference** refers to a point that is implied (as opposed to directly-stated) by the evidence presented. It's necessary to use inference in order to draw conclusions about the meaning of a passage. Authors make implications through character dialogue, thoughts, effects on others, actions, and looks.

When making an inference about a passage, it's important to rely only on the information that is provided in the text itself. This helps readers ensure that their conclusions are valid. Drawing inferences is also discussed in the informational texts and rhetoric section.

Textual Evidence

It's helpful to read a passage a few times, noting details that seem important to the piece. Textual evidence within the details helps readers draw a conclusion about a passage. **Textual evidence** refers to information—facts and examples that support the main idea. Textual evidence will likely come from outside sources and can be in the form of quoted or paraphrased material. In order to draw a conclusion from evidence, it's important to examine the credibility and validity of that evidence as well as how (and if) it relates to the main idea. Effective use of textual evidence should connect to the main idea and support a specific point. Textual evidence is examined further in the informational texts and rhetoric section.

Identifying Literary Theories

A **literary theory** can be considered a methodology for understanding literature. It asks, "What is literature?" and offers readers a working set of principles to understand common themes, ideas, and intent. Classifications of literary theory are often referred to as **schools of thought**. These schools are based on subdivisions in historical perspective and in philosophical thinking across literary analysts and critics.

Romanticism/Aestheticism

Romanticism/Aestheticism spanned the 19th century and developed in response to the idea that enlightenment and reason were the source of all truth and authority in philosophy. Romanticism and Aestheticism embraced the tenet that **aesthetics**—all that is beautiful and natural—in art and literature should be considered the highest-held principle, overriding all others. Popular authors include Oscar Wilde, Edgar Allan Poe, Mary Shelley, and John Keats.

Marxism

Marxism as a literary theory developed in the early twentieth century after the Russian October Revolution of 1917. It loosely embraced the idea that social realism was the highest form of literature and that the social classes' struggle for progress was the most important concept literature could emphasize. Examples of authors include Simone de Beauvoir and Bertolt Brecht.

Structuralism

Structuralism included all aspects of philosophy, linguistics, anthropology, and literary theory. Beginning in the early 1900s, this school of thought focused on ideas surrounding how human culture is understood within its larger structures and how those structures influence people's thoughts and actions. Specifically, structuralism examines how literature is interconnected through structure. It examines common elements in the stories and the myths that contribute to literature as a whole. Popular theorists and writers include Claude Levi-Strauss, Umberto Eco, and Roland Barthes.

Post-Structuralism and Deconstruction

Post-structuralism and **deconstruction** developed out of structuralism in the twentieth century. It expanded on the idea of overall structure in literature, but both theories argue varying analytical concepts of how that structure should be examined and utilized. For example, while structuralism acknowledges oppositional relationships in literature—e.g., male/female, beginning/end, rational/emotional—post-structuralism and deconstruction began de-emphasizing the idea that one idea is always dominant over another. Both also assert that studying text also means studying the knowledge that produced the text. Popular theorists and writers include Roland Barthes and Michel Foucault.

New Criticism

New Criticism dominated American culture in the mid-twentieth century. It purports that close, critical reading was necessary to understanding literary works, especially poetry. Popular theory also focused on the inherent beauty of text itself. New Criticism rejected the previous critical focus of how history, use of language, and the author's experience influence literature, asserting those ideas as being too loosely interpretive in examining literature. As a movement, it tended to separate literature from historical context and an author's intent. It embraced the idea that formal study of structure and text should not be separated. Theorists of note include Stephen Greenblatt and Jonathan Goldberg.

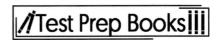

Informational Text

Understanding Development of a Written Argument

Evaluating an Author's Purpose

A reader must be able to evaluate the argument or point the author is trying to make and determine if it is adequately supported. The first step is to determine the main idea. The main idea is what the author wants to say about a specific topic. The next step is to locate the supporting details. An author uses supporting details to illustrate the main idea. These are the details that provide evidence or examples to help make a point. Supporting details often appear in the form of quotations, paraphrasing, or analysis. Test takers should then examine the text to make sure the author connects details and analysis to the main point. These steps are crucial to understanding the text and evaluating how well the author presents his or her argument and evidence. The following graphic demonstrates the connection between the main idea and the supporting details.

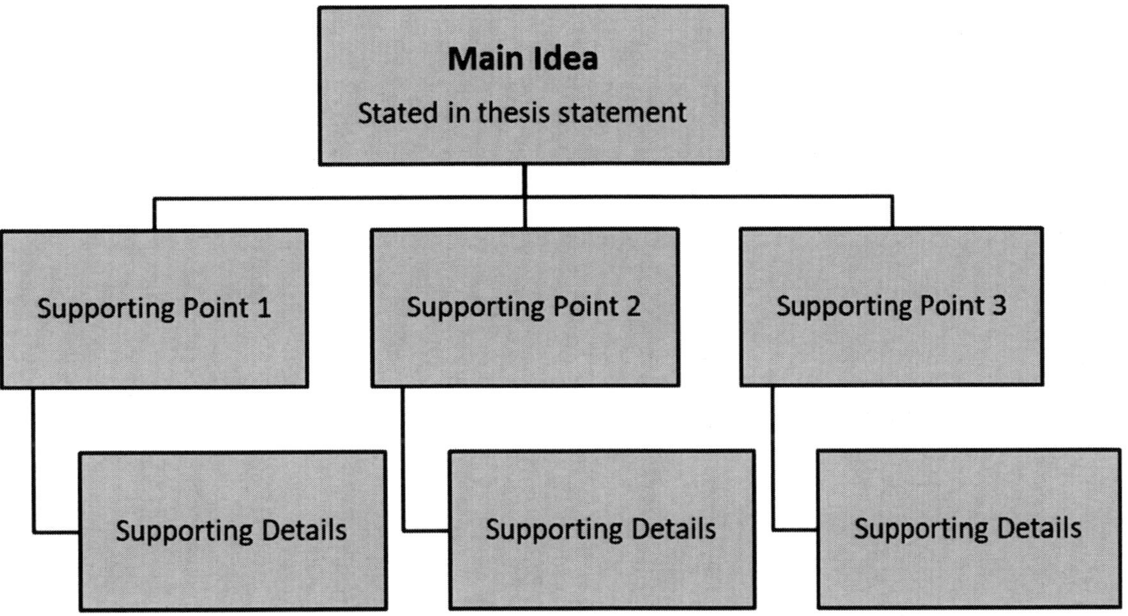

Identifying False Statements

A reader must also be able to identify any **logical fallacies**—logically-flawed statements—that an author may make as those fallacies impact the validity and veracity of the author's claims.

Some of the more common fallacies are shown in the following chart.

Fallacy	Definition
Slippery Slope	A fallacy that is built on the idea that a particular action will lead to a series of events with negative results
Red Herring	The use of an observation or distraction to remove attention from the actual issue
Straw Man	An exaggeration or misrepresentation of an argument so that it is easier to refute
Post Hoc Ergo Propter Hoc	A fallacy that assumes an event to be the consequence of an earlier event merely because it came after it
Bandwagon	A fallacy that assumes because the majority of people feel or believe a certain way then it must be the right way
Ad Hominem	The use of a personal attack on the person or persons associated with a certain argument rather than focusing on the actual argument itself

Readers who are aware of the types of fallacious reasoning are able to weigh the credibility of the author's statements in terms of effective argument. Rhetorical text that contains a myriad of fallacious statements should be considered ineffectual and suspect.

Interpreting Media and Non-Print Text

In the 21st century, rhetoric is evident in a variety of formats. Blogs, vlogs, videos, news footage, advertisements, and live video fill informational feeds, and readers see many shortened images and snapshot texts a day. It's important to note that the majority of these formats use images to appeal to emotion over factual information. Online visuals spread more quickly and are more easily adopted by consumers as fact than printed formats.

Critical readers should be aware that media and non-print text carries some societal weight to the population. In being inundated with pictures and live footage, readers often feel compelled to skip the task of critical reading analysis and accept truth at literal face value. Authors of non-print media are aware of this fact and frequently capitalize on it.

To critically address non-print media requires that the consumer address additional sources and not exclude printed text in order to reach sound conclusions. While it's tempting for consumers to get swept away in the latest viral media, it's important to remember that creators of such have an agenda, and unless the non-print media in question is backed up with sound supporting evidence, any thesis or message cannot be considered valid or factual. Memes, gifs, and looped video cannot tell the whole, truthful story although they may appeal to opinions with which readers already agree. Sharing such non-print media online can precipitate widespread misunderstanding.

When presented with non-print media, critical readers should consider these bits of information as teasers to be investigated for accuracy and veracity. Of course, certain non-print media exists solely for entertainment, but the critical reader should be able to separate out what's generalized for entertainment's sake and what's presented for further verification, before blindly accepting the message. Increasingly, this has become more difficult for readers to do, only because of the onslaught of information to which they are exposed.

If a reader is not to fall prey to strong imagery and non-print media, he or she will need to fact-check. This, of course, requires time and attention on the reader's part, and in current culture, taking the time to fact-check seems counterproductive. However, in order to maintain credibility themselves, readers must be able to evaluate multiple sources of information across media formats and be able to identify the emotional appeal used in the smaller sound bites of non-print media. Readers must view with a discerning eye, listen with a questioning ear, and think with a critical mind.

Interpreting Textual Evidence in Informational Text

Literal and Figurative Meanings

It is important when evaluating informational texts to consider the use of both literal and figurative meanings. The words and phrases an author chooses to include in a text must be evaluated. How does the word choice affect the meaning and tone? By recognizing the use of literal and figurative language, a reader can more readily ascertain the message or purpose of a text. Literal word choice is the easiest to analyze as it represents the usual and intended way a word or phrase is used. It is also more common in informational texts because it is used to state facts and definitions. While figurative language is typically associated with fiction and poetry, it can be found in informational texts as well. The reader must determine not only what is meant by the figurative language in context, but also how the author intended it to shape the overall text.

Inference in Informational Text

Inference refers to the reader's ability to understand the unwritten text, i.e., "read between the lines" in terms of an author's intent or message. The strategy asks that a reader not take everything he or she reads at face value but instead, add his or her own interpretation of what the author seems to be trying to convey. A reader's ability to make inferences relies on his or her ability to think clearly and logically about the text. It does not ask that the reader make wild speculation or guess about the material but demands that he or she be able to come to a sound conclusion about the material.

An author's use of less literal words and phrases requires readers to make more inference when they read. Since inference involves **deduction**—deriving conclusions from ideas assumed to be true—there's more room for interpretation. Still, critical readers who employ inference, if careful in their thinking, can still arrive at the logical, sound conclusions the author intends.

Textual Evidence in Informational Text

Once a reader has determined an author's thesis or main idea, he or she will need to understand how textual evidence supports interpretation of that thesis or main idea. Test takers will be asked direct questions regarding an author's main idea and may be asked to identify evidence that would support those ideas. This will require test takers to comprehend literal and figurative meanings within the text passage, be able to draw inferences from provided information, and be able to separate important evidence from minor supporting detail. It's often helpful to skim test questions and answer options prior to critically reading informational text; however, test takers should avoid the temptation to solely look for the correct answers. Just trying to find the "right answer" may cause test takers to miss important supporting textual evidence. Making mental note of test questions is only helpful as a guide when reading.

After identifying an author's thesis or main idea, a test taker should look at the supporting details that the author provides to back up his or her assertions, identifying those additional pieces of information that help expand the thesis. From there, test takers should examine the additional information and related details for credibility, the author's use of outside sources, and be able to point to direct evidence that supports the author's claims. It's also imperative that test takers be able to identify what is strong support and what is merely additional information that is nice to know but not necessary. Being able to make this differentiation will help test takers effectively answer questions regarding an author's use of supporting evidence within informational text.

Organizational Structure within Informational Texts

Informational text is specifically designed to relate factual information, and although it is open to a reader's interpretation and application of the facts, the structure of the presentation is carefully designed to lead the reader to a particular conclusion or central idea. When reading informational text, it is important that readers are able to understand its organizational structure as the structure often directly relates to an author's intent to inform and/or persuade the reader.

The first step in identifying the text's structure is to determine the thesis or main idea. The thesis statement and organization of a work are closely intertwined. A **thesis statement** indicates the writer's purpose and may include the scope and direction of the text. It may be presented at the beginning of a text or at the end, and it may be explicit or implicit.

Once a reader has a grasp of the thesis or main idea of the text, he or she can better determine its organizational structure. Test takers are advised to read informational text passages more than once in order to comprehend the material fully. It is also helpful to examine any text features present in the text including the table of contents, index, glossary, headings, footnotes, and visuals. The analysis of these features and the information presented within them, can offer additional clues about the central idea and structure of a text. The following questions should be asked when considering structure:

- How does the author assemble the parts to make an effective whole argument?
- Is the passage linear in nature and if so, what is the timeline or thread of logic?
- What is the presented order of events, facts, or arguments? Are these effective in contributing to the author's thesis?
- How can the passage be divided into sections? How are they related to each other and to the main idea or thesis?
- What key terms are used to indicate the organization?

Next, test takers should skim the passage, noting the first line or two of each body paragraph—the **topic sentences**—and the conclusion. Key **transitional terms**, such as *on the other hand*, *also*, *because*, *however*, *therefore*, *most importantly*, and *first*, within the text can also signal organizational structure. Based on these clues, readers should then be able to identify what type of organizational structure is being used.

The following organizational structures are most common:

- **Problem/solution**—organized by an analysis/overview of a problem, followed by potential solution(s)
- **Cause/effect**—organized by the effects resulting from a cause or the cause(s) of a particular effect
- **Spatial order**—organized by points that suggest location or direction—e.g., top to bottom, right to left, outside to inside
- **Chronological/sequence order**—organized by points presented to indicate a passage of time or through purposeful steps/stages
- **Comparison/Contrast**—organized by points that indicate similarities and/or differences between two things or concepts
- **Order of importance**—organized by priority of points, often most significant to least significant or vice versa

Sequential, Comparative, and Cause-Effect Relationships

Ideas within texts should be organized, connected, or related in some way. In **sequential relationships**, ideas or events have a temporal relationship; they occur in some sort of order. Every passage has a plot, whether it is from a short story, a manual, a newspaper article or editorial, or a history text. And each plot has a logical order, which is also known as a sequence. Some of the most straightforward sequences can be found in technology directions, science experiments, instructional materials, and recipes.

These forms of writing list actions that must occur in a proper sequence in order to get sufficient results. Other forms of writing, however, use style and ideas in ways that completely change the sequence of events. Poetry, for instance, may introduce repetitions that make the events seem cyclical. Postmodern writers are famous for experimenting with different concepts of place and time, creating "cut scenes" that distort straightforward sequences and abruptly transport the audience to different contexts or times. Even everyday newspaper articles, editorials, and historical sources may experiment with different sequential forms for stylistic effect.

Most questions that call for test takers to apply their sequential knowledge use key words such as *sequence, sequence of events*, or *sequential order* to cue the test taker in to the task at hand. In social studies or history passages, the test questions might employ key words such as *chronology* or *chronological order* to cue the test taker. In some cases, sequence can be found through comprehension techniques. These literal passages number the sequences, or they use key words such as *firstly, secondly, finally, next*, or *then*. The sequences of these stories can be found by rereading the passage and charting these numbers or key words. In most cases, however, readers have to correctly order events through inferential and evaluative reading techniques; they have to place events in a logical order without explicit cues.

Ideas in a text can also have a **comparative relationship** wherein certain qualities are shown to overlap or be the same between two different things. In comparative relationships, similarities are drawn out. Words like *as, like, also, similarly, in the same way,* and *too* are often used.

Passages that have a **cause-and-effect relationship** demonstrate a specific type of connection between ideas or events wherein one (or multiple) caused another. Words such as *if*, *since*, *because*, *then*, or *consequently* indicate a relationship.

Understanding the Meaning and Purpose of Transition Words

The writer should act as a guide, showing the reader how all the sentences fit together. Consider this example:

> Seat belts save more lives than any other automobile safety feature. Many studies show that airbags save lives as well. Not all cars have airbags. Many older cars don't. Air bags aren't entirely reliable. Studies show that in 15% of accidents, airbags don't deploy as designed. Seat belt malfunctions are extremely rare.

There's nothing wrong with any of these sentences individually, but together they're disjointed and difficult to follow. The best way for the writer to communicate information is through the use of transition words. Here are examples of transition words and phrases that tie sentences together, enabling a more natural flow:

- To show causality: as a result, therefore, and consequently
- To compare and contrast: however, but, and on the other hand
- To introduce examples: for instance, namely, and including
- To show order of importance: foremost, primarily, secondly, and lastly

Note: This is not a complete list of transitions. There are many more that can be used; however, most fit into these or similar categories. The point is that the words should clearly show the relationship between sentences, supporting information, and the main idea.

Here is an update to the previous example using transition words. These changes make it easier to read and bring clarity to the writer's points:

> Seat belts save more lives than any other automobile safety feature. Many studies show that airbags save lives as well; however, not all cars have airbags. For instance, some older cars don't. Furthermore, air bags aren't entirely reliable. For example, studies show that in 15% of accidents, airbags don't deploy as designed; but, on the other hand, seat belt malfunctions are extremely rare.

Also, be prepared to analyze whether the writer is using the best transition word or phrase for the situation. Take this sentence for example: "As a result, seat belt malfunctions are extremely rare." This sentence doesn't make sense in the context above because the writer is trying to show the contrast between seat belts and airbags, not the causality.

Distinguishing Between Fact and Opinion, Biases, and Stereotypes

A **fact** is information that can be proven true. If information can be disproved, it is not a fact. For example, water freezes at or below thirty-two degrees Fahrenheit. An argument stating that water freezes at seventy degrees Fahrenheit cannot be supported by data, and is therefore not a fact. Facts tend to be associated with science, mathematics, and statistics.

Opinions are information open to debate. Opinions are often tied to subjective concepts like equality, morals, and rights. They can also be controversial.

Biases and stereotypes are viewpoints based in opinion and held despite evidence that they are incorrect. A **bias** is an individual prejudice. Biased people ignore evidence that contradicts their position while offering as proof any evidence that supports it. A **stereotype** is a widely held belief projected onto a group. Those who stereotype tend to make assumptions based on what others have told them and usually have little firsthand experience with the group or item in question.

Identifying Primary Sources in Various Media

Primary sources are best defined as records or items that serve as evidence of periods of history. To be considered primary, the source documents or objects must have been created during the time period in which they reference. Examples include diaries, newspaper articles, speeches, government documents, photographs, and historical artifacts. In today's digital age, primary sources, which were once in print, often are embedded in secondary sources. Secondary sources, such as websites, history books, databases, or reviews, contain analysis or commentary on primary sources. Secondary sources borrow information from primary sources through the process of quoting, summarizing, or paraphrasing.

Today's students often complete research online through electronic sources. Electronic sources offer advantages over print, and can be accessed on virtually any computer, where libraries or other research centers are limited to fixed locations and specific catalogs. Electronic sources are also efficient and yield massive amounts of data in seconds. The user can tailor a search based on key words, publication years, and article length. Lastly, many databases provide the user with instant citations, saving the user the trouble of manually assembling sources.

Though electronic sources yield powerful results, researchers must use caution. While there are many reputable and reliable sources on the internet, just as many are unreliable or biased sources. It's up to the researcher to examine and verify the reliability of sources. *Wikipedia*, for example, may or may not be accurate, depending on the contributor. Many databases, such as *EBSCO* or *SIRS*, offer peer-reviewed articles, meaning the publications have been reviewed for the quality of their content.

Credibility

Critical readers examine the facts used to support an author's argument. They check the facts against other sources to be sure those facts are correct. They also check the validity of the sources used to be sure those sources are credible, academic, and/or peer-reviewed. Consider that when an author uses another person's opinion to support their argument, even if it is an expert's opinion, it is still only an opinion and should not be taken as fact. A strong argument uses valid, measurable facts to support ideas. Even then, the reader may disagree with the argument as it may be rooted in their personal beliefs.

An authoritative argument may use the facts to sway the reader. In the example of global warming, many experts differ in their opinions of what alternative fuels can be used to aid in offsetting it. Because of this, a writer may choose to only use the information and expert opinion that supports their viewpoint.

Practice Questions

Questions 1–6 are based on the following passage:

When I got on the coach the driver had not taken his seat, and I saw him talking with the landlady. They were evidently talking of me, for every now and then they looked at me, and some of the people who were sitting on the bench outside the door came and listened, and then looked at me, most of them pityingly. I could hear a lot of words often repeated, queer words, for there were many nationalities in the crowd; so I quietly got my polyglot dictionary from my bag and looked them out. I must say they weren't cheering to me, for amongst them were "Ordog"—Satan, "pokol"—hell, "stregoica"—witch, "vrolok" and "vlkoslak"—both of which mean the same thing, one being Slovak and the other Servian for something that is either were-wolf or vampire.

When we started, the crowd round the inn door, which had by this time swelled to a considerable size, all made the sign of the cross and pointed two fingers towards me. With some difficulty I got a fellow-passenger to tell me what they meant; he wouldn't answer at first, but on learning that I was English, he explained that it was a charm or guard against the evil eye. This was not very pleasant for me, just starting for an unknown place to meet an unknown man; but everyone seemed so kind-hearted, and so sorrowful, and so sympathetic that I couldn't but be touched. I shall never forget the last glimpse which I had of the inn-yard and its crowd of picturesque figures, all crossing themselves, as they stood round the wide archway, with its background of rich foliage of oleander and orange trees in green tubs clustered in the centre of the yard. Then our driver cracked his big whip over his four small horses, which ran abreast, and we set off on our journey.

I soon lost sight and recollection of ghostly fears in the beauty of the scene as we drove along, although had I known the language, or rather languages, which my fellow-passengers were speaking, I might not have been able to throw them off so easily. Before us lay a green sloping land full of forests and woods, with here and there steep hills, crowned with clumps of trees or with farmhouses, the blank gable end to the road. There was everywhere a bewildering mass of fruit blossom—apple, plum, pear, cherry; and as we drove by I could see the green grass under the trees spangled with the fallen petals. In and out amongst these green hills of what they call here the "Mittel Land" ran the road, losing itself as it swept round the grassy curve, or was shut out by the straggling ends of pine woods, which here and there ran down the hillsides like tongues of flame. The road was rugged, but still we seemed to fly over it with a feverish haste. I couldn't understand then what the haste meant, but the driver was evidently bent on losing no time in reaching Borgo Prund.

Dracula by Bram Stoker, 1897

1. What type of narrator is found in this passage?
   a. First person
   b. Second person
   c. Third-person limited
   d. Third-person omniscient

2. Which of the following is true of the traveler?
   a. He wishes the driver would go faster.
   b. He's returning to the country of his birth.
   c. He has some familiarity with the local customs.
   d. He doesn't understand all of the languages being used.

3. How does the traveler's mood change between the second and third paragraphs?
   a. From relaxed to rushed
   b. From fearful to charmed
   c. From confused to enlightened
   d. From comfortable to exhausted

4. Who is the traveler going to meet?
   a. A kind landlady
   b. A distant relative
   c. A friendly villager
   d. A complete stranger

5. Based on the details in this passage, what can readers probably expect to happen in the story?
   a. The traveler will become a farmer.
   b. The traveler will arrive late at his destination.
   c. The traveler will soon encounter danger or evil.
   d. The traveler will have a pleasant journey and make many new friends.

Answer Explanations

1. A: First person. This is a straightforward question that requires readers to know that a first-person narrator speaks from an "I" point of view.

2. D: He doesn't understand all of the languages being used. This can be inferred from the fact that the traveler must refer to his dictionary to understand those around him. Choice *A* isn't a good choice because the traveler seems to wonder why the driver needs to drive so fast. Choice B isn't mentioned in the passage and doesn't seem like a good answer choice because he seems wholly unfamiliar with his surroundings. This is why Choice C can also be eliminated.

3. B: From fearful to charmed. This can be found in the first sentence of the third paragraph, which states, "I soon lost sight and recollection of ghostly fears in the beauty of the scene as we drove along." Also, readers should get a sense of foreboding from the first two paragraphs, where superstitious villagers seem frightened on the traveler's behalf. However, the final paragraph changes to delighted descriptions of the landscape's natural beauty. Choices *A* and *D* can be eliminated because the traveler is anxious, not relaxed or comfortable at the beginning of the passage. Choice *C* can also be eliminated because the traveler doesn't gain any particular insights in the last paragraph, and in fact continues to lament that he cannot understand the speech of those around him.

4. D: A complete stranger. The answer to this reading comprehension question can be found in the second paragraph, when the traveler is "just starting for an unknown place to meet an unknown man"—in other words, a complete stranger.

5. C: The traveler will soon encounter danger or evil. Answering this prediction question requires readers to understand foreshadowing, or hints that the author gives about what will happen next. There are numerous hints scattered throughout this passage: the villager's sorrow and sympathy for the traveler and their superstitious actions; the spooky words that the traveler overhears; the driver's unexplained haste. All of these point to a danger that awaits the protagonist.

Speaking and Listening

Understanding Effective Delivery of a Speech or Presentation

Good public speakers all have several characteristics in common. It is not enough to simply write a speech, but it must also be delivered in a manner that is both engaging and succinct. The following qualities are inherent to good public speaking.

Confidence is possibly the most important attribute a speaker can have. It instills trust in the listener that the person knows what he or she is talking about and that he or she is credible and competent. Confidence is displayed by making brief eye contact—about 2–3 seconds—with different members of the audience to demonstrate that the speaker is engaged. It is also displayed in his or her tone of voice—strong, light-hearted, and natural. A nervous speaker can easily be identified by a small, quivering voice. Confidence is also conveyed by the speaker facing the audience; turning one's back may demonstrate insecurity.

Authenticity is another quality of an effective speaker, as it makes a person more relatable and believable to the audience. Speeches that are memorized word-for-word can give the impression of being inauthentic as the monologue does not flow quite naturally, especially if the speaker accidentally fumbles or forgets. Memorizing speeches can also lead to a monotonous tone, which is sure to put the audience to sleep, or worse, a misinterpreted tone, which can cause the audience to stop listening entirely or even become offended. Therefore, speeches should be practiced with a natural intonation and not be memorized mechanically.

Connection with the audience is another important aspect of public speaking. Speakers should engage with their listeners by the use of storytelling and visual or auditory aids, as well as asking questions that the audience can participate in. Visual and auditory aids could range from an interesting PowerPoint presentation to a short video clip to physical objects the audience can pass around to a soundtrack. The use of appropriate humor also allows the audience to connect with the speaker on a more personal level and will make the speech sound more like a conversation than a one-sided lecture. Speakers who are passionate about their subject inspire their listeners to care about what they're saying; they transfer their energy into the audience. This level of connection will encourage their listeners to want to be there.

Succinctness and purposeful repetition ensure that the audience's attention remains focused on the message at hand. Repeating the overall point of the speech in different ways helps listeners remember what the speaker is trying to tell them, even when the speech is over. A speech that is longer than necessary will cause listeners to become bored and stop absorbing information. Keeping the speech short and sweet and leaving more time for questions at the end will ensure that the audience stays engaged.

There are many different styles a speaker can utilize, but the most important thing speakers should keep in mind is maintaining a connection with the audience. This will help ensure that the audience will remain open and focused enough to hear and absorb the message.

Evaluating the Advantages and Disadvantages of Different Media

Each visual aid has its advantages and disadvantages and should be used sparingly to avoid distracting the audience. Visual aids should be used to emphasize a presentation's message, not overwhelm it.

Microsoft PowerPoint is currently the most commonly used visual aid. It allows for pictures, words, videos, and music to be presented on the same screen and is essentially just a projection of a computer screen, allowing easy and quick access to all forms of media as well as the Internet. However, a PowerPoint presentation should not be overwhelmed with information, such as text-heavy slides, as audience members will spend more time reading the slides than listening to the speaker. Conversely, they may avoid reading it entirely, and the presentation will serve no purpose. A PowerPoint presentation that uses too many animations and visual elements may also detract from the presence of the speaker.

Handouts are a great way for the audience to feel more involved in a presentation. They can present lots of information that may be too much for a PowerPoint, and they can also be taken home and reviewed later. The primary disadvantage of handouts is that the audience may choose to read rather than to listen, thus missing the main points the speaker is trying to make, or they may decide not to read it at all. The best handouts are those that do not contain all the information of a presentation but allow for the audience to take notes and complete the handout by listening or asking questions.

Whiteboards and blackboards are excellent for explaining difficult concepts by allowing the audience to follow along with a process and copy down their own version of what is being written on the board. This visual aid is best used to explain concepts in mathematics and science. The main problem with the board, however, is that there can be limited space, and if the presenter runs out of room, he or she will have to erase the content written on the board and will be unable to refer back to it later. He or she may also have to wait for the entire audience to write the information down, which slows down the presentation.

Overhead projectors are wonderful in that a speaker can use a prepared transparency and draw images or add words to emphasize or explain concepts. They can also erase these additions but still keep the original content if they wish to alter their method to fit the audience or provide further explanations. Similar to PowerPoint presentations, overhead projections should limit the amount of text to keep the audience focused on listening.

Physical objects are a useful way to connect with the audience and allow them to feel more involved. Because people interact with the physical world, physical objects can help solidify understanding of difficult concepts. However, they can be distracting if not properly introduced. If they are presented too early or are visible during the presentation, the audience will focus on the objects, wondering what purpose they may serve instead of listening to the speaker. Objects should instead be hidden until it is time to show them and then collected when they are no longer useful.

Videos are a great way to enliven a presentation by giving it sound, music, flow, and images. They are excellent for emphasizing points, providing evidence for ideas, giving context, or setting tone. The major issue with videos is that the presenter is unable to speak at this point, so this form of media should be used sparingly and purposefully. Also, overly-long videos may lose the audience's attention.

Effective public speakers are aware of the advantages and disadvantages of all forms of media and often choose to utilize a combination of several different types to keep the presentations lively and the audience engaged.

Presenting Information Clearly, Concisely, and Logically

All information should be presented with a clear beginning, middle, and end. Distinct organization always makes any work more clear, concise, and logical. For a presentation, this should involve choosing a primary topic and then discussing it in the following format:

- Introducing the speaker and the main topic
- Providing evidence, supporting details, further explanation of the topic in the main body
- Concluding it with a firm resolution and repetition of the main point

The beginning, middle, and end should also be linked with effective transitions that make the presentation flow well. For example, a presentation should always begin with an introduction by the speaker, including what he/she does and what he/she is there to present. Good transitional introductions may begin with statements such as *For those who do not know me, my name is...*, *As many of you know, I am...* or *Good morning everyone, my name is ___, and I am the new project manager*. A good introduction grabs the attention and interest of the audience.

After an introduction has been made, the speaker will then want to state the purpose of the presentation with a natural transition, such as *I am here to discuss the latest editions to our standard of procedure...* or *This afternoon, I would like to present the results of our latest findings*. Once the purpose has been identified, the speaker will want to adhere to the main idea announced. The presenter should be certain to keep the main idea to one sentence as too much information can confuse an audience; an introduction should be succinct and to the point.

Supporting information should always be presented in concise, easy-to-read formats such as bullet points or lists—if visual aids are presented during the presentation. Good transitions such as *Let's begin with...* or *Now to look at...* make the presentation flow smoothly and logically, helping listeners to keep ideas organized as they are presented. Keeping the material concise is extremely important in a presentation, and visual aids should be used only to emphasize points or explain ideas. All the supporting information should relate back to the main idea, avoiding unnecessary tangents.

Finally, a firm conclusion involves repeating the main point of the presentation by either inspiring listeners to act or by reiterating the most important points made in the speech. It should also include an expression of gratitude to the audience as well as transition to opening the floor for questions.

Grammar and Usage

Understanding the Conventions of Standard English

Parts of Speech

The English language has eight parts of speech, each serving a different grammatical function.

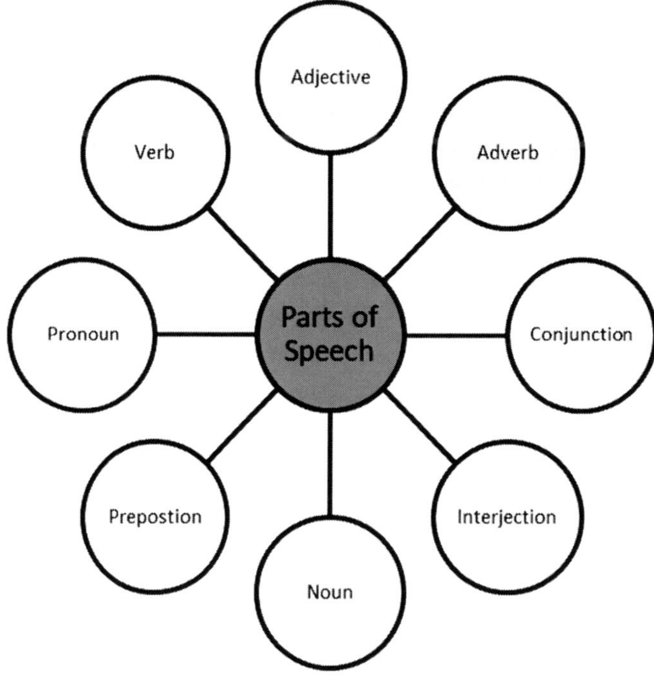

Verb

Verbs describe an action—e.g., *run, play, eat*—or a state of being—e.g., *is, are, was*. It is impossible to make a grammatically-complete sentence without a verb.

He *runs* to the store.

She *is* eight years old.

Noun

Nouns can be a person, place, or thing. They can refer to concrete objects—e.g., chair, apple, house—or abstract things—love, knowledge, friendliness.

Look at the *dog*!

Where are my *keys*?

Some nouns are countable, meaning they can be counted as separate entities—one chair, two chairs, three chairs. They can be either singular or plural. Other nouns, usually substances or concepts, are uncountable—e.g., air, information, wealth—and some nouns can be both countable and uncountable depending on how they are used.

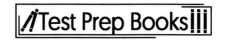

I bought three *dresses*.

Respect is important to me.

I ate way too much *food* last night.

At the international festival, you can sample *foods* from around the world.

Proper nouns are the specific names of people, places, or things and are almost always capitalized.

Marie Curie studied at the *Flying University* in *Warsaw, Poland*.

Pronoun

Pronouns function as substitutes for nouns or noun phrases. Pronouns are often used to avoid constant repetition of a noun or to simplify sentences. **Personal pronouns** are used for people. Some pronouns are **subject pronouns**; they are used to replace the subject in a sentence—*I, we, he, she, they*.

Is *he* your friend?

We work together.

Object pronouns can function as the object of a sentence—*me, us, him, her, them*.

Give the documents to *her*.

Did you call *him* back yet?

Some pronouns can function as either the subject or the object—e.g., *you, it*. The subject of a sentence is the noun of the sentence that is doing or being something.

You should try it.

It tastes great.

Possessive pronouns indicate ownership. They can be used alone—*mine, yours, his, hers, theirs, ours*—or with a noun—*my, your, his, her, their, ours*. In the latter case, they function as a determiner, which is described in detail in the below section on adjectives.

This table is *ours*.

I can't find *my* phone!

Reflexive pronouns refer back to the person being spoken or written about. These pronouns end in -*self/-selves*.

I've heard that New York City is gorgeous in the autumn, but I've never seen it for *myself*.

After moving away from home, young people have to take care of *themselves*.

Indefinite pronouns are used for things that are unknown or unspecified. Some examples are *anybody, something,* and *everything*.

I'm looking for *someone* who knows how to fix computers.

I wanted to buy some shoes today, but I couldn't find *any* that I liked.

Adjective

An **adjective** modifies a noun, making it more precise or giving more information about it. Adjectives answer these questions: What kind? Which one?

I just bought a *red* car.

I don't like *cold* weather.

One special type of word that modifies a noun is a **determiner**. In fact, some grammarians classify determiners as a separate part of speech because whereas adjectives simply describe additional qualities of a noun, a determiner is often a necessary part of a noun phrase, without which the phrase is grammatically incomplete. A determiner indicates whether a noun is definite or indefinite and can identify which noun is being discussed. It also introduces context to the noun in terms of quantity and possession. The most commonly-used determiners are articles—*a, an, the*.

I ordered *a* pizza.

She lives in *the* city.

Possessive pronouns discussed above, such as *my*, *your*, and *our*, are also determiners, along with **demonstratives**—*this, that*—and **quantifiers**—*much, many, some*. These determiners can take the place of an article.

Are you using *this* chair?

I need *some* coffee!

Adverb

Adverbs modify verbs, adjectives, and other adverbs. Words that end in *–ly* are usually adverbs. Adverbs answer these questions: When? Where? In what manner? To what degree?

She talks *quickly*.

The mountains are *incredibly* beautiful!

The students arrived *early*.

Please take your phone call *outside*.

Preposition

Prepositions show the relationship between different elements in a phrase or sentence and connect nouns or pronouns to other words in the sentence. Some examples of prepositions are words such as *after, at, behind, by, during, from, in, on, to,* and *with*.

> Let's go *to* class.
>
> Starry Night was painted *by* Vincent van Gogh *in* 1889.

Conjunction

Conjunctions join words, phrases, clauses, or sentences together, indicating the type of connection between these elements.

> I like pizza, *and* I enjoy spaghetti.
>
> I like to play baseball, *but* I'm allergic to mitts.

Some conjunctions are **coordinating**, meaning they give equal emphasis to two main clauses. Coordinating conjunctions are short, simple words that can be remembered using the mnemonic FANBOYS: *for, and, nor, but, or, yet, so*. Other conjunctions are subordinating. **Subordinating** conjunctions introduce dependent clauses and include words such as *because, since, before, after, if,* and *while*.

Interjection

An **interjection** is a short word that shows greeting or emotion. Examples of interjections include *wow, ouch, hey, oops, alas,* and *hey.*

> *Wow*! Look at that sunset!
>
> Was it your birthday yesterday? *Oops*! I forgot.

Errors in Standard English Grammar, Usage, Syntax, and Mechanics

Sentence Fragments

A **complete sentence** requires a verb and a subject that expresses a complete thought. Sometimes, the subject is omitted in the case of the implied *you*, used in sentences that are the command or imperative form—e.g., "Look!" or "Give me that." It is understood that the subject of the command is *you*, the listener or reader, so it is possible to have a structure without an explicit subject. Without these elements, though, the sentence is incomplete—it is a **sentence fragment**. While sentence fragments often occur in conversational English or creative writing, they are generally not appropriate in academic writing. Sentence fragments often occur when dependent clauses are not joined to an independent clause:

> Sentence fragment: Because the airline overbooked the flight.

The sentence above is a dependent clause that does not express a complete thought. What happened as a result of this cause? With the addition of an independent clause, this now becomes a complete sentence:

> Complete sentence: Because the airline overbooked the flight, several passengers were unable to board.

Sentences fragments may also occur through improper use of conjunctions:

I'm going to the Bahamas for spring break. And to New York City for New Year's Eve.

While the first sentence above is a complete sentence, the second one is not because it is a prepositional phrase that lacks a subject [I] and a verb [am going]. Joining the two together with the coordinating conjunction forms one grammatically-correct sentence:

I'm going to the Bahamas for spring break and to New York City for New Year's Eve.

Run-ons

A **run-on** is a sentence with too many independent clauses that are improperly connected to each other:

This winter has been very cold some farmers have suffered damage to their crops.

The sentence above has two subject-verb combinations. The first is "this winter has been"; the second is "some farmers have suffered." However, they are simply stuck next to each other without any punctuation or conjunction. Therefore, the sentence is a run-on.

Another type of run-on occurs when writers use inappropriate punctuation:

This winter has been very cold, some farmers have suffered damage to their crops.

Though a comma has been added, this sentence is still not correct. When a comma alone is used to join two independent clauses, it is known as a **comma splice**. Without an appropriate conjunction, a comma cannot join two independent clauses by itself.

Run-on sentences can be corrected by either dividing the independent clauses into two or more separate sentences or inserting appropriate conjunctions and/or punctuation. The run-on sentence can be amended by separating each subject-verb pair into its own sentence:

This winter has been very cold. Some farmers have suffered damage to their crops.

The run-on can also be fixed by adding a comma and conjunction to join the two independent clauses with each other:

This winter has been very cold, so some farmers have suffered damage to their crops.

Parallelism

Parallel structure occurs when phrases or clauses within a sentence contain the same structure. Parallelism increases readability and comprehensibility because it is easy to tell which sentence elements are paired with each other in meaning.

Jennifer enjoys cooking, knitting, and to spend time with her cat.

This sentence is not parallel because the items in the list appear in two different forms. Some are **gerunds**, which is the verb + ing: *cooking, knitting*. The other item uses the **infinitive** form, which is to + verb: *to spend*. To create parallelism, all items in the list may reflect the same form:

Jennifer enjoys cooking, knitting, and spending time with her cat.

All of the items in the list are now in gerund forms, so this sentence exhibits parallel structure. Here's another example:

> The company is looking for employees who are responsible and with a lot of experience.

Again, the items that are listed in this sentence are not parallel. "Responsible" is an adjective, yet "with a lot of experience" is a prepositional phrase. The sentence elements do not utilize parallel parts of speech.

> The company is looking for employees who are responsible and experienced.

"Responsible" and "experienced" are both adjectives, so this sentence now has parallel structure.

Dangling and Misplaced Modifiers

Modifiers enhance meaning by clarifying or giving greater detail about another part of a sentence. However, incorrectly-placed modifiers have the opposite effect and can cause confusion. A **misplaced modifier** is a modifier that is not located appropriately in relation to the word or phrase that it modifies:

> Because he was one of the greatest thinkers of Renaissance Italy, John idolized Leonardo da Vinci.

In this sentence, the modifier is "because he was one of the greatest thinkers of Renaissance Italy," and the noun it is intended to modify is "Leonardo da Vinci." However, due to the placement of the modifier next to the subject, John, it seems as if the sentence is stating that John was a Renaissance genius, not Da Vinci.

> John idolized Leonard da Vinci because he was one of the greatest thinkers of Renaissance Italy.

The modifier is now adjacent to the appropriate noun, clarifying which of the two men in this sentence is the greatest thinker.

Dangling modifiers modify a word or phrase that is not readily apparent in the sentence. That is, they "dangle" because they are not clearly attached to anything:

> After getting accepted to college, Amir's parents were proud.

The modifier here, "after getting accepted to college," should modify who got accepted. The noun immediately following the modifier is "Amir's parents"—but they are probably not the ones who are going to college.

> After getting accepted to college, Amir made his parents proud.

The subject of the sentence has been changed to Amir himself, and now the subject and its modifier are appropriately matched.

Inconsistent Verb Tense

Verb tense reflects when an action occurred or a state existed. For example, the tense known as **simple present** expresses something that is happening right now or that happens regularly:

> She *works* in a hospital.

Present continuous tense expresses something in progress. It is formed by to be + verb + -ing.

> Sorry, I can't go out right now. I *am doing* my homework.

Past tense is used to describe events that previously occurred. However, in conversational English, speakers often use present tense or a mix of past and present tense when relating past events because it gives the narrative a sense of immediacy. In formal written English, though, consistency in verb tense is necessary to avoid reader confusion.

> I traveled to Europe last summer. As soon as I stepped off the plane, I feel like I'm in a movie! I'm surrounded by quaint cafes and impressive architecture.

The passage above abruptly switches from past tense—*traveled, stepped*—to present tense—*feel, am surrounded.*

> I *traveled* to Europe last summer. As soon as I *stepped* off the plane, I *felt* like I was in a movie! I *was surrounded* by quaint cafes and impressive architecture.

All verbs are in past tense, so this passage now has consistent verb tense.

Split Infinitives

The **infinitive form** of a verb consists of "to + base verb"—e.g., to walk, to sleep, to approve. A **split infinitive** occurs when another word, usually an adverb, is placed between *to* and the verb:

> I decided *to simply walk* to work to get more exercise every day.

The infinitive *to walk* is split by the adverb *simply.*

> It was a mistake *to hastily approve* the project before conducting further preliminary research.

The infinitive *to approve* is split by *hastily.*

Although some grammarians still advise against split infinitives, this syntactic structure is common in both spoken and written English and is widely accepted in standard usage.

Subject-Verb Agreement

In English, verbs must agree with the subject. The form of a verb may change depending on whether the subject is singular or plural, or whether it is first, second, or third person. For example, the verb *to be* has various forms:

> I <u>am</u> a student.
>
> You <u>are</u> a student.
>
> She <u>is</u> a student.
>
> We <u>are</u> students.
>
> They <u>are</u> students.

Errors occur when a verb does not agree with its subject. Sometimes, the error is readily apparent:

> We is hungry.

Is is not the appropriate form of *to be* when used with the third person plural *we*.

> We are hungry.

This sentence now has correct subject-verb agreement.

However, some cases are trickier, particularly when the subject consists of a lengthy noun phrase with many modifiers:

> Students who are hoping to accompany the anthropology department on its annual summer trip to Ecuador needs to sign up by March 31st.

The verb in this sentence is *needs*. However, its subject is not the noun adjacent to it—Ecuador. The subject is the noun at the beginning of the sentence—students. Because *students* is plural, *needs* is the incorrect verb form.

> *Students* who are hoping to accompany the anthropology department on its annual summer trip to Ecuador *need* to sign up by March 31st.

This sentence now uses correct agreement between *students* and *need*.

Another case to be aware of is a **collective noun**. A collective noun refers to a group of many things or people but can be singular in itself—e.g., *family, committee, army, pair team, council, jury*. Whether or not a collective noun uses a singular or plural verb depends on how the noun is being used. If the noun refers to the group performing a collective action as one unit, it should use a singular verb conjugation:

> The family is moving to a new neighborhood.

The whole family is moving together in unison, so the singular verb form *is* is appropriate here.

> The committee has made its decision.

The verb *has* and the possessive pronoun *its* both reflect the word *committee* as a singular noun in the sentence above; however, when a collective noun refers to the group as individuals, it can take a plural verb:

> The newlywed pair spend every moment together.

This sentence emphasizes the love between two people in a pair, so it can use the plural verb *spend*.

> The council are all newly elected members.

The sentence refers to the council in terms of its individual members and uses the plural verb *are*.

Overall though, American English is more likely to pair a collective noun with a singular verb, while British English is more likely to pair a collective noun with a plural verb.

Grammar, Usage, Syntax, and Mechanics Choices

Colons and Semicolons

In a sentence, **colons** are used before a list, a summary or elaboration, or an explanation related to the preceding information in the sentence:

> There are two ways to reserve tickets for the performance: by phone or in person.
>
> One thing is clear: students are spending more on tuition than ever before.

As these examples show, a colon must be preceded by an independent clause. However, the information after the colon may be in the form of an independent clause or in the form of a list.

Semicolons can be used in two different ways—to join ideas or to separate them. In some cases, semicolons can be used to connect what would otherwise be stand-alone sentences. Each part of the sentence joined by a semicolon must be an independent clause. The use of a semicolon indicates that these two independent clauses are closely related to each other:

> The rising cost of childcare is one major stressor for parents; healthcare expenses are another source of anxiety.
>
> Classes have been canceled due to the snowstorm; check the school website for updates.

Semicolons can also be used to divide elements of a sentence in a more distinct way than simply using a comma. This usage is particularly useful when the items in a list are especially long and complex and contain other internal punctuation.

> Retirees have many modes of income: some survive solely off their retirement checks; others supplement their income through part time jobs, like working in a supermarket or substitute teaching; and others are financially dependent on the support of family members, friends, and spouses.

Its and It's

These pronouns are some of the most confused in the English language as most possessives contain the suffix –'s. However, for *it*, it is the opposite. *Its* is a possessive pronoun:

> The government is reassessing *its* spending plan.

It's is a contraction of the words *it is*:

> *It's* snowing outside.

Saw and Seen

Saw and *seen* are both conjugations of the verb *to see*, but they express different verb tenses. *Saw* is used in the simple past tense. *Seen* is the past participle form of *to see* and can be used in all perfect tenses.

> I seen her yesterday.

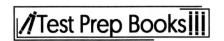

This sentence is incorrect. Because it expresses a completed event from a specified point in time in the past, it should use simple past tense:

> I *saw* her yesterday.

This sentence uses the correct verb tense. Here's how the past participle is used correctly:

> I *have seen* her before.

The meaning in this sentence is slightly changed to indicate an event from an unspecific time in the past. In this case, present perfect is the appropriate verb tense to indicate an unspecified past experience. Present perfect conjugation is created by combining *to have* + past participle.

Then and Than

Then is generally used as an adverb indicating something that happened next in a sequence or as the result of a conditional situation:

> We parked the car and *then* walked to the restaurant.
>
> If enough people register for the event, *then* we can begin planning.

Than is a conjunction indicating comparison:

> This watch is more expensive *than* that one.
>
> The bus departed later *than* I expected.

They're, Their, and There

They're is a contraction of the words *they are*:

> *They're* moving to Ohio next week.

Their is a possessive pronoun:

> The baseball players are training for *their* upcoming season.

There can function as multiple parts of speech, but it is most commonly used as an adverb indicating a location:

> Let's go to the concert! Some great bands are playing *there*.

Insure and Ensure

These terms are both verbs. *Insure* means to guarantee something against loss, harm, or damage, usually through an insurance policy that offers monetary compensation:

> The robbers made off with her prized diamond necklace, but luckily it was *insured* for one million dollars.

Ensure means to make sure, to confirm, or to be certain:

> *Ensure* that you have your passport before entering the security checkpoint.

Accept and Except

Accept is a verb meaning to take or agree to something:

I would like to *accept* your offer of employment.

Except is a preposition that indicates exclusion:

I've been to every state in America *except* Hawaii.

Affect and Effect

Affect is a verb meaning to influence or to have an impact on something:

The amount of rainfall during the growing season *affects* the flavor of wine produced from these grapes.

Effect can be used as either a noun or a verb. As a noun, *effect* is synonymous with a result:

If we implement the changes, what will the *effect* be on our profits?

As a verb, *effect* means to bring about or to make happen:

In just a few short months, the healthy committee has *effected* real change in school nutrition.

Components of Sentences

Clauses

Clauses contain a subject and a verb. An **independent clause** can function as a complete sentence on its own, but it might also be one component of a longer sentence. **Dependent clauses** cannot stand alone as complete sentences. They rely on independent clauses to complete their meaning. Dependent clauses usually begin with a subordinating conjunction. Independent and dependent clauses are sometimes also referred to as **main clauses** and **subordinate clauses**, respectively. The following structure highlights the differences:

Apiculturists raise honeybees because they love insects.

Apiculturists raise honeybees is an independent or main clause. The subject is *apiculturists*, and the verb is *raise*. It expresses a complete thought and could be a standalone sentence.

Because they love insects is a dependent or subordinate clause. If it were not attached to the independent clause, it would be a sentence fragment. While it contains a subject and verb—*they love*—this clause is dependent because it begins with the subordinate conjunction *because*. Thus, it does not express a complete thought on its own.

Another type of clause is a **relative clause**, and it is sometimes referred to as an *adjective clause* because it gives further description about the noun. A relative clause begins with a *relative pronoun*: *that, which, who, whom, whichever, whomever,* or *whoever.* It may also begin with a *relative adverb*: *where, why,* or *when.* Here's an example of a relative clause, functioning as an adjective:

The strawberries that I bought yesterday are already beginning to spoil.

Here, the relative clause is *that I bought yesterday*; the relative pronoun is *that*. The subject is *I*, and the verb is *bought*. The clause modifies the subject *strawberries* by answering the question, "Which strawberries?" Here's an example of a relative clause with an adverb:

> The tutoring center is a place where students can get help with homework.

The relative clause is *where students can get help with homework*, and it gives more information about a place by describing what kind of place it is. It begins with the relative adverb *where* and contains the noun *students* along with its verb phrase *can get*.

Relative clauses may be further divided into two types: essential or nonessential. **Essential clauses** contain identifying information without which the sentence would lose significant meaning or not make sense. These are also sometimes referred to as **restrictive clauses**. The sentence above contains an example of an essential relative clause. Here is what happens when the clause is removed:

> The tutoring center is a place where students can get help with homework.

> The tutoring center is a place.

Without the relative clause, the sentence loses the majority of its meaning; thus, the clause is essential or restrictive.

Nonessential clauses—also referred to as **non-restrictive clauses**—offer additional information about a noun in the sentence, but they do not significantly control the overall meaning of the sentence. The following example indicates a nonessential clause:

> New York City, which is located in the northeastern part of the country, is the most populated city in America.

> New York City is the most populated city in America.

Even without the relative clause, the sentence is still understandable and continues to communicate its central message about New York City. Thus, it is a nonessential clause.

Punctuation differs between essential and nonessential relative clauses, too. Nonessential clauses are set apart from the sentence using commas whereas essential clauses are not separated with commas. Also, the relative pronoun *that* is generally used for essential clauses, while *which* is used for nonessential clauses. The following examples clarify this distinction:

> *Romeo and Juliet* is my favorite play *that Shakespeare wrote*.

The relative clause *that Shakespeare wrote* contains essential, controlling information about the noun *play*, limiting it to those plays by Shakespeare. Without it, it would seem that *Romeo and Juliet* is the speaker's favorite play out of every play ever written, not simply from Shakespeare's repertoire.

> *Romeo and Juliet*, *which Shakespeare wrote*, is my favorite play.

Here, the nonessential relative clause—"which Shakespeare wrote"—modifies *Romeo and Juliet*. It doesn't provide controlling information about the play, but simply offers further background details. Thus, commas are needed.

Phrases

Phrases are groups of words that do not contain the subject-verb combination required for clauses. Phrases are classified by the part of speech that begins or controls the phrase.

A **noun phrase** consists of a noun and all its modifiers—adjectives, adverbs, and determiners. Noun phrases can serve many functions in a sentence, acting as subjects, objects, and object complements:

> *The shallow yellow bowl* sits on the top shelf.
>
> Nina just bought *some incredibly fresh organic produce*.

Prepositional phrases are made up of a preposition and its object. The object of a preposition might be a noun, noun phrase, pronoun, or gerund. Prepositional phrases may function as either an adjective or an adverb:

> Jack picked up the book *in front of him*.

The prepositional phrase *in front of him* acts as an adjective indicating which book Jack picked up.

> The dog ran into the back yard.

The phrase *into the backyard* describes where the dog ran, so it acts as an adverb.

Verb phrases include all of the words in a verb group, even if they are not directly adjacent to each other:

> I *should have woken up* earlier this morning.
>
> The company *is* now *offering* membership discounts for new enrollers.

This sentence's verb phrase is *is offering*. Even though they are separated by the word *now*, they function together as a single verb phrase.

Structures of Sentences

All sentences contain the same basic elements: a subject and a verb. The **subject** is who or what the sentence is about; the **verb** describes the subject's action or condition. However, these elements, subjects and verbs, can be combined in different ways. The following graphic describes the different types of sentence structures.

Sentence Structure	Independent Clauses	Dependent Clauses
Simple	1	0
Compound	2 or more	0
Complex	1	1 or more
Compound-Complex	2 or more	1 or more

A **simple sentence** expresses a complete thought and consists of one subject and verb combination:

> The children ate pizza.

The subject is *children*. The verb is *ate*.

Either the subject or the verb may be **compound**—that is, it could have more than one element:

> *The children and their parents* ate pizza.
>
> The children *ate pizza and watched a movie*.

All of these are still simple sentences. Despite having either compound subjects or compound verbs, each sentence still has only one subject and verb combination.

Compound sentences combine two or more simple sentences to form one sentence that has multiple subject-verb combinations:

> *The children ate pizza,* and *their parents watched a movie.*

This structure is comprised of two independent clauses: (1) *the children ate pizza* and (2) *their parents watched a movie.* Compound sentences join different subject-verb combinations using a comma and a coordinating conjunction.

> I called my mom, *but* she didn't answer the phone.
>
> The weather was stormy, *so* we canceled our trip to the beach.

A **complex sentence** consists of an independent clause and one or more dependent clauses. Dependent clauses join a sentence using **subordinating conjunctions**. Some examples of subordinating conjunctions are *although*, *unless*, *as soon as*, *since*, *while*, *when*, *because*, *if*, and *before*.

> I missed class yesterday *because* my mother was ill.
>
> *Before* traveling to a new country, you need to exchange your money to the local currency.

The order of clauses determines their punctuation. If the dependent clause comes first, it should be separated from the independent clause with a comma. However, if the complex sentence consists of an independent clause followed by a dependent clause, then a comma is not always necessary.

A **compound-complex sentence** can be created by joining two or more independent clauses with at least one dependent clause:

> After the earthquake struck, thousands of homes were destroyed, and many families were left without a place to live.

The first independent clause in the compound structure includes a dependent clause—*after the earthquake struck*. Thus, the structure is both complex and compound.

Context Clues

Familiarity with common prefixes, suffixes, and root words assists tremendously in unraveling the meaning of an unfamiliar word and making an educated guess as to its meaning. However, some words do not contain many easily-identifiable clues that point to their meaning. In this case, rather than looking at the elements within the word, it is useful to consider elements around the word—i.e., its context. **Context** refers to the other words and information within the sentence or surrounding sentences that indicate the unknown word's probable meaning. The following sentences provide context for the potentially-unfamiliar word *quixotic*:

> Rebecca had never been one to settle into a predictable, ordinary life. Her quixotic personality led her to leave behind a job with a prestigious law firm in Manhattan and move halfway around the world to pursue her dream of becoming a sushi chef in Tokyo.

A reader unfamiliar with the word *quixotic* doesn't have many clues to use in terms of affixes or root meaning. The suffix *–ic* indicates that the word is an adjective, but that is it. In this case, then, a reader would need to look at surrounding information to obtain some clues about the word. Other adjectives in the passage include *predictable* and *ordinary*, things that Rebecca was definitely not, as indicated by "Rebecca had never been one to settle." Thus, a first clue might be that *quixotic* means the opposite of predictable.

The second sentence doesn't offer any other modifier of *personality* other than *quixotic*, but it does include a story that reveals further information about her personality. She had a stable, respectable job, but she decided to give it up to follow her dream. Combining these two ideas together, then—*unpredictable* and *dream-seeking*—gives the reader a general idea of what *quixotic* probably means. In fact, the root of the word is the character Don Quixote, a romantic dreamer who goes on an impulsive adventure.

While context clues are useful for making an approximate definition for newly-encountered words, these types of clues also come in handy when encountering common words that have multiple meanings. The word *reservation* is used differently in each the following sentences:

- That restaurant is booked solid for the next month; it's impossible to make a reservation unless you know somebody.
- The hospital plans to open a branch office inside the reservation to better serve Native American patients who cannot easily travel to the main hospital fifty miles away.
- Janet Clark is a dependable, knowledgeable worker, and I recommend her for the position of team leader without reservation.

All three sentences use the word to express different meanings. In fact, most words in English have more than one meaning—sometimes meanings that are completely different from one another. Thus, context can provide clues as to which meaning is appropriate in a given situation. A quick search in the dictionary reveals several possible meanings for *reservation*:

- An exception or qualification
- A tract of public land set aside, such as for the use of American Indian tribes
- An arrangement for accommodations, such as in a hotel, on a plane, or at a restaurant

Sentence A mentions a restaurant, making the third definition the correct one in this case. In sentence B, some context clues include Native Americans, as well as the implication that a reservation is a place—"inside the reservation," both of which indicate that the second definition should be used here. Finally, sentence C uses *without reservation* to mean "completely" or "without exception," so the first definition can be applied here.

Using context clues in this way can be especially useful for words that have multiple, widely varying meanings. If a word has more than one definition and two of those definitions are the opposite of each other, it is known as an **auto-antonym**—a word that can also be its own antonym. In the case of auto-antonyms, context clues are crucial to determine which definition to employ in a given sentence. For example, the word *sanction* can either mean "to approve or allow" or "a penalty." Approving and penalizing have opposite meanings, so *sanction* is an example of an auto-antonym. The following sentences reflect the distinction in meaning:

- In response to North Korea's latest nuclear weapons test, world leaders have called for harsher sanctions to punish the country for its actions.
- The general has sanctioned a withdrawal of troops from the area.

A context clue can be found in sentence A, which mentions "to punish." A punishment is similar to a penalty, so sentence A is using the word *sanction* according to this definition.

Other examples of auto-antonyms include *oversight*—"to supervise something" or "a missed detail," *resign*—"to quit" or "to sign again, as a contract," and *screen*—"to show" or "to conceal." For these types of words, recognizing context clues is an important way to avoid misinterpreting the sentence's meaning.

Syntax

Syntax refers to the arrangement of words, phrases, and clauses to form a sentence. Knowledge of syntax can also give insight into a word's meaning. The section above considered several examples using the word *reservation* and applied context clues to determine the word's appropriate meaning in each sentence. Here is an example of how the placement of a word can impact its meaning and grammatical function:

- The development team has reserved the conference room for today.
- Her quiet and reserved nature is sometimes misinterpreted as unfriendliness when people first meet her.

In addition to using *reserved* to mean different things, each sentence also uses the word to serve a different grammatical function. In sentence A, *reserved* is part of the verb phrase *has reserved*, indicating the meaning "to set aside for a particular use." In sentence B, *reserved* acts as a modifier within the noun phrase "her quiet and reserved nature." Because the word is being used as an adjective to describe a personality characteristic, it calls up a different definition of the word—"restrained or lacking familiarity with others." As this example shows, the function of a word within the overall sentence structure can allude to its meaning. It is also useful to refer to the earlier chart about suffixes and parts of speech as another clue into what grammatical function a word is serving in a sentence.

Analyzing Nuances of Word Meaning and Figures of Speech

By now, it should be apparent that language is not as simple as one word directly correlated to one meaning. Rather, one word can express a vast array of diverse meanings, and similar meanings can be expressed through different words. However, there are very few words that express exactly the same meaning. For this reason, it is important to be able to pick up on the nuances of word meaning.

Many words contain two levels of meaning: connotation and denotation as discussed previously in the informational texts and rhetoric section. A word's **denotation** is its most literal meaning—the definition that can readily be found in the dictionary. A word's **connotation** includes all of its emotional and cultural associations.

In literary writing, authors rely heavily on connotative meaning to create mood and characterization. The following are two descriptions of a rainstorm:

- The rain slammed against the windowpane and the wind howled through the fireplace. A pair of hulking oaks next to the house cast eerie shadows as their branches trembled in the wind.

- The rain pattered against the windowpane and the wind whistled through the fireplace. A pair of stately oaks next to the house cast curious shadows as their branches swayed in the wind.

Description A paints a creepy picture for readers with strongly emotional words like *slammed*, connoting force and violence. *Howled* connotes pain or wildness, and *eerie* and *trembled* connote fear. Overall, the connotative language in this description serves to inspire fear and anxiety.

However, as can be seen in description B, swapping out a few key words for those with different connotations completely changes the feeling of the passage. *Slammed* is replaced with the more cheerful *pattered*, and *hulking* has been swapped out for *stately*. Both words imply something large, but *hulking* is more intimidating whereas *stately* is more respectable. *Curious* and *swayed* seem more playful than the language used in the earlier description. Although both descriptions represent roughly the same situation, the nuances of the emotional language used throughout the passages create a very different sense for readers.

Selective choice of connotative language can also be extremely impactful in other forms of writing, such as editorials or persuasive texts. Through connotative language, writers reveal their biases and opinions while trying to inspire feelings and actions in readers:

- Parents won't stop complaining about standardized tests.
- Parents continue to raise concerns about standardized tests.

Readers should be able to identify the nuance in meaning between these two sentences. The first one carries a more negative feeling, implying that parents are being bothersome or whiny. Readers of the second sentence, though, might come away with the feeling that parents are concerned and involved in their children's education. Again, the aggregate of even subtle cues can combine to give a specific emotional impression to readers, so from an early age, students should be aware of how language can be used to influence readers' opinions.

Another form of non-literal expression can be found in **figures of speech**. As with connotative language, figures of speech tend to be shared within a cultural group and may be difficult to pick up on for learners outside of that group. In some cases, a figure of speech may be based on the literal denotation of the words it contains, but in other cases, a figure of speech is far removed from its literal meaning. A case in point is **irony**, where what is said is the exact opposite of what is meant:

> The new tax plan is poorly planned, based on faulty economic data, and unable to address the financial struggles of middle-class families. Yet legislators remain committed to passing this brilliant proposal.

When the writer refers to the proposal as brilliant, the opposite is implied—the plan is "faulty" and "poorly planned." By using irony, the writer means that the proposal is anything but brilliant by using the word in a non-literal sense.

Another figure of speech is **hyperbole**—extreme exaggeration or overstatement. Statements like, "I love you to the moon and back" or "Let's be friends for a million years" utilize hyperbole to convey a greater depth of emotion, without literally committing oneself to space travel or a life of immortality.

Figures of speech may sometimes use one word in place of another. **Synecdoche**, for example, uses a part of something to refer to its whole. The expression "Don't hurt a hair on her head!" implies protecting more than just an individual hair, but rather her entire body. "The art teacher is training a class of Picassos" uses Picasso, one individual notable artist, to stand in for the entire category of talented artists. Another figure of speech using word replacement is **metonymy**, where a word is replaced with something closely associated to it. For example, news reports may use the word "Washington" to refer to the American government or "the crown" to refer to the British monarch.

Using Print and Digital Reference Materials

Appropriate Print or Digital Reference Material

Reference materials are indispensable tools for beginners and experts alike. Becoming a competent English communicator doesn't necessarily mean memorizing every single rule about spelling, grammar, or punctuation—it means knowing where and how to find accurate information about the rules of English usage. Students of English have a wide variety of references materials available to them, and, in an increasingly digitized world, more and more of these materials can be found online or as easily-accessible phone applications. Educators should introduce students to different types of reference materials as well as when and how to use them.

Spell Check

Most word processing software programs come equipped with a spell-checking feature. Web browsers and personal devices like smartphones and tablets may also have a spell checker enabled. **Spell check** automatically detects misspelled words and suggests alternate spellings. Many writers have come to rely on spell check due to its convenience and ease of use. However, there are some caveats to using spell check—it only checks whether a word is spelled correctly, not if it is used correctly. As discussed above, there are numerous examples of commonly-confused words in English, the misuse of which may not be detected by a spell checker. Many word processing programs do integrate spell checking and grammar checking functions, however. Thus, although running a spell check is an important part of reviewing any piece of writing, it should not be the only step of the review process. Further, spell checkers recommend correctly-spelled words based on an approximation of the misspelled word, so writers need to be somewhat close to the correct spelling in order for spell check to be useful.

Dictionary

Dictionaries are readily available in print, digital formats, and as mobile apps. A dictionary offers a wealth of information to users. First, in the absence of spell-checking software, a dictionary can be used to identify correct spelling and to determine the word's pronunciation—often written using the International Phonetic Alphabet (IPA). Perhaps the best-known feature of a dictionary is that its explanation of a word's meanings as a single word can have multiple definitions. A dictionary organizes these definitions based on their parts of speech and then arranges them from most to least commonly used meanings or from oldest to most modern usage. Many dictionaries also offer information about a word's etymology and usage. With all these functions, then, a dictionary is a basic, essential tool in many situations. Students can turn to a dictionary when they encounter an unfamiliar word or when they see a familiar word used in a new way.

There are many dictionaries to choose from, but perhaps the most highly respected source is the *Oxford English Dictionary* (OED). The OED is a historical dictionary, and as such, all entries include quotes of the word as it has been used throughout history. Users of the OED can get a deeper sense of a word's evolution over time and in different parts of the world. Another standard dictionary in America is *Merriam-Webster*.

Thesaurus

Whereas a dictionary entry lists a word's definitions, a **thesaurus** entry lists a word's **synonyms** and **antonyms**—i.e., words with similar and opposite meanings, respectively. A dictionary can be used to find out what a word means and where it came from, and a thesaurus can be used to understand a word's relationship to other words. A thesaurus can be a powerful vocabulary-building tool. By becoming familiar with synonyms and antonyms, students will be more equipped to use a broad range of vocabulary in their speech and writing. Of course, one thing to be aware of when using a thesaurus is that most words do not have exact synonyms. Rather, there are slight nuances of meaning that can make one word more appropriate than another in a given context. In this case, it is often to the user's advantage to consult a thesaurus side-by-side with a dictionary to confirm any differences in usage between two synonyms. Some digital sources, such as *Dictionary.com*, integrate a dictionary and a thesaurus.

Generally, though, a thesaurus is a useful tool to help writers add variety and precision to their word choice. Consulting a thesaurus can help students elevate their writing to an appropriate academic level by replacing vague or overused words with more expressive or academic ones. Also, word processors often offer a built-in thesaurus, making it easy for writers to look up synonyms and vary word choice as they work.

Glossary

A **glossary** is similar to a dictionary in that it offers an explanation of terms. However, while a dictionary attempts to cover every word in a language, a glossary only focuses on those terms relevant to a specific field. Also, a glossary entry is more likely to offer a longer explanation of a term and its relevance within that field. Glossaries are often found at the back of textbooks or other nonfiction publications in order to explain new or unfamiliar terms to readers. A glossary may also be an entire book on its own that covers all of the essential terms and concepts within a particular profession, field, or other specialized area of knowledge. For learners seeking general definitions of terms from any context, then, a dictionary is an appropriate reference source, but for students of specialized fields, a glossary will usually provide more in-depth information.

Style Manual

Many rules of English usage are standard, but other rules may be more subjective. An example can be seen in the following structures:

- I went to the store and bought eggs, milk, and bread.
- I went to the store and bought eggs, milk and bread.

The final comma in a list before *and* or *or* is known as an Oxford comma or serial comma. To determine the appropriate use of the Oxford comma, writers can consult a style manual.

A **style manual** is a comprehensive collection of guidelines for language use and document formatting. Some fields refer to a common style guide—e.g., the Associated Press or *AP Stylebook*, a standard in American journalism. Individual organizations may rely on their own house style. Regardless, the purpose of a style manual is to ensure uniformity across all documents. Style manuals explain things such as how to format titles, when to write out numbers or use numerals, and how to cite sources. Because there are many different style guides, students should know how and when to consult an appropriate guide. The Chicago Manual of Style is common in the publication of books and academic journals. The Modern Language Association style (MLA) is another commonly used academic style format, while the American Psychological Association style (APA) may be used for scientific publications. Familiarity with using a style guide is particularly important for students who are college bound or pursuing careers in academic or professional writing.

In the examples above, the Oxford comma is recommended by the Chicago Manual of Style, so sentence A would be correct if the writer is using this style. But the comma is not recommended by the *AP Stylebook*, so sentence B would be correct if the writer is using the AP style.

General Grammar and Style References

Any language arts textbook should offer general grammatical and stylistic advice to students, but there are a few well-respected texts that can also be used for reference. *Elements of Style* by William Strunk is regularly assigned to students as a guide on effective written communication, including how to avoid common usage mistakes and how to make the most of parallel structure. *Garner's Modern American Usage* by Bryan Garner is another text that guides students on how to achieve precision and understandability in their writing. Whereas other reference sources discussed above tend to address specific language concerns, these types of texts offer a more holistic approach to cultivating effective language skills.

Electronic Resources

With print texts, it is easy to identify the authors and their credentials, as well as the publisher and their reputation. With electronic resources like websites, though, it can be trickier to assess the reliability of information. Students should be alert when gathering information from the Internet. Understanding the significance of website **domains**—which include identification strings of a site—can help. Website domains ending in *.edu* are educational sites and tend to offer more reliable research in their field. A *.org* ending tends to be used by nonprofit organizations and other community groups, *.com* indicates a privately-owned website, and a *.gov* site is run by the government. Websites affiliated with official organizations, research groups, or institutes of learning are more likely to offer relevant, fact-checked, and reliable information.

Identifying Dialect and Diction

Identifying Variation in Dialect and Diction

Language arts educators often seem to be in the position of teaching the "right" way to use English, particularly in lessons about grammar and vocabulary. However, all it takes is back-to-back viewings of speeches by the queen of England and the president of the United States or side-by-side readings of a contemporary poem and one written in the 1600s to come to the conclusion that there is no single, fixed, correct form of spoken or written English. Instead, language varies and evolves across different regions and time periods. It also varies between cultural groups depending on factors such as race, ethnicity, age, and socioeconomic status. Students should come away from a language arts class with more than a strictly prescriptive view of language; they should have an appreciation for its rich diversity.

It is important to understand some key terms in discussing linguistic variety.

Language is a tool for communication. It may be spoken, unspoken—as with body language—written, or codified in other ways. Language is symbolic in the sense that it can describe objects, ideas, and events that are not actually present, have not actually occurred, or only exist in the mind of the speaker. All languages are governed by systematic rules of grammar and semantics. These rules allow speakers to manipulate a finite number of elements, such as sounds or written symbols, to create an infinite number of meanings.

A **dialect** is a distinct variety of a language in terms of patterns of grammar, vocabulary, and/or **phonology**—the sounds used by its speakers—that distinguish it from other forms of that language. Two dialects are not considered separate languages if they are mutually intelligible—if speakers of each dialect are able to understand one another. A dialect is not a subordinate version of a language. Examples of English dialects include Scottish English and American Southern English.

By definition, Standard English is a dialect. It is one variety of English with its own usage of grammar, vocabulary, and pronunciation. Given that Standard English is taught in schools and used in places like government, journalism, and other professional workplaces, it is often elevated above other English dialects. Linguistically, though, there is nothing that makes Standard English more correct or advanced than other dialects.

A **pidgin** is formed when speakers of different languages begin utilizing a simplified mixture of elements from both languages to communicate with each other. In North America, pidgins occurred when Africans were brought to European colonies as slaves, leading to a mixture of African and European languages. Historically, pidgins also sprung up in areas of international trade. A pidgin is communication born of necessity and lacks the full complexity or standardized rules that govern a language.

When a pidgin becomes widely used and is taught to children as their native language, it becomes a Creole. An example is Haitian Creole, a language based on French and including elements of West African languages.

An **accent** is a unique speech pattern, particularly in terms of tone or intonation. Speakers from different regions tend to have different accents, as do learners of English from different native languages. In some cases, accents are mutually intelligible, but in other cases, speakers with different accents might have some difficulty in understanding one another.

Colloquial language is language that is used conversationally or familiarly—e.g., "What's up?"—in contrast to formal, professional, or academic language—"How are you this evening?"

Vernacular refers to the native, everyday language of a place. Historically, for instance, Bibles and religious services across Europe were primarily offered in Latin, even centuries after the fall of the Roman Empire. After the revolution of the printing press and the widespread availability of vernacular translations of the Bible in the fifteenth and sixteenth centuries, everyday citizens were able to study from Bibles in their own language without needing specialized training in Latin.

A **regionalism** is a word or expression used in a particular region. In the United States, for instance, examples of regionalisms might be *soda*, *pop*, or *Coke*—terms that vary in popularity according to region.

Jargon is vocabulary used within a specialized field, such as computer programming or mechanics. Jargon may consist of specialized words or of everyday words that have a different meaning in this specialized context.

Slang refers to non-standard expressions that are not used in elevated speech and writing. Slang creates linguistic in-groups and out-groups of people, those who can understand the slang terms and those who can't. Slang is often tied to a specific time period. For example, "groovy" and "far out" are connected to the 1970s, and "as if!" and "4-1-1-" are connected to the 1990s.

A language arts classroom should demonstrate the history and evolution of language, rather than presenting fixed, unchangeable linguistic regulations. Particularly for students who feel intimidated or excluded by Standard English, instructors can make lessons more relatable or inclusive by allowing students to share or explore their own patterns of language. Students can be encouraged to act as linguists or anthropologists by getting involved in projects. Some examples include asking them to identify and compare slang in their generation to slang from their parents' generation, to exchange information about their dialect with students who come from different cultural backgrounds, or to conduct a linguistic survey of their friends, family, or neighbors. Language arts class can also be integrated with history topics by having students research unfamiliar slang or words that have shifted in meaning from the past until now—a type of study particularly useful when reading a text from a past era.

Understanding Dialect and its Appropriateness

While students should come away from class feeling supported in their linguistic diversity, the reality is that certain forms of language are viewed differently depending on the context. Lessons learned in the classroom have a real-life application to a student's future, so he or she should know where, when, and how to utilize different forms of language.

For students preparing for college, knowledge of the conventions of Standard English is essential. The same is true for students who plan to enter professional job fields. Without necessarily having a word for it, many students are already familiar with the concept of **code-switching**—altering speech patterns depending upon context. For example, a person might use a different accent or slang with neighborhood friends than with coworkers or pick up new vocabulary and speech patterns after moving to a new region, either unconsciously or consciously. In this way, speakers have an innate understanding of how their language use helps them fit into any given situation.

Instructors can design activities that help students pay attention to their language use in a given context. When discussing a novel in class, students might be encouraged to spend a few minutes freewriting in a journal to generate ideas and express their unedited thoughts. Later, though, students will then be asked to present those thoughts in a formal writing assignment that requires adherence to Standard English grammar, employing academic vocabulary and expressions appropriate to literary discussions. Alternatively, students might design an advertisement that appeals to teenagers and another one that appeals to adults, utilizing different language in each. In this way, students can learn how to reformulate their thoughts using the language appropriate to the task at hand.

Awareness of dialect can also help students as readers, too. Many writers of literary fiction and nonfiction utilize dialect and colloquialisms to add verisimilitude to their writing. This is especially true for authors who focus on a particular region or cultural group in their works, also known as **regionalism** or **local color literature**. Examples include Zora Neale Hurston's *Their Eyes Were Watching God* and the short stories of Kate Chopin. Students can be asked to consider how the speech patterns in a text affect a reader's understanding of the characters—how the pattern reflects a character's background and place in society. They might consider a reader's impression of the region—how similar or different it is from the reader's region or what can be inferred about the region based on how people speak. In some cases, unfamiliar dialect may be very difficult for readers to understand on the page but becomes much more intelligible when read aloud—as in the reading of Shakespeare.

Reading passages together in class and then finding recordings or videos of the dialect presented in the text can help familiarize students with different speech patterns. And of course, students should also consider how use of dialect affects the audience or if it is directed to a specific audience. Who was the intended audience for *Their Eyes Were Watching God*, a novel that recreates the speech patterns of African Americans in early 1900s Florida? How might the novel be understood differently by readers who recognize that dialect than by readers who are encountering it for the first time? What would be lost if the characters didn't converse in their local dialect? Being alert to these questions creates students who are attuned to the nuances of language use in everyday life.

Understanding the Use of Affixes, Context, and Syntax

Affixes

Individual words are constructed from building blocks of meaning. An **affix** is an element that is added to a root or stem word that can change the word's meaning.

For example, the stem word *fix* is a verb meaning *to repair*. When the ending *–able* is added, it becomes the adjective *fixable*, meaning "capable of being repaired." Adding *un–* to the beginning changes the word to *unfixable*, meaning "incapable of being repaired." In this way, affixes attach to the word stem to create a new word and a new meaning. Knowledge of affixes can assist in deciphering the meaning of unfamiliar words.

Affixes are also related to inflection. **Inflection** is the modification of a base word to express a different grammatical or syntactical function. For example, countable nouns such as *car* and *airport* become plural with the addition of *–s* at the end: *cars* and *airports*.

Verb tense is also expressed through inflection. *Regular verbs*—those that follow a standard inflection pattern—can be changed to past tense using the affixes *–ed*, *–d*, or *–ied*, as in *cooked* and *studied*. Verbs can also be modified for continuous tenses by using *–ing*, as in *working* or *exploring*. Thus, affixes are used not only to express meaning but also to reflect a word's grammatical purpose.

A **prefix** is an affix attached to the beginning of a word. The meanings of English prefixes mainly come from Greek and Latin origins. The chart below contains a few of the most commonly used English prefixes.

Prefix	**Meaning**	**Example**
a-	not	amoral, asymptomatic
anti-	against	antidote, antifreeze
auto-	self	automobile, automatic
circum-	around	circumference, circumspect
co-, com-, con-	together	coworker, companion
contra-	against	contradict, contrary
de-	negation or reversal	deflate, deodorant
extra-	outside, beyond	extraterrestrial, extracurricular
in-, im-, il-, ir-	not	impossible, irregular
inter-	between	international, intervene
intra-	within	intramural, intranet
mis-	wrongly	mistake, misunderstand
mono-	one	monolith, monopoly
non-	not	nonpartisan, nonsense
pre-	before	preview, prediction
re-	again	review, renew
semi-	half	semicircle, semicolon
sub-	under	subway, submarine
super-	above	superhuman, superintendent
trans-	across, beyond, through	trans-Siberian, transform
un-	not	unwelcome, unfriendly

While the addition of a prefix alters the meaning of the base word, the addition of a **suffix** may also affect a word's part of speech. For example, adding a suffix can change the noun *material* into the verb *materialize* and back to a noun again in *materialization*.

Suffix	Part of Speech	Meaning	Example
-able, -ible	adjective	having the ability to	honorable, flexible
-acy, -cy	noun	state or quality	intimacy, dependency
-al, -ical	adjective	having the quality of	historical, tribal
-en	verb	to cause to become	strengthen, embolden
-er, -ier	adjective	comparative	happier, longer
-est, -iest	adjective	superlative	sunniest, hottest
-ess	noun	female	waitress, actress
-ful	adjective	full of, characterized by	beautiful, thankful
-fy, -ify	verb	to cause, to come to be	liquefy, intensify
-ism	noun	doctrine, belief, action	Communism, Buddhism
-ive, -ative, -itive	adjective	having the quality of	creative, innovative
-ize	verb	to convert into, to subject to	Americanize, dramatize
-less	adjective	without, missing	emotionless, hopeless
-ly	adverb	in the manner of	quickly, energetically
-ness	noun	quality or state	goodness, darkness
-ous, -ious, -eous	adjective	having the quality of	spontaneous, pious
-ship	noun	status or condition	partnership, ownership
-tion	noun	action or state	renovation, promotion
-y	adjective	characterized by	smoky, dreamy

Through knowledge of prefixes and suffixes, a student's vocabulary can be instantly expanded with an understanding of **etymology**—the origin of words. This, in turn, can be used to add sentence structure variety to academic writing.

Practice Questions

1. Read this paragraph.

   (1) *Romeo and Juliet*'s a well known tragedy written by William Shakespeare. (2) The drama depicts a story of two teenagers from families of different social classes. (3) Romeo and Juliet fall in love at a masquerade ball and, soon after, run away to get married. (4) Tragically, their love story quickly ends when a series of events leads to their deaths.

How should the paragraph be revised?

a. Sentence 1: Change ***Juliet's*** to **Juliet** *is* AND ***well known*** to **well-known**.
b. Sentence 2: Change ***two*** to **too** AND ***from*** to **of**.
c. Sentence 3: Change ***fall*** to **fell** AND ***run*** to **ran**.
d. Sentence 4: Delete the comma after ***Tragically*** AND change ***ends*** to **end**.

2. Read this paragraph.

   (1) The respiratory system is vital to the human body. (2) When air is inhaled the lungs extract oxygen from the air and send it into the blood. (3) The heart then pumps the blood through a series of veins and arteries to deliver the oxygen to the body. (4) Once the oxygen has been removed from the blood, carbon dioxide is exhaled.

Which sentence should be revised to correct an error in sentence structure?

a. Sentence 1
b. Sentence 2
c. Sentence 3
d. Sentence 4

3. Read these sentences.

   People who text while driving look away from the road for a minimum of five seconds.

   Driving fifty-five miles per hour, it takes at least five seconds to travel the length of a football field.

What is the best way to combine the sentences to clarify the relationship between the ideas?

a. It takes five seconds to travel the length of a football field, which is the same amount of time it takes to send a text while driving.
b. It is as dangerous to text and drive as it is to drive fifty-five miles per hour, the length of a football field.
c. Sending a text while driving is equivalent to taking your eyes off the road while driving the length of a football field at fifty-five miles per hour.
d. It takes five seconds to travel the length of a football field without looking, so texting while driving only takes about five seconds.

4. Read this sentence.

Mr. Wilkinson arrived late to work due to the fact that he felt it necessary to stop and purchase an assortment of breakfast items for the class as a reward for their excellent test scores last week.

Which revision uses the most concise language?

a. Mr. Wilkinson arrived late to work due to the fact that he felt it necessary to stop and get breakfast for the class.
b. He felt it necessary to stop and purchase breakfast items for the class as a reward for their excellent test scores last week.
c. Mr. Wilkinson stopped to purchase breakfast for the class as a reward.
d. Mr. Wilkinson was late to work because he stopped to buy breakfast for his class as a reward for their good test scores last week.

5. Read this paragraph.

(1) The American Flag is a symbol of unity strength and courage for the United States. (2) The flag design consists of thirteen red and white horizontal stripes and fifty white stars against a blue background. (3) The original design of the flag only had thirteen stars to represent the original thirteen colonies. (4) However, after the Civil War, the design was revised to display fifty white stars to represent the fifty states.

How should the paragraph be revised?

a. Sentence 1: Change ***Flag*** to **flag** AND ***unity strength and courage*** to **unity, strength, and courage**.
b. Sentence 2: Insert a comma after ***red*** AND insert a comma after ***stripes***.
c. Sentence 3: Change ***had*** to **has** AND ***represent*** to **represented**.
d. Sentence 4: Remove the comma after ***War*** AND insert a comma after ***stars***.

Answer Explanations

1. A: Choice *A* is the correct answer. The *'s* in *Juliet's* suggests a contraction using the word *is*. Proper nouns cannot be part of a contraction, so *Juliet's* should be changed to *Juliet is*. The word *well* is an adverb that modifies known, and *known* is an adjective. They should be joined with a hyphen to describe the word, *tragedy*.

2. B: Choice *B* is correct because sentence 2 is punctuated incorrectly. This sentence is a complex sentence, or a sentence consisting of a dependent and independent clause. The phrase, *When air is inhaled*, is a clause because it starts with the subordinating conjunction, *when*. The phrase cannot stand alone as a complete sentence, so a comma is needed after the word *inhaled*.

3. C: Choice *C* is correct. These two sentences aim to provide a visual of how far a driver can travel while reading a text. Combining these sentences clarifies the idea that the amount of time it takes to drive the length of a football field is the minimum amount of time it takes to read or send a text while driving.

4. D: Choice *D* is the most concise way to convey the idea presented in the sentence. Choice *A* is incorrect because the revision only eliminates some of the wordiness in the sentence. Choice *B* is incorrect because it eliminates too much information, such as Mr. Wilkinson's name and the fact that he was late to work. Choice *C* is also incorrect because it leaves out some important information, such as the fact that Mr. Wilkinson was late to work, and the class was being rewarded for good test grades.

5. A: Choice *A* is correct because the word *Flag* does not need to be capitalized, and commas are needed to separate three or more words in a list, such as *unity, strength, and courage*.

Writing

Text Types and Purposes

Text Types

Depending on what the author is attempting to accomplish, certain formats or text structures work better than others. For example, a sequence structure might work for narration but not when identifying similarities and differences between dissimilar concepts. Similarly, a comparison-contrast structure is not useful for narration. It's the author's job to put the right information in the correct format.

Readers should be familiar with the five main literary structures:

1. **Sequence structure** (sometimes referred to as the order structure) is when the order of events proceeds in a predictable manner. In many cases, this means the text goes through the plot elements: exposition, rising action, climax, falling action, and resolution. Readers are introduced to characters, setting, and conflict in the exposition. In the rising action, there's an increase in tension and suspense. The climax is the height of tension and the point of no return. Tension decreases during the falling action. In the resolution, any conflicts presented in the exposition are solved, and the story concludes. An informative text that is structured sequentially will often go in order from one step to the next.

2. In the **problem-solution structure**, authors identify a potential problem and suggest a solution. This form of writing is usually divided into two paragraphs and can be found in informational texts. For example, cell phone, cable, and satellite providers use this structure in manuals to help customers troubleshoot or identify problems with services or products.

3. When authors want to discuss similarities and differences between separate concepts, they arrange thoughts in a **comparison-contrast paragraph structure**. **Venn diagrams** are an effective graphic organizer for comparison-contrast structures, because they feature two overlapping circles that can be used to organize and group similarities and differences. A comparison-contrast essay organizes one paragraph based on similarities and another based on differences. A comparison-contrast essay can also be arranged with the similarities and differences of individual traits addressed within individual paragraphs. Words such as *however*, *but*, and *nevertheless* help signal a contrast in ideas.

4. The **descriptive writing structure** is designed to appeal to one's senses. Much like an artist who constructs a painting, good descriptive writing builds an image in the reader's mind by appealing to the five senses: sight, hearing, taste, touch, and smell. However, overly descriptive writing can become tedious; whereas sparse descriptions can make settings and characters seem flat. Good authors strike a balance by applying descriptions only to passages, characters, and settings that are integral to the plot.

5. Passages that use the **cause and effect structure** are simply asking *why* by demonstrating some type of connection between ideas. Words such as *if*, *since*, *because*, *then*, or *consequently* indicate relationship. By switching the order of a complex sentence, the writer can rearrange the emphasis on different clauses. Saying *If Sheryl is late, we'll miss the dance* is different from saying, *We'll miss*

the dance if Sheryl is late. One emphasizes Sheryl's tardiness while the other emphasizes missing the dance. Paragraphs can also be arranged in a cause and effect format. Since the format—before and after—is sequential, it is useful when authors wish to discuss the impact of choices. Researchers often apply this paragraph structure to the scientific method.

Production and Distribution of Writing

Organization

Good writing is not merely a random collection of sentences. No matter how well written, sentences must relate and coordinate appropriately to one another. If not, the writing seems random, haphazard, and disorganized. Therefore, good writing must be organized (where each sentence fits a larger context and relates to the sentences around it).

Logical Sequence

Even if the writer includes plenty of information to support their point, the writing is only effective when the information is in a logical order. **Logical sequencing** is really just common sense, but it's an important writing technique. First, the writer should introduce the main idea, whether for a paragraph, a section, or the entire piece. Then they should present evidence to support the main idea by using transitional language. This shows the reader how the information relates to the main idea and to the sentences around it. The writer should then take time to interpret the information, making sure necessary connections are obvious to the reader. Finally, the writer can summarize the information in a closing section.

Although most writing follows this pattern, it isn't a set rule. Sometimes writers change the order for effect. For example, the writer can begin with a surprising piece of supporting information to grab the reader's attention, and then transition to the main idea. Thus, if a passage doesn't follow the logical order, don't immediately assume it's wrong. However, most writing usually settles into a logical sequence after a nontraditional beginning.

Focus

Good writing stays focused and on topic. During the test, determine the main idea for each passage and then look for times when the writer strays from the point they're trying to make. Let's go back to the seat belt example. If the writer suddenly begins talking about how well airbags, crumple zones, or other safety features work to save lives, they might be losing focus from the topic of "safety belts."

Focus can also refer to individual sentences. Sometimes the writer does address the main topic, but in a confusing way. For example:

> Thanks to seat belt usage, survival in serious car accidents has shown a consistently steady increase since the development of the retractable seat belt in the 1950s.

This statement is definitely on topic, but it's not easy to follow. A simpler, more focused version of this sentence might look like this:

> Seat belts have consistently prevented car fatalities since the 1950s.

Providing adequate information is another aspect of focused writing. Statements like "seat belts are important" and "many people drive cars" are true, but they're so general that they don't contribute much to the writer's case. When reading a passage, watch for these kinds of unfocused statements.

Introductions and Conclusions

Examining the writer's strategies for introductions and conclusions puts the reader in the right mindset to interpret the rest of the passage. Look for methods the writer might use for introductions such as:

- Stating the main point immediately, followed by outlining how the rest of the piece supports this claim.
- Establishing important, smaller pieces of the main idea first, and then grouping these points into a case for the main idea.
- Opening with a quotation, anecdote, question, seeming paradox, or other piece of interesting information, and then using it to lead to the main point.

Whatever method the writer chooses, the introduction should make their intention clear, establish their voice as a credible one, and encourage a person to continue reading.

Conclusions tend to follow a similar pattern. In them, the writer restates their main idea a final time, often after summarizing the smaller pieces of that idea. If the introduction uses a quote or anecdote to grab the reader's attention, the conclusion often makes reference to it again. Whatever way the writer chooses to arrange the conclusion, the final restatement of the main idea should be clear and simple for the reader to interpret.

Finally, conclusions shouldn't introduce any new information.

Precision

People often think of **precision** in terms of math, but precise word choice is another key to successful writing. Since language itself is imprecise, it's important for the writer to find the exact word or words to convey the full, intended meaning of a given situation. For example:

> The number of deaths has gone down since seat belt laws started.

There are several problems with this sentence. First, the word *deaths* is too general. From the context, it's assumed that the writer is referring only to *deaths* caused by car accidents. However, without clarification, the sentence lacks impact and is probably untrue. The phrase "gone down" might be accurate, but a more precise word could provide more information and greater accuracy. Did the numbers show a slow and steady decrease of highway fatalities or a sudden drop? If the latter is true, the writer is missing a chance to make their point more dramatically. Instead of "gone down" they could substitute *plummeted*, *fallen drastically*, or *rapidly diminished* to bring the information to life. Also, the phrase "seat belt laws" is unclear. Does it refer to laws requiring cars to include seat belts or to laws requiring drivers and passengers to use them? Finally, *started* is not a strong verb. Words like *enacted* or *adopted* are more direct and make the content more real. When put together, these changes create a far more powerful sentence:

> The number of highway fatalities has plummeted since laws requiring seat belt usage were enacted.

However, it's important to note that precise word choice can sometimes be taken too far. If the writer of the sentence above takes precision to an extreme, it might result in the following:

> The incidence of high-speed, automobile accident related fatalities has decreased 75% and continued to remain at historical lows since the initial set of federal legislations requiring seat belt use were enacted in 1992.

This sentence is extremely precise, but it takes so long to achieve that precision that it suffers from a lack of clarity. Precise writing is about finding the right balance between information and flow. This is also an issue of **conciseness** (discussed in the next section).

The last thing to consider with precision is a word choice that's not only unclear or uninteresting, but also confusing or misleading. For example:

> The number of highway fatalities has become hugely lower since laws requiring seat belt use were enacted.

In this case, the reader might be confused by the word *hugely*. Huge means large, but here the writer uses *hugely* to describe something small. Though most readers can decipher this, doing so disconnects them from the flow of the writing and makes the writer's point less effective.

On the test, there can be questions asking for alternatives to the writer's word choice. In answering these questions, always consider the context and look for a balance between precision and flow.

Conciseness

"Less is more" is a good rule to follow when writing a sentence. Unfortunately, writers often include extra words and phrases that seem necessary at the time, but add nothing to the main idea. This confuses the reader and creates unnecessary repetition. Writing that lacks conciseness is usually guilty of excessive wordiness and redundant phrases. Here's an example containing both of these issues:

> When legislators decided to begin creating legislation making it mandatory for automobile drivers and passengers to make use of seat belts while in cars, a large number of them made those laws for reasons that were political reasons.

There are several empty or "fluff" words here that take up too much space. These can be eliminated while still maintaining the writer's meaning. For example:

- "decided to begin" could be shortened to "began"
- "making it mandatory for" could be shortened to "requiring"
- "make use of" could be shortened to "use"
- "a large number" could be shortened to "many"

In addition, there are several examples of redundancy that can be eliminated:

- "legislators decided to begin creating legislation" and "made those laws"
- "automobile drivers and passengers" and "while in cars"
- "reasons that were political reasons"

These changes are incorporated as follows:

> When legislators began requiring drivers and passengers to use seat belts, many of them did so for political reasons.

There are many examples of redundant phrases, such as "complete and total," "time schedule," and "transportation vehicle." If asked to identify a redundant phrase on the test, look for words that are close together with the same (or similar) meanings.

Proposition

The **proposition** (also called the **claim** since it can be true or false) is a clear statement of the point or idea the writer is trying to make. The length or format of a proposition can vary, but it often takes the form of a **topic sentence**. A good topic sentence is:

- Clear: does not weave a complicated web of words for the reader to decode or unwrap
- Concise: presents only the information needed to make the claim and doesn't clutter up the statement with unnecessary details
- Precise: clarifies the exact point the writer wants to make and doesn't use broad, overreaching statements

Look at the following example:

> The civil rights movement, from its genesis in the Emancipation Proclamation to its current struggles with de facto discrimination, has changed the face of the United States more than any other factor in its history.

Is the statement clear? Yes, the statement is fairly clear, although other words can be substituted for "genesis" and "de facto" to make it easier to understand.

Is the statement concise? No, the statement is not concise. Details about the Emancipation Proclamation and the current state of the movement are unnecessary for a topic sentence. Those details should be saved for the body of the text.

Is the statement precise? No, the statement is not precise. What exactly does the writer mean by "changed the face of the United States"? The writer should be more specific about the effects of the movement. Also, suggesting that something has a greater impact than anything else in U.S. history is far too ambitious a statement to make.

A better version might look like this:

> The civil rights movement has greatly increased the career opportunities available for African-Americans.

The unnecessary language and details are removed, and the claim can now be measured and supported.

Effective Language Use

Language can be analyzed in a variety of ways. But one of the primary ways is its effectiveness in communicating and especially convincing others.

Rhetoric is a literary technique used to make the writing (or speaking) more effective or persuasive. Rhetoric makes use of other effective language devices such as irony, metaphors, allusion, and repetition. An example of the rhetorical use of repetition would be: "Let go, I say, let go!!!".

Figures of Speech

A **figure of speech** (sometimes called an **idiom**) is a rhetorical device. It's a phrase that's not intended to be taken literally.

When the writer uses a figure of speech, their intention must be clear if it's to be used effectively. Some phrases can be interpreted in a number of ways, causing confusion for the reader. Some test questions may ask for an alternative to a problematic word or phrase. Look for clues to the writer's true intention to determine the best replacement. Likewise, some figures of speech may seem out of place in a more formal piece of writing. To show this, here is the previous seat belt example but with one slight change:

> Seat belts save more lives than any other automobile safety feature. Many studies show that airbags save lives as well. However, not all cars have airbags. For instance, some older cars don't. In addition, air bags aren't entirely reliable. For example, studies show that in 15% of accidents, airbags don't deploy as designed. But, on the other hand, seat belt malfunctions happen once in a blue moon.

Most people know that "once in a blue moon" refers to something that rarely happens. However, because the rest of the paragraph is straightforward and direct, using this figurative phrase distracts the reader. In this example, the earlier version is much more effective.

Now it's important to take a moment and review the meaning of the word *literally*. This is because it's one of the most misunderstood and misused words in the English language. *Literally* means that something is exactly what it says it is, and there can be no interpretation or exaggeration. Unfortunately, *literally* is often used for emphasis as in the following example:

> This morning, I literally couldn't get out of bed.

This sentence meant to say that the person was extremely tired and wasn't able to get up. However, the sentence can't *literally* be true unless that person was tied down to the bed, paralyzed, or affected by a strange situation that the writer (most likely) didn't intend. Here's another example:

> I literally died laughing.

The writer tried to say that something was very funny. However, unless they're writing this from beyond the grave, it can't *literally* be true.

Rhetorical Fallacies

A **rhetorical fallacy** is an argument that doesn't make sense. It usually involves distracting the reader from the issue at hand in some way. There are many kinds of rhetorical fallacies. Here are just a few, along with examples of each:

- **Ad Hominem**: Makes an irrelevant attack against the person making the claim, rather than addressing the claim itself.
  - Senator Wilson opposed the new seat belt legislation, but should we really listen to someone who's been divorced four times?

- **Exaggeration**: Represents an idea or person in an obviously excessive manner.
    - Senator Wilson opposed the new seat belt legislation. Maybe she thinks if more people die in car accidents, it will help with overpopulation.
- **Stereotyping** (or Categorical Claim): Claims that all people of a certain group are the same in some way.
    - Senator Wilson still opposes the new seat belt legislation. You know women can never admit when they're wrong.

When examining a possible rhetorical fallacy, carefully consider the point the writer is trying to make and if the argument directly relates to that point. If something feels wrong, there's a good chance that a fallacy is at play.

Style, Tone, and Mood

Style, tone, and mood are often thought to be the same thing. Though they're closely related, there are important differences to keep in mind. The easiest way to do this is to remember that style "creates and affects" tone and mood. More specifically, style is *how the writer uses words* to create the desired tone and mood for their writing.

Style

Style can include any number of technical writing choices, and some may have to be analyzed on the test. A few examples of style choices include:

- Sentence Construction: When presenting facts, does the writer use shorter sentences to create a quicker sense of the supporting evidence, or do they use longer sentences to elaborate and explain the information?
- Technical Language: Does the writer use jargon to demonstrate their expertise in the subject, or do they use ordinary language to help the reader understand things in simple terms?
- Formal Language: Does the writer refrain from using contractions such as *won't* or *can't* to create a more formal tone, or do they use a colloquial, conversational style to connect to the reader?
- Formatting: Does the writer use a series of shorter paragraphs to help the reader follow a line of argument, or do they use longer paragraphs to examine an issue in great detail and demonstrate their knowledge of the topic?

On the test, examine the writer's style and how their writing choices affect the way the passage comes across.

Tone

Tone refers to the writer's attitude toward the subject matter. Tone is usually explained in terms of a work of fiction. For example, the tone conveys how the writer feels about their characters and the situations in which they're involved. Nonfiction writing is sometimes thought to have no tone at all, but this is incorrect.

A lot of nonfiction writing has a neutral tone, which is an extremely important tone for the writer to take. A neutral tone demonstrates that the writer is presenting a topic impartially and letting the information speak for itself. On the other hand, nonfiction writing can be just as effective and appropriate if the tone isn't neutral. For instance, take the previous examples involving seat belt use. In them, the writer mostly chooses to retain a neutral tone when presenting information. If the writer would instead include their own personal experience of losing a friend or family member in a car accident, the tone would change dramatically. The tone would no longer be neutral. Now it would show that the writer has a personal stake in the content, allowing them to interpret the information in a different way. When analyzing tone, consider what the writer is trying to achieve in the passage, and how they *create* the tone using style.

Mood

Mood refers to the feelings and atmosphere that the writer's words create for the reader. Like tone, many nonfiction pieces can have a neutral mood. To return to the previous example, if the writer would choose to include information about a person they know being killed in a car accident, the passage would suddenly carry an emotional component that is absent in the previous examples. Depending on how they present the information, the writer can create a sad, angry, or even hopeful mood. When analyzing the mood, consider what the writer wants to accomplish and whether the best choice was made to achieve that end.

Consistency

Whatever style, tone, and mood the writer uses, good writing should remain consistent throughout. If the writer chooses to include the tragic, personal experience above, it would affect the style, tone, and mood of the entire piece. It would seem out of place for such an example to be used in the middle of a neutral, measured, and analytical piece. To adjust the rest of the piece, the writer needs to make additional choices to remain consistent. For example, the writer might decide to use the word *tragedy* in place of the more neutral *fatality*, or they could describe a series of car-related deaths as an *epidemic*. Adverbs and adjectives such as *devastating* or *horribly* could be included to maintain this consistent attitude toward the content. When analyzing writing, look for sudden shifts in style, tone, and mood, and consider whether the writer would be wiser to maintain the prevailing strategy.

Syntax

Syntax is the order of words in a sentence. While most of the writing on the test has proper syntax, there may be questions on ways to vary the syntax for effectiveness. One of the easiest writing mistakes to spot is repetitive sentence structure. For example:

> Seat belts are important. They save lives. People don't like to use them. We have to pass seat belt laws. Then more people will wear seat belts. More lives will be saved.

What's the first thing that comes to mind when reading this example? The short, choppy, and repetitive sentences! In fact, most people notice this syntax issue more than the content itself. By combining some sentences and changing the syntax of others, the writer can create a more effective writing passage:

> Seat belts are important because they save lives. Since people don't like to use seat belts, though, more laws requiring their usage need to be passed. Only then will more people wear them and only then will more lives be saved.

Many rhetorical devices can be used to vary syntax (more than can possibly be named here). These often have intimidating names like *anadiplosis*, *metastasis*, and *paremptosis*. The test questions don't ask for definitions of these tricky techniques, but they can ask how the writer plays with the words and what effect that has on the writing. For example, *anadiplosis* is when the last word (or phrase) from a sentence is used to begin the next sentence:

> Cars are driven by people. People cause accidents. Accidents cost taxpayers money.

The test doesn't ask for this technique by name, but be prepared to recognize what the writer is doing and why they're using the technique in this situation. In this example, the writer is probably using *anadiplosis* to demonstrate causation.

Support

Once the main idea or proposition is stated, the writer attempts to prove or support the claim with text evidence and supporting details.

Take for example the sentence, "Seat belts save lives." Though most people can't argue with this statement, its impact on the reader is much greater when supported by additional content. The writer can support this idea by:

- Providing statistics on the rate of highway fatalities alongside statistics for estimated seat belt usage.
- Explaining the science behind a car accident and what happens to a passenger who doesn't use a seat belt.
- Offering anecdotal evidence or true stories from reliable sources on how seat belts prevent fatal injuries in car crashes.

However, using only one form of supporting evidence is not nearly as effective as using a variety to support a claim. Presenting only a list of statistics can be boring to the reader, but providing a true story that's both interesting and humanizing helps. In addition, one example isn't always enough to prove the writer's larger point, so combining it with other examples is extremely effective for the writing. Thus, when reading a passage, don't just look for a single form of supporting evidence.

Another key aspect of supporting evidence is a reliable source. Does the writer include the source of the information? If so, is the source well known and trustworthy? Is there a potential for bias? For example, a seat belt study done by a seat belt manufacturer may have its own agenda to promote.

Quantitative Information

Some writing in the test contains **infographics** such as charts, tables, or graphs. In these cases, interpret the information presented and determine how well it supports the claims made in the text. For example, if the writer makes a case that seat belts save more lives than other automobile safety measures, they might want to include a graph (like the one below) showing the number of lives saved by seat belts versus those saved by air bags.

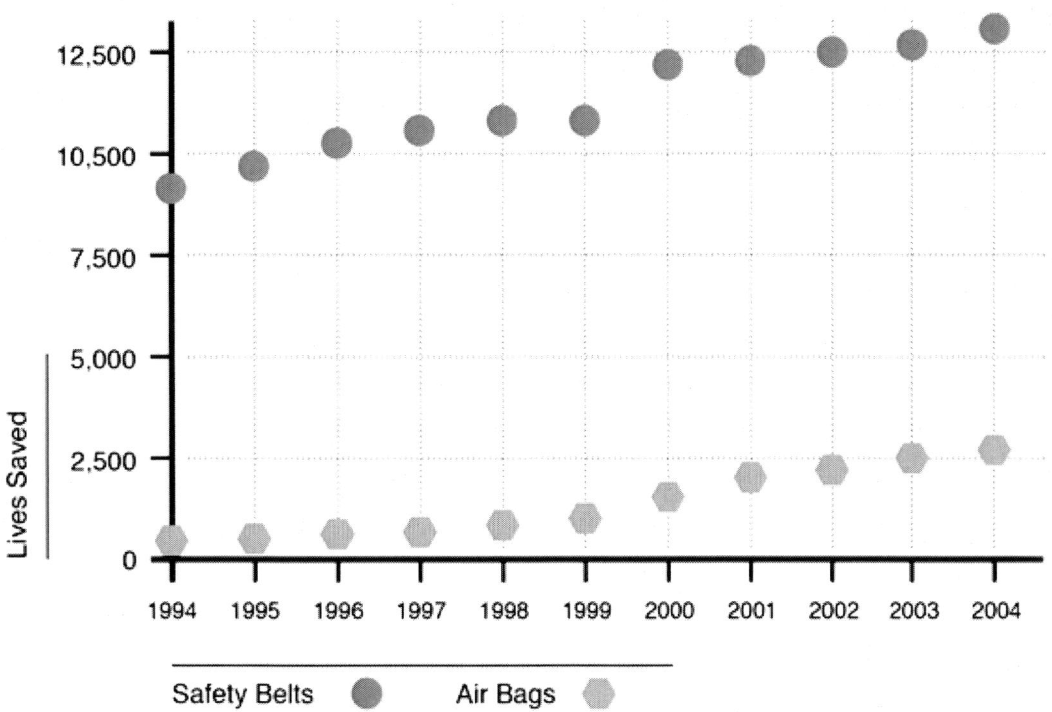

Based on data from the National Highway Traffic Safety Administration

If the graph clearly shows a higher number of lives are saved by seat belts, then it's effective. However, if the graph shows air bags save more lives than seat belts, then it doesn't support the writer's case.

Finally, graphs should be easy to understand. Their information should immediately be clear to the reader at a glance. Here are some basic things to keep in mind when interpreting infographics:

- In a **bar graph**, higher bars represent larger numbers. Lower bars represent smaller numbers.
- **Line graphs** are the same but often show trends over time. A line that consistently ascends from left to right shows a steady increase over time. A line that consistently descends from left to right shows a steady decrease over time. If the line bounces up and down, this represents instability or inconsistency in the trend. When interpreting a line graph, determine the point the writer is trying to make, and then see if the graph supports that point.
- **Pie charts** are used to show proportions or percentages of a whole but are less effective in showing change over time.
- **Tables** present information in numerical form, not as graphics. When interpreting a table, make sure to look for patterns in the numbers.

There can also be timelines, illustrations, or maps on the test. When interpreting these, keep in mind the writer's intentions and determine whether or not the graphic supports the case.

Evaluating and Integrating Data from Multiple Source in Various Formats, Including Media

Finding Relevant Information

With a wealth of information at your fingertips in this digital age, it's important to know not only the type of information you're looking for, but also in what medium you're most likely to find it. Information needs to be specific and reliable. For example, if you're repairing a car, an encyclopedia would be mostly useless. While an encyclopedia might include information about cars, an owner's manual will contain the specific information needed for repairs. Information must also be reliable or credible so that it can be trusted. A well-known newspaper may have reliable information, but a peer-reviewed journal article will have likely gone through a more rigorous check for validity. Determining bias can be helpful in determining credibility. If the information source (person, organization, or company) has something to gain from the reader forming a certain view on a topic, it's likely the information is skewed. For example, if you are trying to find the unemployment rate, the Bureau of Labor Statistics is a more credible source than a politician's speech.

Evaluating the Credibility of a Print or Digital Source

There are several additional criteria that need to be examined before using a source for a research topic. The following questions will help determine whether a source is credible:

- Author—Who is he or she?
- Does he or she have the appropriate credentials—e.g., M.D, PhD?
- Is this person authorized to write on the matter through his/her job or personal experiences?
- Is he or she affiliated with any known credible individuals or organizations?
- Has he or she written anything else?
- Publisher—Who published/produced the work? Is it a well-known journal, like National Geographic, or a tabloid, like The National Enquirer?
- Is the publisher from a scholarly, commercial, or government association?
- Do they publish works related to specific fields?
- Have they published other works?
- If a digital source, what kind of website hosts the text? Does it end in .edu, .org, or .com?
- Bias—Is the writing objective? Does it contain any loaded or emotional language?
- Does the publisher/producer have a known bias, such as Fox News or CNN?
- Does the work include diverse opinions or perspectives?
- Does the author have any known bias—e.g., Michael Moore, Bill O'Reilly, or the Pope? Is he or she affiliated with any organizations or individuals that may have a known bias—e.g., Citizens United or the National Rifle Association?
- Does the magazine, book, journal, or website contain any advertising?
- References—Are there any references?
- Are the references credible? Do they follow the same criteria as stated above?
- Are the references from a related field?
- Accuracy/reliability—Has the article, book, or digital source been peer reviewed?
- Are all of the conclusions, supporting details, or ideas backed with published evidence?

- If a digital source, is it free of grammatical errors, poor spelling, and improper English?
- Do other published individuals have similar findings?
- Coverage—Is the topic successfully addressed and appropriate for the intended audience?
- Does the work add new information or theories to those of their sources?

Integrate Data

It's important to find multiple relevant and credible sources for data. Rather than just reading one article from a credible newspaper regarding a current event, read several articles from different newspapers. Journalists will differ in how they report a story, and in which details they choose to include.

The same principle holds true for scientific or academic research. Multiple sources help give one a more thorough and balanced perspective. Be sure to find data from multiple types of sources as well. For instance, if you were to research the results of U.S. presidential elections it would be helpful to combine books with graphs and articles to get a comprehensive understanding.

Always consider the data from one source or type of source in light of data from our sources. A chart may convince you to think one way until you read a book that goes more into depth about the factors affecting the data.

Writing Prompt

Please read the prompt below and answer in an essay format.

> Science fiction has been a part of the American fabric for a long time. During the Great Depression, many Americans were looking for an escape from dismal circumstances, and their escape often took the form of reading. Outlandish stories of aliens and superheroes were printed on cheap, disposable paper stock, hence the name *pulp* (as in paper) *fiction*. Iconic heroes like Buck Rogers, the Shadow, and Doc Rogers got their start in throwaway magazines and pulp novels.

1. Analyze and evaluate the passage given.

2. State and develop your own perspective.

3. Explain the relationship between your perspective and the one given.

Practice Test #1

Reading Comprehension

Questions 1–10 are based upon the following passage:

"Did you ever come across a protégé of his—one Hyde?" He asked.

"Hyde?" repeated Lanyon. "No. Never heard of him. Since my time."

That was the amount of information that the lawyer carried back with him to the great, dark bed on which he tossed to and fro until the small hours of the morning began to grow large. It was a night of little ease to his toiling mind, toiling in mere darkness and besieged by questions.

Six o'clock struck on the bells of the church that was so conveniently near to Mr. Utterson's dwelling, and still he was digging at the problem. Hitherto it had touched him on the intellectual side alone; but; but now his imagination also was engaged, or rather enslaved; and as he lay and tossed in the gross darkness of the night in the curtained room, Mr. Enfield's tale went by before his mind in a scroll of lighted pictures. He would be aware of the great field of lamps in a nocturnal city; then of the figure of a man walking swiftly; then of a child running from the doctor's; and then these met, and that human Juggernaut trod the child down and passed on regardless of her screams. Or else he would see a room in a rich house, where his friend lay asleep, dreaming and smiling at his dreams; and then the door of that room would be opened, the curtains of the bed plucked apart, the sleeper recalled, and, lo! There would stand by his side a figure to whom power was given, and even at that dead hour he must rise and do its bidding. The figure in these two phrases haunted the lawyer all night; and if at anytime he dozed over, it was but to see it glide more stealthily through sleeping houses, or move the more swiftly, and still the more smoothly, even to dizziness, through wider labyrinths of lamplighted city, and at every street corner crush a child and leave her screaming. And still the figure had no face by which he might know it; even in his dreams it had no face, or one that baffled him and melted before his eyes; and thus there it was that there sprung up and grew apace in the lawyer's mind a singularly strong, almost an inordinate, curiosity to behold the features of the real Mr. Hyde. If he could but once set eyes on him, he thought the mystery would lighten and perhaps roll altogether away, as was the habit of mysterious things when well examined. He might see a reason for his friend's strange preference or bondage, and even for the startling clauses of the will. And at least it would be a face worth seeing: the face of a man who was without bowels of mercy: a face which had but to show itself to raise up, in the mind of the unimpressionable Enfield, a spirit of enduring hatred.

> From that time forward, Mr. Utterson began to haunt the door in the by-street of shops. In the morning before office hours, at noon when business was plenty and time scarce, at night under the face of the full city moon, by all lights and at all hours of solitude or concourse, the lawyer was to be found on his chosen post.
>
> "If he be Mr. Hyde," he had thought, "I should be Mr. Seek."

Excerpt from The Strange Case of Dr. Jekyll and Mr. Hyde by Robert Louis Stevenson

1. What is the purpose of the use of repetition in the following passage?

> It was a night of little ease to his toiling mind, toiling in mere darkness and besieged by questions.

a. It serves as a demonstration of the mental state of Mr. Lanyon.
b. It is reminiscent of the church bells that are mentioned in the story.
c. It mimics Mr. Utterson's ambivalence.
d. It emphasizes Mr. Utterson's anguish in failing to identify Hyde's whereabouts.

2. What is the setting of the story in this passage?
a. In the city
b. On the countryside
c. In a jail
d. In a mental health facility

3. What can one infer about the meaning of the word *Juggernaut* from the author's use of it in the passage?
a. It is an apparition that appears at daybreak.
b. It scares children.
c. It is associated with space travel.
d. Mr. Utterson finds it soothing.

4. What is the definition of the word *haunt* in the following passage?

> From that time forward, Mr. Utterson began to *haunt* the door in the by-street of shops. In the morning before office hours, at noon when business was plenty and time scarce, at night under the face of the full city moon, by all lights and at all hours of solitude or concourse, the lawyer was to be found on his chosen post.

a. To levitate
b. To constantly visit
c. To terrorize
d. To daunt

5. The phrase *labyrinths of lamplighted city* contains an example of what?
a. Hyperbole
b. Simile
c. Juxtaposition
d. Alliteration

6. What can one reasonably conclude from the final comment of this passage?

> "If he be Mr. Hyde," he had thought, "I should be Mr. Seek."

a. The speaker is considering a name change.
b. The speaker is experiencing an identity crisis.
c. The speaker has mistakenly been looking for the wrong person.
d. The speaker intends to continue to look for Hyde.

7. The author's attitude toward the main subject of this passage can be described as:
a. Intrigue
b. Elation
c. Animosity
d. Rigidity

8. According to the passage, what is Mr. Utterson struggling with as he tosses and turns in bed?
a. A murderer who is stalking Mr. Utterson since he moved to the city.
b. The mystery surrounding a dark figure and the terrible crimes he commits.
c. The cases he is involved in as a detective.
d. A chronic illness that is causing Mr. Utterson to hallucinate.

9. According to the passage, why did Mr. Utterson start to haunt the doors by the street shops?
a. He was looking for a long, lost love who he kept dreaming about.
b. He was recently homeless, and the street shops offered him food to eat when he was hungry.
c. He was looking for the dark, mysterious figure who he had been obsessing over in his sleep.
d. He was looking for a thief that would regularly steal out of stores.

10. What point of view is the passage written in?
a. First person
b. Second person
c. Third person limited
d. Third person omniscient

Questions 11–20 are based on the following passages:

Passage I

Lethal force, or deadly force, is defined as the physical means to cause death or serious harm to another individual. The law holds that lethal force is only accepted when you or another person are in immediate and unavoidable danger of death or severe bodily harm. For example, a person could be beating a weaker person in such a way that they are suffering severe enough trauma that could result in death or serious harm. This would be an instance where lethal force would be acceptable and possibly the only way to save that person from irrevocable damage.

Another example of when to use lethal force would be when someone enters your home with a deadly weapon. The intruder's presence and possession of the weapon indicate mal-intent and the ability to inflict death or severe injury to you and your loved ones. Again, lethal force can be used in this situation. Lethal force can also be applied to prevent the harm of another individual. If a woman is being brutally assaulted and is unable to fend off an attacker, lethal force can be used to defend her as a last-ditch effort. If she is in immediate jeopardy of rape, harm, and/or death, lethal force could be the only response that could effectively deter the assailant.

The key to understanding the concept of lethal force is the term *last resort*. Deadly force cannot be taken back; it should be used only to prevent severe harm or death. The law does distinguish whether the means of one's self-defense is fully warranted, or if the individual goes out of control in the process. If you continually attack the assailant after they are rendered incapacitated, this would be causing unnecessary harm, and the law can bring charges against you. Likewise, if you kill an attacker unnecessarily after defending yourself, you can be charged with murder. This would move lethal force beyond necessary defense, making it no longer a last resort but rather a use of excessive force.

Passage II

Assault is the unlawful attempt of one person to apply apprehension on another individual by an imminent threat or by initiating offensive contact. Assaults can vary, encompassing physical strikes, threatening body language, and even provocative language. In the case of the latter, even if a hand has not been laid, it is still considered an assault because of its threatening nature.

Let's look at an example: A homeowner is angered because his neighbor blows fallen leaves into his freshly mowed lawn. Irate, the homeowner gestures a fist to his fellow neighbor and threatens to bash his head in for littering on his lawn. The homeowner's physical motions and verbal threat heralds a physical threat against the other neighbor. These factors classify the homeowner's reaction as an assault. If the angry neighbor hits the threatening homeowner in retaliation, that would constitute an assault as well because he physically hit the homeowner.

Assault also centers on the involvement of weapons in a conflict. If someone fires a gun at another person, this could be interpreted as an assault unless the shooter acted in self-defense. If an individual drew a gun or a knife on someone with the intent to harm them, that would be considered assault. However, it's also considered an assault if someone simply aimed a weapon, loaded or not, at another person in a threatening manner.

11. What is the purpose of the second passage?
    a. To inform the reader about what assault is and how it is committed
    b. To inform the reader about how assault is a minor example of lethal force
    c. To disprove the previous passage concerning lethal force
    d. The author is recounting an incident in which they were assaulted

12. Which of the following situations, according to the passages, would not constitute an illegal use of lethal force?
    a. A disgruntled cashier yells obscenities at a customer.
    b. A thief is seen running away with stolen cash.
    c. A man is attacked in an alley by another man with a knife.
    d. A woman punches another woman in a bar.

13. Given the information in the passages, which of the following must be true about assault?
  a. Assault charges are more severe than unnecessary use of force charges.
  b. There are various forms of assault.
  c. Smaller, weaker people cannot commit assaults.
  d. Assault is justified only as a last resort.

14. Which of the following, if true, would most seriously undermine the explanation proposed by the author of Passage I in the third paragraph?
  a. An instance of lethal force in self-defense is not absolutely absolved from blame. The law considers the necessary use of force at the time it is committed.
  b. An individual who uses lethal force under necessary defense is in direct compliance of the law under most circumstances.
  c. Lethal force in self-defense should be forgiven in all cases for the peace of mind of the primary victim.
  d. The use of lethal force is not evaluated on the intent of the user, but rather the severity of the primary attack that warranted self-defense.

15. Based on the passages, what can be inferred about the relationship between assault and lethal force?
  a. An act of lethal force always leads to a type of assault.
  b. An assault will result in someone using lethal force.
  c. An assault with deadly intent can lead to an individual using lethal force to preserve their well-being.
  d. If someone uses self-defense in a conflict, it is called deadly force; if actions or threats are intended, it is called assault.

16. Which of the following best describes the way the passages are structured?
  a. Both passages open by defining a legal concept and then continue to describe situations that further explain the concept.
  b. Both passages begin with situations, introduce accepted definitions, and then cite legal ramifications.
  c. Passage I presents a long definition while the Passage II begins by showing an example of assault.
  d. Both cite specific legal doctrines, then proceed to explain the rulings.

17. What can be inferred about the role of intent in lethal force and assault?
  a. Intent is irrelevant. The law does not take intent into account.
  b. Intent is vital for determining the lawfulness of using lethal force.
  c. Intent is very important for determining both lethal force and assault; intent is examined in both parties and helps determine the severity of the issue.
  d. The intent of the assailant is the main focus for determining legal ramifications; it is used to determine if the defender was justified in using force to respond.

18. The author uses the example in the second paragraph of Passage II in order to do what?
    a. To demonstrate two different types of assault by showing how each specifically relates to the other
    b. To demonstrate a single example of two different types of assault, then adding in the third type of assault in the example's conclusion
    c. To prove that the definition of lethal force is altered when the victim in question is a homeowner and his property is threatened
    d. To suggest that verbal assault can be an exaggerated crime by the law and does not necessarily lead to physical violence

19. As it is used in the second passage, the word *apprehension* most nearly means:
    a. Pain
    b. Exhaustion
    c. Fear
    d. Honor

20. One of the main purposes of the last paragraph in the first passage is to state:
    a. How assault is different when used in the home versus when it is used out in public.
    b. A specific example of lethal force so that the audience will know what it looks like.
    c. Why police officers defend those who use lethal force but do not defend those who use assault.
    d. The concept of lethal force as a last resort and the point at which it can cross a line from defense to manslaughter.

Questions 21–30 are based upon the following passage:

> My Good Friends,—When I first imparted to the committee of the projected Institute my particular wish that on one of the evenings of my readings here the main body of my audience should be composed of working men and their families, I was animated by two desires; first, by the wish to have the great pleasure of meeting you face to face at this Christmas time, and accompany you myself through one of my little Christmas books; and second, by the wish to have an opportunity of stating publicly in your presence, and in the presence of the committee, my earnest hope that the Institute will, from the beginning, recognise one great principle—strong in reason and justice—which I believe to be essential to the very life of such an Institution. It is, that the working man shall, from the first unto the last, have a share in the management of an Institution which is designed for his benefit, and which calls itself by his name.
>
> I have no fear here of being misunderstood—of being supposed to mean too much in this. If there ever was a time when any one class could of itself do much for its own good, and for the welfare of society—which I greatly doubt—that time is unquestionably past. It is in the fusion of different classes, without confusion; in the bringing together of employers and employed; in the creating of a better common understanding among those whose interests are identical, who depend upon each other, who are vitally essential to each other, and who never can be in unnatural antagonism without deplorable results, that one of the chief principles of a Mechanics' Institution should consist. In this world, a great deal of the bitterness among us arises from an imperfect understanding of one another. Erect in Birmingham a great Educational Institution, properly educational; educational of the feelings as well as of the reason; to which all orders of Birmingham men contribute; in which all orders of

Birmingham men meet; wherein all orders of Birmingham men are faithfully represented—and you will erect a Temple of Concord here which will be a model edifice to the whole of England.

Contemplating as I do the existence of the Artisans' Committee, which not long ago considered the establishment of the Institute so sensibly, and supported it so heartily, I earnestly entreat the gentlemen—earnest I know in the good work, and who are now among us—by all means to avoid the great shortcoming of similar institutions; and in asking the working man for his confidence, to set him the great example and give him theirs in return. You will judge for yourselves if I promise too much for the working man, when I say that he will stand by such an enterprise with the utmost of his patience, his perseverance, sense, and support; that I am sure he will need no charitable aid or condescending patronage; but will readily and cheerfully pay for the advantages which it confers; that he will prepare himself in individual cases where he feels that the adverse circumstances around him have rendered it necessary; in a word, that he will feel his responsibility like an honest man, and will most honestly and manfully discharge it. I now proceed to the pleasant task to which I assure you I have looked forward for a long time.

From Charles Dickens' speech in Birmingham in England on December 30, 1853 on behalf of the Birmingham and Midland Institute.

21. Which word is most closely synonymous with the word *patronage* as it appears in the following statement?

...that I am sure he will need no charitable aid or condescending patronage

a. Auspices
b. Aberration
c. Acerbic
d. Adulation

22. Which term is most closely aligned with the definition of the term *working man* as it is defined in the following passage?

> You will judge for yourselves if I promise too much for the working man, when I say that he will stand by such an enterprise with the utmost of his patience, his perseverance, sense, and support...

a. Plebian
b. Viscount
c. Entrepreneur
d. Bourgeois

23. Which of the following statements most closely correlates with the definition of the term *working man* as it is defined in Question 22?

a. A working man is not someone who works for institutions or corporations, but someone who is well-versed in the workings of the soul.
b. A working man is someone who is probably not involved in social activities because the physical demand for work is too high.
c. A working man is someone who works for wages among the middle class.
d. The working man has historically taken to the field, to the factory, and now to the screen.

24. Based upon the contextual evidence provided in the passage above, what is the meaning of the term *enterprise* in the third paragraph?

a. Company
b. Courage
c. Game
d. Cause

25. The speaker addresses his audience as *My Good Friends.* What kind of credibility does this salutation give to the speaker?

a. The speaker is an employer addressing his employees, so the salutation is a way for the boss to bridge the gap between himself and his employees.
b. The speaker's salutation is one from an entertainer to his audience and uses the friendly language to connect to his audience before a serious speech.
c. The salutation is used ironically to give a somber tone to the serious speech that follows.
d. The speech is one from a politician to the public, so the salutation is used to grab the audience's attention.

26. According to the passage, what is the speaker's second desire for his time in front of the audience?

a. To read a Christmas story
b. For the working man to have a say in his institution, which is designed for his benefit
c. To have an opportunity to stand in their presence
d. For the life of the institution to be essential to the audience as a whole

27. The speaker's tone in the passage can be described as:

a. Happy and gullible
b. Lazy and entitled
c. Confident and informed
d. Angry and frustrated

28. One of the main purposes of the last paragraph is:

a. To persuade the audience to support the Institute no matter what since it provided so much support to the working class.
b. To market the speaker's new book while at the same time supporting the activities of the Institute.
c. To inform the audience that the Institute is corrupt and will not help them out when the time comes to give them compensation.
d. To provide credibility to the working man and share confidence in their ability to take on responsibilities if they are compensated appropriately.

29. According to the passage, what does the speaker wish to erect in Birmingham?
    a. An Educational Institution
    b. The Temple of Concord
    c. A Writing Workshop
    d. A VA Hospital

30. As it is used in the second paragraph, the word *antagonism* most nearly means:
    a. Conformity
    b. Opposition
    c. Affluence
    d. Scarcity

Questions 31–40 are based upon the following passage:

Three years ago, I think there were not many bird-lovers in the United States who believed it possible to prevent the total extinction of both egrets from our fauna. All the known rookeries accessible to plume-hunters had been totally destroyed. Two years ago, the secret discovery of several small, hidden colonies prompted William Dutcher, President of the National Association of Audubon Societies, and Mr. T. Gilbert Pearson, Secretary, to attempt the protection of those colonies. With a fund contributed for the purpose, wardens were hired and duly commissioned. As previously stated, one of those wardens was shot dead in cold blood by a plume hunter. The task of guarding swamp rookeries from the attacks of money-hungry desperadoes to whom the accursed plumes were worth their weight in gold, is a very chancy proceeding. There is now one warden in Florida who says that "before they get my rookery they will first have to get me."

Thus far the protective work of the Audubon Association has been successful. Now there are twenty colonies, which contain all told, about 5,000 egrets and about 120,000 herons and ibises which are guarded by the Audubon wardens. One of the most important is on Bird Island, a mile out in Orange Lake, central Florida, and it is ably defended by Oscar E. Baynard. To-day, the plume hunters who do not dare to raid the guarded rookeries are trying to study out the lines of flight of the birds, to and from their feeding-grounds, and shoot them in transit. Their motto is—"Anything to beat the law, and get the plumes." It is there that the state of Florida should take part in the war.

The success of this campaign is attested by the fact that last year a number of egrets were seen in eastern Massachusetts—for the first time in many years. And so to-day the question is, can the wardens continue to hold the plume-hunters at bay?

Excerpt from Our Vanishing Wildlife by William T. Hornaday

31. The author's use of first-person pronouns in the following text does NOT have which of the following effects?

> Three years ago, I think there were not many bird-lovers in the United States who believed it possible to prevent the total extinction of both egrets from our fauna.

a. The phrase *I think* acts as a sort of hedging, where the author's tone is less direct and/or absolute.
b. It allows the reader to more easily connect with the author.
c. It encourages the reader to empathize with the egrets.
d. It distances the reader from the text by overemphasizing the story.

32. What purpose does the quote serve at the end of the first paragraph?
a. The quote shows proof of a hunter threatening one of the wardens.
b. The quote lightens the mood by illustrating the colloquial language of the region.
c. The quote provides an example of a warden protecting one of the colonies.
d. The quote provides much needed comic relief in the form of a joke.

33. What is the meaning of the word *rookeries* in the following text?

> To-day, the plume hunters who do not dare to raid the guarded rookeries are trying to study out the lines of flight of the birds, to and from their feeding-grounds, and shoot them in transit.

a. Houses in a slum area
b. A place where hunters gather to trade tools
c. A place where wardens go to trade stories
d. A colony of breeding birds

34. What is on Bird Island?
a. Hunters selling plumes
b. An important bird colony
c. Bird Island Battle between the hunters and the wardens
d. An important egret with unique plumes

35. What is the main purpose of the passage?
a. To persuade the audience to act in preservation of the bird colonies
b. To show the effect hunting egrets has had on the environment
c. To argue that the preservation of bird colonies has had a negative impact on the environment
d. To demonstrate the success of the protective work of the Audubon Association

36. According to the passage, why are hunters trying to study the lines of flight of the birds?
a. To study ornithology, one must know the lines of flight that birds take.
b. To help wardens preserve the lives of the birds
c. To have a better opportunity to hunt the birds
d. To build their homes under the lines of flight because they believe it brings good luck

37. A year before the passage was written, where were a number of egrets seen?
a. California
b. Florida
c. Eastern Massachusetts
d. Western Texas

38. As it is used in the first paragraph, the word *commissioned* most nearly means:
    a. Appointed
    b. Compelled
    c. Beguiled
    d. Fortified

39. What happened two years before the passage was written?
    a. The plume hunters didn't dare to raid the rookeries, as they are heavily guarded.
    b. Twenty colonies have emerged as thousands of egrets are protected and make their homes in safe havens.
    c. The plume hunters tried to shoot the birds in their line of flight.
    d. Several hidden colonies were found which prompted Dutcher and Pearson to protect them.

40. As it is used in the second paragraph, the phrase *in transit* most nearly means:
    a. On a journey or trip
    b. To give authority to
    c. On the way to the destination
    d. To make angry

English Language

Questions 1–9 are based on the following passage:

While all dogs (1) descend through gray wolves, it's easy to notice that dog breeds come in a variety of shapes and sizes. With such a (2) drastic range of traits, appearances and body types dogs are one of the most variable and adaptable species on the planet. (3) But why so many differences. The answer is that humans have actually played a major role in altering the biology of dogs. (4) This was done through a process called selective breeding.

(5) Selective breeding which is also called artificial selection is the processes in which animals with desired traits are bred in order to produce offspring that share the same traits. In natural selection, (6) animals must adapt to their environments increase their chance of survival. Over time, certain traits develop in animals that enable them to thrive in these environments. Those animals with more of these traits, or better versions of these traits, gain an (7) advantage over others of their species. Therefore, the animal's chances to mate are increased and these useful (8) genes are passed into their offspring. With dog breeding, humans select traits that are desired and encourage more of these desired traits in other dogs by breeding dogs that already have them.

The reason for different breeds of dogs is that there were specific needs that humans wanted to fill with their animals. For example, scent hounds are known for their extraordinary ability to track game through scent. These breeds are also known for their endurance in seeking deer and other prey. Therefore, early hunters took dogs that displayed these abilities and bred them to encourage these traits. Later, these generations took on characteristics that aided these desired traits. (9) For example, Bloodhounds have broad snouts and droopy ears that fall to the ground when they smell. These physical qualities not only define the look of the Bloodhound, but also contribute to their amazing tracking ability. The broad snout is able to define and hold onto scents longer than many other breeds. The long, floppy ears serve to collect and hold the scents the earth holds so that the smells are clearer and able to be distinguished.

1. Which of the following would be the best choice for this sentence (reproduced below)?

While all dogs (1) descend through gray wolves, it's easy to notice that dog breeds come in a variety of shapes and sizes.

a. NO CHANGE
b. descend by gray wolves
c. descend from gray wolves
d. descended through gray wolves

2. Which of the following would be the best choice for this sentence (reproduced below)?

With such a (2) drastic range of traits, appearances and body types, dogs are one of the most variable and adaptable species on the planet.

a. NO CHANGE
b. drastic range of traits, appearances, and body types,
c. drastic range of traits and appearances and body types,
d. drastic range of traits, appearances, as well as body types,

3. Which of the following would be the best choice for this sentence (reproduced below)?

(3) But why so many differences.

a. NO CHANGE
b. But are there so many differences?
c. But why so many differences are there.
d. But why so many differences?

4. Which of the following would be the best choice for this sentence (reproduced below)?

(4) This was done through a process called selective breeding.

a. NO CHANGE
b. This was done, through a process called selective breeding.
c. This was done, through a process, called selective breeding.
d. This was done through selective breeding, a process.

5. Which of the following would be the best choice for this sentence (reproduced below)?

(5) Selective breeding which is also called artificial selection is the processes in which animals with desired traits are bred in order to produce offspring that share the same traits.

a. NO CHANGE
b. Selective breeding, which is also called artificial selection is the processes
c. Selective breeding which is also called, artificial selection, is the processes
d. Selective breeding, which is also called artificial selection, is the processes

6. Which of the following would be the best choice for this sentence (reproduced below)?

In natural selection, (6) animals must adapt to their environments increase their chance of survival.

a. NO CHANGE
b. animals must adapt to their environments to increase their chance of survival.
c. animals must adapt to their environments, increase their chance of survival.
d. animals must adapt to their environments, increasing their chance of survival.

7. Which of the following would be the best choice for this sentence (reproduced below)?

Those animals with more of these traits, or better versions of these traits, gain an (7) advantage over others of their species.

a. NO CHANGE
b. advantage over others, of their species.
c. advantages over others of their species.
d. advantage over others.

8. Which of the following would be the best choice for this sentence (reproduced below)?

Therefore, the animal's chances to mate are increased and these useful (8) genes are passed into their offspring.

a. NO CHANGE
b. genes are passed onto their offspring.
c. genes are passed on to their offspring.
d. genes are passed within their offspring.

9. Which of the following would be the best choice for this sentence (reproduced below)?

(9) For example, Bloodhounds have broad snouts and droopy ears that fall to the ground when they smell.

a. NO CHANGE
b. For example, Bloodhounds,
c. For example Bloodhounds
d. For example, bloodhounds

Questions 10–18 are based on the following passage:

I'm not alone when I say that it's hard to pay attention sometimes. I can't count how many times I've sat in a classroom, lecture, speech, or workshop and (10) been bored to tears or rather sleep. (11) Usually I turn to doodling in order to keep awake. This never really helps; I'm not much of an artist. Therefore, after giving up on drawing a masterpiece, I would just concentrate on keeping my eyes open and trying to be attentive. This didn't always work because I wasn't engaged in what was going on.

(12) Sometimes in particularly dull seminars, I'd imagine comical things going on in the room or with the people trapped in the room with me. Why? (13) Because I wasn't invested in what was going on I wasn't motivated to listen. I'm not going to write about how I conquered the difficult task of actually paying attention in a difficult or unappealing class—it can be done, sure. I have

sat through the very epitome of boredom (in my view at least) several times and come away learning something. (14) Everyone probably has had to at one time do this. What I want to talk about is that profound moment when curiosity is sparked (15) in another person drawing them to pay attention to what is before them and expand their knowledge.

What really makes people pay attention? (16) Easy it's interest. This doesn't necessarily mean (17) embellishing subject matter drawing people's attention. This won't always work. However, an individual can present material in a way that is clear to understand and actually engages the audience. Asking questions to the audience or class will make them a part of the topic at hand. Discussions that make people think about the content and (18) how it applies to there lives world and future is key. If math is being discussed, an instructor can explain the purpose behind the equations or perhaps use real-world applications to show how relevant the topic is. When discussing history, a lecturer can prompt students to imagine themselves in the place of key figures and ask how they might respond. The bottom line is to explore the ideas rather than just lecture. Give people the chance to explore material from multiple angles, and they'll be hungry to keep paying attention for more information.

10. Which of the following would be the best choice for this sentence (reproduced below)?

I can't count how many times I've sat in a classroom, lecture, speech, or workshop and (10) been bored to tears or rather sleep.

a. NO CHANGE
b. been bored to, tears, or rather sleep.
c. been bored, to tears or rather sleep.
d. been bored to tears or, rather, sleep.

11. Which of the following would be the best choice for this sentence (reproduced below)?

(11) Usually I turn to doodling in order to keep awake.

a. NO CHANGE
b. Usually, I turn to doodling in order to keep awake.
c. Usually I turn to doodling, in order, to keep awake.
d. Usually I turned to doodling in order to keep awake.

12. Which of the following would be the best choice for this sentence (reproduced below)?

(12) Sometimes in particularly dull seminars, I'd imagine comical things going on in the room or with the people trapped in the room with me.

a. NO CHANGE
b. Sometimes, in particularly, dull seminars,
c. Sometimes in particularly dull seminars
d. Sometimes in particularly, dull seminars,

13. Which of the following would be the best choice for this sentence (reproduced below)?

(13) Because I wasn't invested in what was going on I wasn't motivated to listen.

a. NO CHANGE
b. Because I wasn't invested, in what was going on, I wasn't motivated to listen.
c. Because I wasn't invested in what was going on. I wasn't motivated to listen.
d. I wasn't motivated to listen because I wasn't invested in what was going on.

14. Which of the following would be the best choice for this sentence (reproduced below)?

(14) Everyone probably has had to at one time do this.

a. NO CHANGE
b. Everyone probably has had to, at one time. Do this.
c. Everyone's probably had to do this at some time.
d. At one time everyone probably has had to do this.

15. Which of the following would be the best choice for this sentence (reproduced below)?

What I want to talk about is that profound moment when curiosity is sparked (15) in another person drawing them to pay attention to what is before them and expand their knowledge.

a. NO CHANGE
b. in another person, drawing them to pay attention
c. in another person; drawing them to pay attention to what is before them.
d. in another person, drawing them to pay attention to what is before them.

16. Which of the following would be the best choice for this sentence (reproduced below)?

(16) Easy it's interest.

a. NO CHANGE
b. Easy it is interest.
c. Easy. It's interest.
d. Easy—it's interest.

17. Which of the following would be the best choice for this sentence (reproduced below)?

This doesn't necessarily mean (17) embellishing subject matter drawing people's attention.

a. NO CHANGE
b. embellishing subject matter which draws people's attention.
c. embellishing subject matter to draw people's attention.
d. embellishing subject matter for the purpose of drawing people's attention.

18. Which of the following would be the best choice for this sentence (reproduced below)?

> Discussions that make people think about the content and (18) how it applies to there lives world and future is key.
>
> a. NO CHANGE
> b. how it applies to their lives, world, and future is key.
> c. how it applied to there lives world and future is key.
> d. how it applies to their lives, world and future is key.

Questions 19–27 are based on the following passage:

> Since the first discovery of dinosaur bones, (19) scientists has made strides in technological development and methodologies used to investigate these extinct animals. We know more about dinosaurs than ever before and are still learning fascinating new things about how they looked and lived. However, one has to ask, (20) how if earlier perceptions of dinosaurs continue to influence people's understanding of these creatures? Can these perceptions inhibit progress towards further understanding of dinosaurs?
>
> (21) The biggest problem with studying dinosaurs is simply that there are no living dinosaurs to observe. All discoveries associated with these animals are based on physical remains. To gauge behavioral characteristics, scientists cross-examine these (22) finds with living animals that seem similar in order to gain understanding. While this method is effective, these are still deductions. Some ideas about dinosaurs can't be tested and confirmed simply because humans can't replicate a living dinosaur. For example, a Spinosaurus has a large sail, or a finlike structure that grows from its back. Paleontologists know this sail exists and have ideas for the function of (23) the sail however they are uncertain of which idea is the true function. Some scientists believe (24) the sail serves to regulate the Spinosaurus' body temperature and yet others believe its used to attract mates. Still, other scientists think the sail is used to intimidate other predatory dinosaurs for self-defense. These are all viable explanations, but they are also influenced by what scientists know about modern animals. (25) Yet, it's quite possible that the sail could hold a completely unique function.
>
> While it's (26) plausible, even likely that dinosaurs share many traits with modern animals, there is the danger of overattributing these qualities to a unique, extinct species. For much of the early nineteenth century, when people first started studying dinosaur bones, the assumption was that they were simply giant lizards. (27) For the longest time this image was the prevailing view on dinosaurs, until evidence indicated that they were more likely warm blooded. Scientists have also discovered that many dinosaurs had feathers and actually share many traits with modern birds.

19. Which of the following would be the best choice for this sentence (reproduced below)?

Since the first discovery of dinosaur bones, (19) scientists has made strides in technological development and methodologies used to investigate these extinct animals.

a. NO CHANGE
b. scientists has made strides in technological development, and methodologies, used to investigate
c. scientists have made strides in technological development and methodologies used to investigate
d. scientists, have made strides in technological development and methodologies used, to investigate

20. Which of the following would be the best choice for this sentence (reproduced below)?

However, one has to ask, (20) how if earlier perceptions of dinosaurs continue to influence people's understanding of these creatures?

a. NO CHANGE
b. how perceptions of dinosaurs
c. how, if, earlier perceptions of dinosaurs
d. whether earlier perceptions of dinosaurs

21. Which of the following would be the best choice for this sentence (reproduced below)?

(21) The biggest problem with studying dinosaurs is simply that there are no living dinosaurs to observe.

a. NO CHANGE
b. The biggest problem with studying dinosaurs is simple, that there are no living dinosaurs to observe.
c. The biggest problem with studying dinosaurs is simple. There are no living dinosaurs to observe.
d. The biggest problem with studying dinosaurs, is simply that there are no living dinosaurs to observe.

22. Which of the following would be the best choice for this sentence (reproduced below)?

To gauge behavioral characteristics, scientists cross-examine these (22) finds with living animals that seem similar in order to gain understanding.

a. NO CHANGE
b. finds with living animals to explore potential similarities.
c. finds with living animals to gain understanding of similarities.
d. finds with living animals that seem similar, in order, to gain understanding.

23. Which of the following would be the best choice for this sentence (reproduced below)?

Paleontologists know this sail exists and have ideas for the function of (23) the sail however they are uncertain of which idea is the true function.

a. NO CHANGE
b. the sail however, they are uncertain of which idea is the true function.
c. the sail however they are, uncertain, of which idea is the true function.
d. the sail; however, they are uncertain of which idea is the true function.

24. Which of the following would be the best choice for this sentence (reproduced below)?

Some scientists believe (24) the sail serves to regulate the Spinosaurus' body temperature and yet others believe its used to attract mates.

a. NO CHANGE
b. the sail serves to regulate the Spinosaurus' body temperature, yet others believe it's used to attract mates.
c. the sail serves to regulate the Spinosaurus' body temperature and yet others believe it's used to attract mates.
d. the sail serves to regulate the Spinosaurus' body temperature however others believe it's used to attract mates.

25. Which of the following would be the best choice for this sentence (reproduced below)?

(25) Yet, it's quite possible that the sail could hold a completely unique function.

a. NO CHANGE
b. Yet, it's quite possible,
c. It's quite possible,
d. Its quite possible

26. Which of the following would be the best choice for this sentence (reproduced below)?

While it's (26) plausible, even likely that dinosaurs share many traits with modern animals, there is the danger of over attributing these qualities to a unique, extinct species.

a. NO CHANGE
b. plausible, even likely that, dinosaurs share many
c. plausible, even likely, that dinosaurs share many
d. plausible even likely that dinosaurs share many

27. Which of the following would be the best choice for this sentence (reproduced below)?

(27) For the longest time this image was the prevailing view on dinosaurs, until evidence indicated that they were more likely warm blooded.

a. NO CHANGE
b. For the longest time this was the prevailing view on dinosaurs
c. For the longest time, this image, was the prevailing view on dinosaurs
d. For the longest time this was the prevailing image of dinosaurs

Questions 28–36 are based on the following passage:

Everyone has heard the (28) idea of the end justifying the means; that would be Weston's philosophy. Weston is willing to cross any line, commit any act no matter how heinous, to achieve success in his goal. (29) Ransom is reviled by this fact, seeing total evil in Weston's plan. To do an evil act in order (30) to gain a result that's supposedly good would ultimately warp the final act. (31) This opposing viewpoints immediately distinguishes Ransom as the hero. In the conflict with Un-man, Ransom remains true to his moral principles, someone who refuses to be compromised by power. Instead, Ransom makes it clear that by allowing such processes as murder and lying dictate how one attains a positive outcome, (32) the righteous goal becomes corrupted. The good end would not be truly good, but a twisted end that conceals corrupt deeds.

(33) This idea of allowing necessary evils to happen, is very tempting, it is what Weston fell prey to. (34) The temptation of the evil spirit Un-man ultimately takes over Weston and he is possessed. However, Ransom does not give into temptation. He remains faithful to the truth of what is right and incorrect. This leads him to directly face Un-man for the fate of Perelandra and its inhabitants.

Just as Weston was corrupted by the Un-man, (35) Un-man after this seeks to tempt the Queen of Perelandra to darkness. Ransom must literally (36) show her the right path, to accomplish this, he does this based on the same principle as the "means to an end" argument—that good follows good, and evil follows evil. Later in the plot, Weston/Un-man seeks to use deceptive reasoning to turn the queen to sin, pushing the queen to essentially ignore Melildil's rule to satisfy her own curiosity. In this sense, Un-man takes on the role of a false prophet, a tempter. Ransom must shed light on the truth, but this is difficult; his adversary is very clever and uses brilliant language. Ransom's lack of refinement heightens the weight of Un-man's corrupted logic, and so the Queen herself is intrigued by his logic.

Based on an excerpt from *Perelandra* by C.S. Lewis

28. Which of the following would be the best choice for this sentence (reproduced below)?

Everyone has heard the (28) idea of the end justifying the means; that would be Weston's philosophy.

a. NO CHANGE
b. idea of the end justifying the means; this is Weston's philosophy.
c. idea of the end justifying the means, this is the philosophy of Weston
d. idea of the end justifying the means. That would be Weston's philosophy.

29. Which of the following would be the best choice for this sentence (reproduced below)?

(29) Ransom is reviled by this fact, seeing total evil in Weston's plan.

a. NO CHANGE
b. Ransom is reviled by this fact; seeing total evil in Weston's plan.
c. Ransom, is reviled by this fact, seeing total evil in Weston's plan.
d. Ransom reviled by this, sees total evil in Weston's plan.

30. Which of the following would be the best choice for this sentence (reproduced below)?

To do an evil act in order (30) to gain a result that's supposedly good would ultimately warp the final act.

a. NO CHANGE
b. for an outcome that's for a greater good would ultimately warp the final act.
c. to gain a final act would warp its goodness.
d. to achieve a positive outcome would ultimately warp the goodness of the final act.

31. Which of the following would be the best choice for this sentence (reproduced below)?

(31) This opposing viewpoints immediately distinguishes Ransom as the hero.

a. NO CHANGE
b. This opposing viewpoints immediately distinguishes Ransom, as the hero.
c. This opposing viewpoint immediately distinguishes Ransom as the hero.
d. Those opposing viewpoints immediately distinguishes Ransom as the hero.

32. Which of the following would be the best choice for this sentence (reproduced below)?

Instead, Ransom makes it clear that by allowing such processes as murder and lying dictate how one attains a positive outcome, (32) the righteous goal becomes corrupted.

a. NO CHANGE
b. the goal becomes corrupted and no longer righteous.
c. the righteous goal becomes, corrupted.
d. the goal becomes corrupted, when once it was righteous.

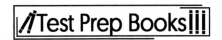

33. Which of the following would be the best choice for this sentence (reproduced below)?

(33) This idea of allowing necessary evils to happen, is very tempting, it is what Weston fell prey to.

a. NO CHANGE
b. This idea of allowing necessary evils to happen, is very tempting. This is what Weston fell prey to.
c. This idea, allowing necessary evils to happen, is very tempting, it is what Weston fell prey to.
d. This tempting idea of allowing necessary evils to happen is what Weston fell prey to.

34. Which of the following would be the best choice for this sentence (reproduced below)?

(34) The temptation of the evil spirit Un-man ultimately takes over Weston and he is possessed.

a. NO CHANGE
b. The temptation of the evil spirit Un-man ultimately takes over and possesses Weston.
c. Weston is possessed as a result of the temptation of the evil spirit Un-man ultimately, who takes over.
d. The temptation of the evil spirit Un-man takes over Weston and he is possessed ultimately.

35. Which of the following would be the best choice for this sentence (reproduced below)?

Just as Weston was corrupted by the Un-man, (35) Un-man after this seeks to tempt the Queen of Perelandra to darkness.

a. NO CHANGE
b. Un-man, after this, would tempt the Queen of Perelandra
c. Un-man, after this, seeks to tempt the Queen of Perelandra
d. Un-man then seeks to tempt the Queen of Perelandra

36. Which of the following would be the best choice for this sentence (reproduced below)?

Ransom must literally (36) show her the right path, to accomplish this, he does this based on the same principle as the "means to an end" argument—that good follows good, and evil follows evil.

a. NO CHANGE
b. show her the right path. To accomplish this, he uses the same principle as the "means to an end" argument
c. show her the right path; to accomplish this he uses the same principle as the "means to an end" argument
d. show her the right path, to accomplish this, the same principle as the "means to an end" argument is applied

Questions 37–45 are based on the following passage:

(37) What's clear about the news is today is that the broader the media the more ways there are to tell a story. Even if different news groups cover the same story, individual newsrooms can interpret or depict the story differently than other counterparts. Stories can also change depending on the type of (38) media in question incorporating different styles and unique ways to approach the news. (39) It is because of these respective media types that ethical and news-

related subject matter can sometimes seem different or altered. But how does this affect the narrative of the new story?

I began by investigating a written newspaper article from the Baltimore Sun. Instantly striking are the bolded headlines. (40) These are clearly meant for direct the viewer to the most exciting and important stories the paper has to offer. What was particularly noteworthy about this edition was that the first page dealt with two major ethical issues. (41) On a national level there was a story on the evolving Petraeus scandal involving his supposed affair. The other article was focused locally in Baltimore, a piece questioning the city's Ethics Board and their current director. Just as a television newscaster communicates the story through camera and dialogue, the printed article applies intentional and targeted written narrative style. More so than any of the mediums, a news article seems to be focused specifically on a given story without need to jump to another. Finer details are usually expanded on (42) in written articles, usually people who read newspapers or go online for web articles want more than a quick blurb. The diction of the story is also more precise and can be either straightforward or suggestive (43) depending in earnest on the goal of the writer. However, there's still plenty of room for opinions to be inserted into the text.

Usually, all news (44) outlets have some sort of bias, it's just a question of how much bias clouds the reporting. As long as this bias doesn't withhold information from the reader, it can be considered credible. (45) However an over use of bias, opinion, and suggestive language can rob readers of the chance to interpret the news events for themselves.

37. Which of the following would be the best choice for this sentence (reproduced below)?

(37) What's clear about the news today is that the broader the media the more ways there are to tell a story.

a. NO CHANGE
b. What's clear, about the news today, is that the broader the media
c. What's clear about today's news is that the broader the media
d. The news today is broader than earlier media

38. Which of the following would be the best choice for this sentence (reproduced below)?

Stories can also change depending on the type of (38) media in question incorporating different styles and unique ways to approach the news.

a. NO CHANGE
b. media in question; each incorporates unique styles and unique
c. media in question. To incorporate different styles and unique
d. media in question, incorporating different styles and unique

39. Which of the following would be the best choice for this sentence (reproduced below)?

(39) It is because of these respective media types that ethical and news-related subject matter can sometimes seem different or altered.

a. NO CHANGE
b. It is because of these respective media types, that ethical and news-related subject matter, can sometimes seem different or altered.
c. It is because of these respective media types, that ethical and news-related subject matter can sometimes seem different or altered.
d. It is because of these respective media types that ethical and news-related subject matter can sometimes seem different. Or altered.

40. Which of the following would be the best choice for this sentence (reproduced below)?

(40) These are clearly meant for direct the viewer to the most exciting and important stories the paper has to offer.

a. NO CHANGE
b. These are clearly meant for the purpose of giving direction to the viewer
c. These are clearly meant to direct the viewer
d. These are clearly meant for the viewer to be directed

41. Which of the following would be the best choice for this sentence (reproduced below)?

(41) On a national level there was a story on the evolving Petraeus scandal involving his supposed affair.

a. NO CHANGE
b. On a national level a story was there
c. On a national level; there was a story
d. On a national level, there was a story

42. Which of the following would be the best choice for this sentence (reproduced below)?

Finer details are usually expanded on (42) in written articles, usually people who read newspapers or go online for web articles want more than a quick blurb.

a. NO CHANGE
b. in written articles. People who usually
c. in written articles, usually, people who
d. in written articles usually people who

43. Which of the following would be the best choice for this sentence (reproduced below)?

The diction of the story is also more precise and can be either straightforward or suggestive (43) depending in earnest on the goal of the writer.

a. NO CHANGE
b. depending; in earnest on the goal of the writer.
c. depending, in earnest, on the goal of the writer.
d. the goal of the writer, in earnest, depends on the goal of the writer.

44. Which of the following would be the best choice for this sentence (reproduced below)?

Usually, all news (44) outlets have some sort of bias, it's just a question of how much bias clouds the reporting.

a. NO CHANGE
b. outlets have some sort of bias. Just a question of how much
c. outlets have some sort of bias it can just be a question of how much
d. outlets have some sort of bias, its just a question of how much

45. Which of the following would be the best choice for this sentence (reproduced below)?

(45) However an over use of bias, opinion, and suggestive language can rob readers of the chance to interpret the news events for themselves.

a. NO CHANGE
b. However, an over use of bias,
c. However, with too much bias,
d. However, an overuse of bias,

Questions 46–54 are based on the following passage:

(46) One of the icon's of romantic and science fiction literature remains Mary Shelley's classic, *Frankenstein, or The Modern Prometheus*. Schools throughout the world still teach the book in literature and philosophy courses. Scientific communities also engage in discussion on the novel. But why? Besides the novel's engaging (47) writing style the story's central theme remains highly relevant in a world of constant discovery and moral dilemmas. Central to the core narrative is the (48) struggle between enlightenment and the cost of overusing power.

The subtitle, *The Modern Prometheus*, encapsulates the inner theme of the story more than the main title of *Frankenstein*. As with many romantic writers, Shelley invokes the classical myths and (49) symbolism of Ancient Greece and Rome to high light core ideas. Looking deeper into the myth of Prometheus sheds light not only on the character of Frankenstein (50) but also poses a psychological dilemma to the audience. Prometheus is the titan who gave fire to mankind. (51) However, more than just fire he gave people knowledge and power. The power of fire advanced civilization. Yet, for giving fire to man, Prometheus is (52) punished by the gods bound to a rock and tormented for his act. This is clearly a parallel to Frankenstein—he is the modern Prometheus.

Frankenstein's quest for knowledge becomes an obsession. It leads him to literally create new life, breaking the bounds of conceivable science to illustrate that man can create life out of nothing. (53) Yet he ultimately faltered as a creator, abandoning his progeny in horror of what he created. Frankenstein then suffers his creature's wrath, (54) the result of his pride, obsession for power and lack of responsibility.

Shelley isn't condemning scientific achievement. Rather, her writing reflects that science and discovery are good things, but, like all power, it must be used wisely. The text alludes to the message that one must have reverence for nature and be mindful of the potential consequences. Frankenstein did not take responsibility or even consider how his actions would affect others. His scientific brilliance ultimately led to suffering.

Based on an excerpt from *Frankenstein* by Mary Shelley

46. Which of the following would be the best choice for this sentence (reproduced below)?

(46) One of the icon's of romantic and science fiction literature remains Mary Shelley's classic, *Frankenstein, or The Modern Prometheus*.

a. NO CHANGE
b. One of the icons of romantic and science fiction literature
c. One of the icon's of romantic, and science fiction literature,
d. The icon of romantic and science fiction literature

47. Which of the following would be the best choice for this sentence (reproduced below)?

Besides the novel's engaging (47) writing style the story's central theme remains highly relevant in a world of constant discovery and moral dilemmas.

a. NO CHANGE
b. writing style the central theme of the story
c. writing style, the story's central theme
d. the story's central theme's writing style

48. Which of the following would be the best choice for this sentence (reproduced below)?

Central to the core narrative is the (48) struggle between enlightenment and the cost of overusing power.

a. NO CHANGE
b. struggle between enlighten and the cost of overusing power.
c. struggle between enlightenment's cost of overusing power.
d. struggle between enlightening and the cost of overusing power.

49. Which of the following would be the best choice for this sentence (reproduced below)?

As with many romantic writers, Shelley invokes the classical myths and (49) symbolism of Ancient Greece and Rome to high light core ideas.

a. NO CHANGE
b. symbolism of Ancient Greece and Rome to highlight core ideas.
c. symbolism of ancient Greece and Rome to highlight core ideas.
d. symbolism of Ancient Greece and Rome highlighting core ideas.

50. Which of the following would be the best choice for this sentence (reproduced below)?

Looking deeper into the myth of Prometheus sheds light not only on the character of Frankenstein (50) but also poses a psychological dilemma to the audience.

a. NO CHANGE
b. but also poses a psychological dilemma with the audience.
c. but also poses a psychological dilemma for the audience.
d. but also poses a psychological dilemma there before the audience.

51. Which of the following would be the best choice for this sentence (reproduced below)?

(51) However, more than just fire he gave people knowledge and power.

a. NO CHANGE
b. However, more than just fire he gave people, knowledge, and power.
c. However, more than just fire, he gave people knowledge and power.
d. Besides actual fire, Prometheus gave people knowledge and power.

52. Which of the following would be the best choice for this sentence (reproduced below)?

Yet, for giving fire to man, Prometheus is (52) punished by the gods bound to a rock and tormented for his act.

a. NO CHANGE
b. punished by the gods, bound to a rock and tormented for his act.
c. bound to a rock and tormented as punishment by the gods.
d. punished for his act by being bound to a rock and tormented as punishment from the gods.

53. Which of the following would be the best choice for this sentence (reproduced below)?

(53) Yet he ultimately faltered as a creator, abandoning his progeny in horror of what he created.

a. NO CHANGE
b. Yet, he ultimately falters as a creator by
c. Yet, he ultimately faltered as a creator,
d. Yet he ultimately falters as a creator by

54. Which of the following would be the best choice for this sentence (reproduced below)?

Frankenstein then suffers his creature's wrath, (54) the result of his pride, obsession for power and lack of responsibility.

a. NO CHANGE
b. the result of his pride, obsession for power and lacking of responsibility.
c. the result of his pride, obsession for power, and lack of responsibility.
d. the result of his pride and also his obsession for power and lack of responsibility.

Questions 55–63 are based on the following passage:

The power of legends continues to enthrall our imagination, provoking us both to wonder and explore. (55) Who doesnt love a good legend? Some say legends never (56) die and this is certainly the case for the most legendary creature of all, Bigfoot. To this day, people still claim sightings of the illusive cryptid. Many think of Bigfoot as America's monster, yet many nations have legends of a similar creature. In my own research I have found that Australia has the Yowie, China has the Yerin, and Russia has the Almas. (57) Their all over the world, the bigfoots and the legends tied to them. Does this mean they could exist?

There are many things to consider when addressing (58) this question but the chief factor is whether there is credible evidence. (59) For science to formally recognize that such a species exists, there needs to be physical proof. While people have found supposed footprints and even (60) captured photos and film of the creature, this validity of such evidence is up for debate. There is room for uncertainty. Most visual evidence is out of focus, thus (61) there is often skepticism whether such images are real. Some researchers have even claimed to have hair and blood samples, but still there is doubt in the scientific community. The reason is simple: there needs to be a body or living specimen found and actively studied in order to prove the Bigfoots' existence.

Yet, one cannot ignore the fact that (62) hundreds of witnesses continuing to describe a creature with uniform features all over the world. These bigfoot sightings aren't a modern occurrence either. Ancient civilizations have reported (63) seeing Bigfoot as well including Native Americans. It is from Native Americans that we gained the popular term Sasquatch, which is the primary name for the North American bigfoot. How does their testimony factor in? If indigenous people saw these animals, could they not have existed at some point? After all, when Europeans first arrived in Africa, they disbelieved the native accounts of the gorilla. But sure enough, Europeans eventually found gorillas and collected a body.

55. Which of the following would be the best choice for this sentence (reproduced below)?

(55) Who doesnt love a good legend?

a. NO CHANGE
b. Who does not love a good legend?
c. A good legend, who doesn't love one?
d. Who doesn't love a good legend?

56. Which of the following would be the best choice for this sentence (reproduced below)?

Some say legends never (56) die and this is certainly the case for the most legendary creature of all, Bigfoot.

a. NO CHANGE
b. die, and this is certainly the case
c. die; this is certainly the case
d. die. This is certainly the case

57. Which of the following would be the best choice for this sentence (reproduced below)?

(57) Their all over the world, the bigfoots and the legends tied to them.

a. NO CHANGE
b. There all over the world, the
c. They're all over the world, the
d. All over the world they are, the

58. Which of the following would be the best choice for this sentence (reproduced below)?

There are many things to consider when addressing (58) this question but the chief factor is whether there is credible evidence.

a. NO CHANGE
b. this question, but the chief factor
c. this question however the chief factor
d. this question; but the chief factor

59. Which of the following would be the best choice for this sentence (reproduced below)?

(59) For science to formally recognize that such a species exists, there needs to be physical proof.

a. NO CHANGE
b. Physical proof are needed in order for science to formally recognize that such a species exists.
c. For science to formally recognize that such a species exists there needs to be physical proof.
d. For science, to formally recognize that such a species exists, there needs to be physical proof.

60. Which of the following would be the best choice for this sentence (reproduced below)?

While people have found supposed footprints and even (60) captured photos and film of the creature, this validity of such evidence is up for debate.

a. NO CHANGE
b. captured photos and film of the creature. This validity of such evidence is up for debate.
c. captured photos and film of the creature, the validities of such evidence is up for debate.
d. captured photos and film of the creature, the validity of such evidence is up for debate.

61. Which of the following would be the best choice for this sentence (reproduced below)?

Most visual evidence is out of focus, thus there is (61) often skepticism whether such images are real.

a. NO CHANGE
b. often skepticism whether such images are real.
c. there is often skepticism, whether such images are real.
d. there is often skepticism weather such images are real.

62. Which of the following would be the best choice for this sentence (reproduced below)?

Yet, one cannot ignore the fact that (62) hundreds of witnesses continuing to describe a creature with uniform features all over the world.

a. NO CHANGE
b. hundreds of witnesses continuing to describing a creature
c. hundreds of witnesses continue to describe a creature
d. hundreds of the witnesses continue to described a creature

63. Which of the following would be the best choice for this sentence (reproduced below)?

Ancient civilizations have reported (63) seeing Bigfoot as well including Native Americans.

a. NO CHANGE
b. seeing Bigfoot, Native Americans as well.
c. seeing Bigfoot also the Native Americans.
d. seeing Bigfoot, including Native Americans.

Questions 64–70 are based on the following passage:

I have to admit that when my father bought a recreational vehicle (RV), I thought he was making a huge mistake. I didn't really know anything about RVs, but I knew that my dad was as big a "city slicker" as there was. (64) In fact, I even thought he might have gone a little bit crazy. On trips to the beach, he preferred to swim at the pool, and whenever he went hiking, he avoided touching any plants for fear that they might be poison ivy. Why would this man, with an almost irrational fear of the outdoors, want a 40-foot camping behemoth?

(65) The RV was a great purchase for our family and brought us all closer together. Every morning (66) we would wake up, eat breakfast, and broke camp. We laughed at our own comical attempts to back The Beast into spaces that seemed impossibly small. (67) We rejoiced as "hackers." When things inevitably went wrong and we couldn't solve the problems on our own, we discovered the incredible helpfulness and friendliness of the RV community. (68) We even made some new friends in the process.

(69) Above all, it allowed us to share adventures. While traveling across America, which we could not have experienced in cars and hotels. Enjoying a campfire on a chilly summer evening with the mountains of Glacier National Park in the background or waking up early in the morning to see the sun rising over the distant spires of Arches National Park are memories that

will always stay with me and our entire family. (70) Those are also memories that my siblings and me have now shared with our own children.

64. Which of the following would be the best choice for this sentence (reproduced below)?

(64) In fact, I even thought he might have gone a little bit crazy.

a. NO CHANGE
b. Move the sentence so that it comes before the preceding sentence.
c. Move the sentence to the end of the first paragraph.
d. Omit the sentence.

65. In context, which is the best version of the underlined portion of this sentence (reproduced below)?

(65) The RV was a great purchase for our family and brought us all closer together.

a. NO CHANGE
b. Not surprisingly, the RV
c. Furthermore, the RV
d. As it turns out, the RV

66. Which is the best version of the underlined portion of this sentence (reproduced below)?

Every morning (66) we would wake up, eat breakfast, and broke camp.

a. NO CHANGE
b. we would wake up, eat breakfast, and break camp.
c. would we wake up, eat breakfast, and break camp?
d. we are waking up, eating breakfast, and breaking camp.

67. Which is the best version of the underlined portion of this sentence (reproduced below)?

(67) We rejoiced as "hackers."

a. NO CHANGE
b. To a nagging problem of technology, we rejoiced as "hackers."
c. We rejoiced when we figured out how to "hack" a solution to a nagging technological problem.
d. To "hack" our way to a solution, we had to rejoice.

68. Which is the best version of the underlined portion of this sentence (reproduced below)?

(68) We even made some new friends in the process.

a. NO CHANGE
b. In the process was the friends we were making.
c. We are even making some new friends in the process.
d. We will make new friends in the process.

69. Which is the best version of the underlined portion of this sentence (reproduced below)?

> (69) Above all, it allowed us to share adventures. While traveling across America, which we could not have experienced in cars and hotels.

a. NO CHANGE
b. Above all, it allowed us to share adventures while traveling across America
c. Above all, it allowed us to share adventures; while traveling across America
d. Above all, it allowed us to share adventures—while traveling across America

70. Which is the best version of the underlined portion of this sentence (reproduced below)?

> (70) Those are also memories that my siblings and me have now shared with our own children.

a. NO CHANGE
b. Those are also memories that me and my siblings
c. Those are also memories that my siblings and I
d. Those are also memories that I and my siblings

Questions 71–75 are based on the following passage:

> We live in a savage world; that's just a simple fact. It is a time of violence, when the need for self-defense is imperative. (71) Martial arts, like Jiu-Jitsu, still play a vital role in ones survival. (72) Jiu-Jitsu, however doesn't justify kicking people around, even when being harassed or attacked. Today, laws prohibit the (73) use of unnecessary force in self-defense; these serve to eliminate beating someone to a pulp once they have been neutralized. Such laws are needed. Apart from being unnecessary to continually strike a person when (74) their down, its immoral. Such over-aggressive retaliation turns the innocent into the aggressor. Jiu-Jitsu provides a way for defending oneself while maintaining the philosophy of restraint and self-discipline. (75) Integrated into its core philosophy, Jiu-Jitsu tempers the potential to do great physical harm with respect for that power and for life.

71. Which of the following would be the best choice for this sentence (reproduced below)?

> (71) Martial arts, like Jiu-Jitsu, still play a vital role in ones survival.

a. NO CHANGE
b. Martial arts, like Jiu-Jitsu, still play a vital role in one's survival.
c. Martial arts, like Jiu-Jitsu still play a vital role in ones survival.
d. Martial arts, like Jiu-Jitsu, still plays a vital role in one's survival.

72. Which of the following would be the best choice for this sentence (reproduced below)?

> (72) Jiu-Jitsu, however doesn't justify kicking people around, even when being harassed or attacked.

a. NO CHANGE
b. Jiu-Jitsu, however, isn't justified by kicking people around,
c. However, Jiu-Jitsu doesn't justify kicking people around,
d. Jiu-Jitsu however doesn't justify kicking people around,

73. Which of the following would be the best choice for this sentence (reproduced below)?

Today, laws prohibit the (73) use of unnecessary force in self-defense; these serve to eliminate beating someone to a pulp once they have been neutralized.

a. NO CHANGE
b. use of unnecessary force in self-defense serving to eliminate
c. use of unnecessary force, in self-defense, these serve to eliminate
d. use of unnecessary force. In self-defense, these serve to eliminate

74. Which of the following would be the best choice for this sentence (reproduced below)?

Apart from being unnecessary to continually strike a person when (74) their down, its immoral.

a. NO CHANGE
b. their down, it's immoral.
c. they're down, its immoral.
d. they're down, it's immoral.

75. Which of the following would be the best choice for this sentence (reproduced below)?

(75) Integrated into its core philosophy, Jiu-Jitsu tempers the potential to do great physical harm with respect for that power, and for life.

a. NO CHANGE
b. Integrated into its core philosophy
c. Integrated into it's core philosophy,
d. Integrated into its' core philosophy,

Writing

Please read the prompt below and answer in an essay format.

Some people feel that sharing their lives on social media sites such as Facebook, Instagram, and Snapchat is fine. They share every aspect of their lives, including pictures of themselves and their families, what they ate for lunch, who they are dating, and when they are going on vacation. They even say that if it's not on social media, it didn't happen. Other people believe that sharing so much personal information is an invasion of privacy and could prove dangerous. They think sharing personal pictures and details invites predators, cyberbullying, and identity theft.

1. Analyze and evaluate the passage given.

2. State and develop your own perspective.

3. Explain the relationship between your perspective and the one given.

Answer Explanations #1

Reading Comprehension

1. D: It emphasizes Mr. Utterson's anguish in failing to identify Hyde's whereabouts. Context clues indicate that Choice *D* is correct because the passage provides great detail of Mr. Utterson's feelings about locating Hyde. Choice *A* does not fit because there is no mention of Mr. Lanyon's mental state. Choice *B* is incorrect; although the text does make mention of bells, Choice *B* is not the *best* answer overall. Choice *C* is incorrect because the passage clearly states that Mr. Utterson was determined, not unsure.

2. A: In the city. The word *city* appears in the passage several times, thus establishing the location for the reader.

3. B: It scares children. The passage states that the Juggernaut causes the children to scream. Choices *A* and *D* don't apply because the text doesn't mention either of these instances specifically. Choice *C* is incorrect because there is nothing in the text that mentions space travel.

4. B: To constantly visit. The mention of *morning*, *noon*, and *night* make it clear that the word *haunt* refers to frequent appearances at various locations. Choice *A* doesn't work because the text makes no mention of levitating. Choices *C* and *D* are not correct because the text makes mention of Mr. Utterson's anguish and disheartenment because of his failure to find Hyde but does not make mention of Mr. Utterson's feelings negatively affecting anyone else.

5. D: This is an example of alliteration. Choice *D* is the correct answer because of the repetition of the *L*-words. Hyperbole is an exaggeration, so Choice *A* doesn't work. No comparison is being made, so no simile or juxtaposition is being used, thus eliminating Choices *B* and *C*.

6. D: The speaker intends to continue to look for Hyde. Choices *A* and *B* are not possible answers because the text doesn't refer to any name changes or an identity crisis, despite Mr. Utterson's extreme obsession with finding Hyde. The text also makes no mention of a mistaken identity when referring to Hyde, so Choice *C* is also incorrect.

7. A: The author's attitude toward the main subject can be described as *intrigue*. Although this is fiction and we are seeing the passage through the eyes of a character, the author still is in control of word choice and tone. *Intrigue* means to arouse curiosity, so we are confronted with words and phrases such as "besieged by questions," "digging," "imagination," and "haunt." Choice *B*, elation, means joy. Choice *C*, animosity, means strong dislike. Choice *D*, rigidity, means stiff or unyielding.

8. B: Mr. Utterson is struggling with the mystery surrounding a dark figure and the terrible crimes he commits. As Mr. Utterson tosses and turns in bed in the long paragraph, we see him wanting to discern the figure's face as he imagines him committing the crimes, but Mr. Utterson has no idea who the figure is.

9. C: Choice *C* is the best answer because of the chronological aspect of the passage. By the transition "From that time forward," we know that Mr. Utterson haunted storefronts *after* his night visions of the mysterious figure, and we also see that Mr. Utterson's dialogue at the very end is a promise to find "Mr. Hyde," whoever he may be.

10. C: The passage is in third person limited, which means we see the thoughts of one character only by the use of the pronouns "he" or "she." First person is characterized by the use of "I." Second person is characterized by the use of "you." Third person omniscient is when we see the thoughts of all the characters in the story, and the author uses the pronouns "he" or "she."

11. A: The purpose is to inform the reader about what assault is and how it is committed. Choice *B* is incorrect because the passage does not state that assault is a lesser form of lethal force, only that an assault can use lethal force, or alternatively, lethal force can be utilized to counter a dangerous assault. Choice *C* is incorrect because the passage is informative and does not have a set agenda. Finally, Choice *D* is incorrect because although the author uses an example in order to explain assault, it is not indicated that this is the author's personal account.

12. C: If the man being attacked in an alley by another man with a knife used self-defense by lethal force, it would not be considered illegal. The presence of a deadly weapon indicates mal-intent and because the individual is isolated in an alley, lethal force in self-defense may be the only way to preserve his life. Choices *A* and *B* can be ruled out because in these situations, no one is in danger of immediate death or bodily harm by someone else. Choice *D* is an assault and does exhibit intent to harm, but this situation isn't severe enough to merit lethal force; there is no intent to kill.

13. B: As discussed in the second passage, there are several forms of assault, like assault with a deadly weapon, verbal assault, or threatening posture or language. Choice *A* is incorrect because the author does mention what the charges are on assaults; therefore, we cannot assume that they are more or less than unnecessary use of force charges. Choice *C* is incorrect because anyone is capable of assault; the author does not state that one group of people cannot commit assault. Choice *D* is incorrect because assault is never justified. Self-defense resulting in lethal force can be justified.

14. D: The use of lethal force is not evaluated on the intent of the user, but rather on the severity of the primary attack that warranted self-defense. This statement most undermines the last part of the passage because it directly contradicts how the law evaluates the use of lethal force. Choices *A* and *B* are stated in the paragraph, so they do not undermine the explanation from the author. Choice *C* does not necessarily undermine the passage, but it does not support the passage either. It is more of an opinion that does not offer strength or weakness to the explanation.

15. C: An assault with deadly intent can lead to an individual using lethal force to preserve their well-being. Choice *C* is correct because it clearly establishes what both assault and lethal force are and gives the specific way in which the two concepts meet. Choice *A* is incorrect because lethal force doesn't necessarily result in assault. This is also why Choice *B* is incorrect. Not all assaults would necessarily be life-threatening to the point where lethal force is needed for self-defense. Choice *D* is compelling but ultimately too vague; the statement touches on aspects of the two ideas but fails to present the concrete way in which the two are connected to each other.

16. A: Both passages open by defining a legal concept and then continue to describe situations in order to further explain the concept. Choice *D* is incorrect because while the passages utilize examples to help explain the concepts discussed, the author doesn't indicate that they are specific court cases. It's also clear that the passages don't open with examples, but instead, they begin by defining the terms addressed in each passage. This eliminates Choice *B,* and ultimately reveals Choice *A* to be the correct answer. Choice *A* accurately outlines the way both passages are structured. Because the passages follow a nearly identical structure, the Choice *C* can easily be ruled out.

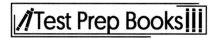

17. C: Intent is very important for determining both lethal force and assault; intent is examined in both parties and helps determine the severity of the issue. Choices *A* and *B* are incorrect because it is clear in both passages that intent is a prevailing theme in both lethal force and assault. Choice *D* is compelling, but if a person uses lethal force to defend himself or herself, the intent of the defender is also examined in order to help determine if there was excessive force used. Choice *C* is correct because it states that intent is important for determining both lethal force and assault, and that intent is used to gauge the severity of the issues. Remember, just as lethal force can escalate to excessive use of force, there are different kinds of assault. Intent dictates several different forms of assault.

18. B: The example is used to demonstrate a single example of two different types of assault, then adding in a third type of assault to the example's conclusion. The example mainly provides an instance of "threatening body language" and "provocative language" with the homeowner gesturing threats to his neighbor. It ends the example by adding a third type of assault: physical strikes. This example is used to show the variant nature of assaults. Choice *A* is incorrect because it doesn't mention the "physical strike" assault at the end and is not specific enough. Choice *C* is incorrect because the example does not say anything about the definition of lethal force or how it might be altered. Choice *D* is incorrect, as the example mentions nothing about cause and effect.

19. C: The word *apprehension* most nearly means fear. The passage indicates that "assault is the unlawful attempt of one person to apply fear/anxiety on another individual by an imminent threat." The creation of fear in another individual seems to be a property of assault.

20. D: Choice *D* is the best answer, "The concept of lethal force as a last resort and the point at which it can cross a line from defense to manslaughter." The last paragraph of the first passage states what the term "last resort" means and how it's distinguished in the eyes of the law.

21. A: The word *patronage* most nearly means *auspices*, which means *protection* or *support*. Choice *B*, *aberration*, means *deformity* and does not make sense within the context of the sentence. Choice *C*, *acerbic,* means *bitter* and also does not make sense in the sentence. Choice *D*, *adulation*, is a positive word meaning *praise*, and thus does not fit with the word *condescending* in the sentence.

22. D: *Working man* is most closely aligned with Choice *D*, *bourgeois.* In the context of the speech, the word *bourgeois* means *working* or *middle class*. Choice *A*, *plebian*, does suggest *common people*; however, this is a term that is specific to ancient Rome. Choice *B*, *viscount*, is a European title used to describe a specific degree of nobility. Choice *C*, *entrepreneur*, is a person who operates their own business.

23. C: In the context of the speech, the term *working man* most closely correlates with Choice *C*, "A working man is someone who works for wages among the middle class." Choice *A* is not mentioned in the passage and is off-topic. Choice *B* may be true in some cases, but it does not reflect the sentiment described for the term *working man* in the passage. Choice *D* may also be arguably true. However, it is not given as a definition but as *acts* of the working man, and the topics of *field, factory,* and *screen* are not mentioned in the passage.

24. D: *Enterprise* most closely means *cause*. Choices *A, B,* and *C* are all related to the term *enterprise*. However, Dickens speaks of a *cause* here, not a company, courage, or a game. "He will stand by such an enterprise" is a call to stand by a cause to enable the working man to have a certain autonomy over his own economic standing. The very first paragraph ends with the statement that the working man "shall . . . have a share in the management of an institution which is designed for his benefit."

25. B: The speaker's salutation is one from an entertainer to his audience and uses the friendly language to connect to his audience before a serious speech. Recall in the first paragraph that the speaker is there to "accompany [the audience] . . . through one of my little Christmas books," making him an author there to entertain the crowd with his own writing. The speech preceding the reading is the passage itself, and, as the tone indicates, a serious speech addressing the "working man." Although the passage speaks of employers and employees, the speaker himself is not an employer of the audience, so Choice *A* is incorrect. Choice *C* is also incorrect, as the salutation is not used ironically, but sincerely, as the speech addresses the well-being of the crowd. Choice *D* is incorrect because the speech is not given by a politician, but by a writer.

26. B: Choice *A* is incorrect because that is the speaker's *first* desire, not his second. Choices *C* and *D* are tricky because the language of both of these is mentioned after the word *second*. However, the speaker doesn't get to the second wish until the next sentence. Choices *C* and *D* are merely prepositions preparing for the statement of the main clause, Choice *B,* for the working man to have a say in his institution which is designed for his benefit.

27. C: The speaker's tone can best be described as *confident and informed.* The speaker addresses the audience as "My good friends," and says, "I have no fear of being misunderstood," which implies confidence. Additionally, the speaker's knowledge of the proposal and topic can be seen in the text as well, especially in the second paragraph.

28. D: To provide credibility to the working man and share confidence in their ability to take on responsibilities if they are compensated appropriately. The speaker provides credibility by saying "he will stand by such an enterprise with the utmost of his patience," and displays their responsibilities by saying "he will feel his responsibility like an honest man."

29. A: The speaker says to "Erect in Birmingham a great Education Institution, properly educational." Choice *B* is close, but the speaker uses the name "Temple of Concord" in the passage as a metaphor, so this is incorrect. The other two choices aren't mentioned in the passage.

30. B: The word *antagonism* most nearly means opposition. Choice *A*, *conformity*, is the opposite of antagonism. Choice *C*, *affluence*, means abundance. Choice *D*, *scarcity*, means being deficient in something.

31. D: The use of "I" could have all of the effects for the reader; it could serve to have a "hedging" effect, allow the reader to connect with the author in a more personal way, and cause the reader to empathize more with the egrets. However, it doesn't distance the reader from the text, thus eliminating Choice *D*.

32. C: The quote provides an example of a warden protecting one of the colonies. Choice *A* is incorrect because the speaker of the quote is a warden, not a hunter. Choice *B* is incorrect because the quote does not lighten the mood but shows the danger of the situation between the wardens and the hunters. Choice *D* is incorrect because there is no humor found in the quote.

33. D: A *rookery* is a colony of breeding birds. Although *rookery* could mean Choice *A*, houses in a slum area, it does not make sense in this context. Choices *B* and *C* are both incorrect, as this is not a place for hunters to trade tools or for wardens to trade stories.

34. B: An important bird colony. The previous sentence is describing "twenty colonies" of birds, so what follows should be a bird colony. Choice *A* may be true, but we have no evidence of this in the text.

Choice *C* does touch on the tension between the hunters and wardens, but there is no official "Bird Island Battle" mentioned in the text. Choice *D* does not exist in the text.

35. D: To demonstrate the success of the protective work of the Audubon Association. The text mentions several different times how and why the association has been successful and gives examples to back this fact. Choice *A* is incorrect because although the article, in some instances, calls certain people to act, it is not the purpose of the entire passage. There is no way to tell if Choices *B* and *C* are correct, as they are not mentioned in the text.

36. C: To have a better opportunity to hunt the birds. Choice *A* might be true in a general sense, but it is not relevant to the context of the text. Choice *B* is incorrect because the hunters are not studying lines of flight to help wardens, but to hunt birds. Choice *D* is incorrect because nothing in the text mentions that hunters are trying to build homes underneath lines of flight of birds for good luck.

37. C: The passage states in the third paragraph that a year before, "a number of egrets were seen in eastern Massachusetts." Florida is mentioned in the passage as a place where bird colonies reside. The other two locations are not mentioned in the passage.

38. A: The word *commissioned* most nearly means *appointed*. Choice *B*, *compelled*, means forced. Choice *C*, *beguiled*, means entertained. Choice *D*, *fortified*, means defended.

39. D: Several hidden colonies were found which prompted Dutcher and Pearson to protect them. This information is presented in the first paragraph starting with the sentence "Two years ago." The other answer choices are current to the passage.

40. C: *In transit* means on the way to the destination. Choice *A* is the definition of *travelling*. Choice *B* is the definition of *delegate*. Choice *D* is the definition of *provoke*.

English Language

1. C: Choice *C* correctly uses *from* to describe the fact that dogs are related to wolves. The word *through* is incorrectly used here, so Choice *A* is incorrect. Choice *B* makes no sense. Choice *D* unnecessarily changes the verb tense in addition to incorrectly using *through*.

2. B: Choice *B* is correct because the Oxford comma is applied, clearly separating the specific terms. Choice *A* lacks this clarity. Choice *C* is correct but too wordy since commas can be easily applied. Choice *D* doesn't flow with the sentence's structure.

3. D: Choice *D* correctly uses the question mark, fixing the sentence's main issue. Thus, Choice *A* is incorrect because questions do not end with periods. Choice *B*, although correctly written, changes the meaning of the original sentence. Choice *C* is incorrect because it completely changes the direction of the sentence, disrupts the flow of the paragraph, and lacks the crucial question mark.

4. A: Choice *A* is correct since there are no errors in the sentence. Choices *B* and *C* both have extraneous commas, disrupting the flow of the sentence. Choice *D* unnecessarily rearranges the sentence.

5. D: Choice *D* is correct because the commas serve to distinguish that *artificial selection* is just another term for *selective breeding* before the sentence continues. The structure is preserved, and the sentence can flow with more clarity. Choice *A* is incorrect because the sentence needs commas to avoid being a run-on. Choice *B* is close but still lacks the required comma after *selection*, so this is incorrect. Choice *C* is incorrect because the comma to set off the aside should be placed after *breeding* instead of *called*.

6. B: Choice *B* is correct because the sentence is talking about a continuing process. Therefore, the best modification is to add the word *to* in front of *increase*. Choice *A* is incorrect because this modifier is missing. Choice *C* is incorrect because with the additional comma, the present tense of *increase* is inappropriate. Choice *D* makes more sense, but the tense is still not the best to use.

7. A: The sentence has no errors, so Choice *A* is correct. Choice *B* is incorrect because it adds an unnecessary comma. Choice *C* is incorrect because *advantage* should not be plural in this sentence without the removal of the singular *an*. Choice *D* is very tempting. While this would make the sentence more concise, this would ultimately alter the context of the sentence, which would be incorrect.

8. C: Choice *C* correctly uses *on to*, describing the way genes are passed generationally. The use of *into* is inappropriate for this context, which makes Choice *A* incorrect. Choice *B* is close, but *onto* refers to something being placed on a surface. Choice *D* doesn't make logical sense.

9. D: Choice *D* is correct, since only proper names should be capitalized. Because the name of a dog breed is not a proper name, Choice *A* is incorrect. In terms of punctuation, only one comma after *example* is needed, so Choices *B* and *C* are incorrect.

10. D: Choice *D* is the correct answer because "rather" acts as an interrupting word here and thus should be separated by commas. Choices *A, B,* and *C* all use commas unwisely, breaking the flow of the sentence.

11. B: Since the sentence can stand on its own without *Usually*, separating it from the rest of the sentence with a comma is correct. Choice *A* needs the comma after *Usually*, while Choice *C* uses commas incorrectly. Choice *D* is tempting, but changing *turn* to past tense goes against the rest of the paragraph.

12. A: In Choice *A*, the dependent clause *Sometimes in particularly dull seminars* is seamlessly attached with a single comma after *seminars*. Choice *B* contains too many commas. Choice *C* does not correctly combine the dependent clause with the independent clause. Choice *D* introduces too many unnecessary commas.

13. D: Choice *D* rearranges the sentence to be more direct and straightforward, so it is correct. Choice *A* needs a comma after *on*. Choice *B* introduces unnecessary commas. Choice *C* creates an incomplete sentence, since *Because I wasn't invested in what was going on* is a dependent clause.

14. C: Choice *C* is fluid and direct, making it the best revision. Choice *A* is incorrect because the construction is awkward and lacks parallel structure. Choice *B* is incorrect because of the unnecessary comma and period. Choice *D* is close, but its sequence is still awkward and overly complicated.

15. B: Choice *B* correctly adds a comma after *person* and cuts out the extraneous writing, making the sentence more streamlined. Choice *A* is poorly constructed, lacking proper grammar to connect the sections of the sentence correctly. Choice *C* inserts an unnecessary semicolon and doesn't enable this section to flow well with the rest of the sentence. Choice *D* is better but still unnecessarily long.

16. D: This sentence, though short, is a complete sentence. The only thing the sentence needs is an em-dash after "Easy." In this sentence the em-dash works to add emphasis to the word "Easy" and also acts in place of a colon, but in a less formal way. Therefore, Choice *D* is correct. Choices *A* and *B* lack the crucial comma, while Choice *C* unnecessarily breaks the sentence apart.

17. C: Choice *C* successfully fixes the construction of the sentence, changing *drawing* into *to draw*. Keeping the original sentence disrupts the flow, so Choice *A* is incorrect. Choice *B*'s use of *which* offsets the whole sentence. Choice *D* is incorrect because it unnecessarily expands the sentence content and makes it more confusing.

18. B: Choice *B* fixes the homophone issue. Because the author is talking about people, *their* must be used instead of *there*. This revision also appropriately uses the Oxford comma, separating and distinguishing *lives, world, and future*. Choice *A* uses the wrong homophone and is missing commas. Choice *C* neglects to fix these problems and unnecessarily changes the tense of *applies*. Choice *D* fixes the homophone but fails to properly separate *world* and *future*.

19. C: Choice *C* is correct because it fixes the core issue with this sentence: the singular *has* should not describe the plural *scientists*. Thus, Choice *A* is incorrect. Choices *B* and *D* add unnecessary commas.

20. D: Choice *D* correctly conveys the writer's intention of asking if, or *whether*, early perceptions of dinosaurs are still influencing people. Choice *A* makes no sense as worded. Choice *B* is better, but *how* doesn't coincide with the context. Choice *C* adds unnecessary commas.

21. A: Choice *A* is correct, as the sentence does not require modification. Choices *B* and *C* implement extra punctuation unnecessarily, disrupting the flow of the sentence. Choice *D* incorrectly adds a comma in an awkward location.

22. B: Choice *B* is the strongest revision, as adding *to explore* is very effective in both shortening the sentence and maintaining, even enhancing, the point of the writer. To explore is to seek understanding in order to gain knowledge and insight, which coincides with the focus of the overall sentence. Choice *A* is not technically incorrect, but it is overcomplicated. Choice *C* is a decent revision, but the sentence could still be more condensed and sharpened. Choice *D* fails to make the sentence more concise and inserts unnecessary commas.

23. D: Choice *D* correctly applies a semicolon to introduce a new line of thought while remaining in a single sentence. The comma after *however* is also appropriately placed. Choice *A* is a run-on sentence. Choice *B* is also incorrect because the single comma is not enough to fix the sentence. Choice *C* adds commas around *uncertain* which are unnecessary.

24. B: Choice *B* not only fixes the homophone issue from *its*, which is possessive, to *it's*, which is a contraction of *it is*, but also streamlines the sentence by adding a comma and eliminating *and*. Choice *A* is incorrect because of these errors. Choices *C* and *D* only fix the homophone issue.

25. A: Choice *A* is correct, as the sentence is fine the way it is. Choices *B* and *C* add unnecessary commas, while Choice *D* uses the possessive *its* instead of the contraction *it's*.

26. C: Choice *C* is correct because the phrase *even likely* is flanked by commas, creating a kind of aside, which allows the reader to see this separate thought while acknowledging it as part of the overall sentence and subject at hand. Choice *A* is incorrect because it seems to ramble after *even* due to a missing comma after *likely*. Choice *B* is better but inserting a comma after *that* warps the flow of the writing. Choice *D* is incorrect because there must be a comma after *plausible*.

27. D: Choice *D* strengthens the overall sentence structure while condensing the words. This makes the subject of the sentence, and the emphasis of the writer, much clearer to the reader. Thus, while Choice *A* is technically correct, the language is choppy and over-complicated. Choice *B* is better but lacks the reference to a specific image of dinosaurs. Choice *C* introduces unnecessary commas.

28. B: Choice *B* correctly joins the two independent clauses. Choice *A* is decent, but *that would be* is too verbose for the sentence. Choice *C* incorrectly changes the semicolon to a comma. Choice *D* splits the clauses effectively but is not concise enough.

29. A: Choice *A* is correct, as the original sentence has no error. Choices *B* and *C* employ unnecessary semicolons and commas. Choice *D* would be an ideal revision, but it lacks the comma after *Ransom* that would enable the sentence structure to flow.

30. D: By reorganizing the sentence, the context becomes clearer with Choice *D*. Choice *A* has an awkward sentence structure. Choice *B* offers a revision that doesn't correspond well with the original sentence's intent. Choice *C* cuts out too much of the original content, losing the full meaning.

31. C: Choice *C* fixes the disagreement between the singular *this* and the plural *viewpoints*. Choice *A*, therefore, is incorrect. Choice *B* introduces an unnecessary comma. In Choice *D*, *those* agrees with *viewpoints*, but neither agrees with *distinguishes*.

32. A: Choice *A* is direct and clear, without any punctuation errors. Choice *B* is well-written but too wordy. Choice *C* adds an unnecessary comma. Choice *D* is also well-written but much less concise than Choice *A*.

33. D: Choice *D* rearranges the sentence to improve clarity and impact, with *tempting* directly describing *idea*. On its own, Choice *A* is a run-on. Choice *B* is better because it separates the clauses, but it keeps an unnecessary comma. Choice *C* is also an improvement but still a run-on.

34. B: Choice *B* is the best answer simply because the sentence makes it clear that Un-man takes over and possesses Weston. In Choice *A*, these events sounded like two different things, instead of an action and result. Choices *C* and *D* make this relationship clearer, but the revisions don't flow very well grammatically.

35. D: Changing the phrase *after this* to *then* makes the sentence less complicated and captures the writer's intent, making Choice *D* correct. Choice *A* is awkwardly constructed. Choices *B* and *C* misuse their commas and do not adequately improve the clarity.

36. B: By starting a new sentence, the run-on issue is eliminated, and a new line of reasoning can be seamlessly introduced, making Choice *B* correct. Choice *A* is thus incorrect. While Choice *C* fixes the run-on via a semicolon, a comma is still needed after *this*. Choice *D* contains a comma splice. The independent clauses must be separated by more than just a comma, even with the rearrangement of the second half of the sentence.

37. C: Choice *C* condenses the original sentence while being more active in communicating the emphasis on changing times/media that the author is going for, so it is correct. Choice *A* is clunky because it lacks a comma after *today* to successfully transition into the second half of the sentence. Choice *B* inserts unnecessary commas. Choice *D* is a good revision of the underlined section, but not only does it not fully capture the original meaning, it also does not flow into the rest of the sentence.

38. B: Choice *B* clearly illustrates the author's point, with a well-placed semicolon that breaks the sentence into clearer, more readable sections. Choice *A* lacks punctuation. Choice *C* is incorrect because the period inserted after *question* forms an incomplete sentence. Choice *D* is a very good revision but does not make the author's point clearer than the original.

39. A: Choice *A* is correct: while the sentence seems long, it actually doesn't require any commas. The conjunction *that* successfully combines the two parts of the sentence without the need for additional punctuation. Choices *B* and *C* insert commas unnecessarily, incorrectly breaking up the flow of the sentence. Choice *D* alters the meaning of the original text by creating a new sentence, which is only a fragment.

40. C: Choice *C* correctly replaces *for* with *to*, the correct preposition for the selected area. Choice *A* is not the answer because of this incorrect preposition. Choice *B* is unnecessarily long and disrupts the original sentence structure. Choice *D* is also too wordy and lacks parallel structure.

41. D: Choice *D* is the answer because it inserts the correct punctuation to fix the sentence, linking the dependent and independent clauses. Choice *A* is therefore incorrect. Choice *B* is also incorrect since this revision only adds content to the sentence while lacking grammatical precision. Choice *C* overdoes the punctuation; only a comma is needed, not a semicolon.

42. B: Choice *B* correctly separates the section into two sentences and changes the word order to make the second part clearer. Choice *A* is incorrect because it is a run-on. Choice *C* adds an extraneous comma, while Choice *D* makes the run-on worse and does not coincide with the overall structure of the sentence.

43. C: Choice *C* is the best answer because of how the commas are used to flank *in earnest*. This distinguishes the side thought (*in earnest*) from the rest of the sentence. Choice *A* needs punctuation. Choice *B* inserts a semicolon in a spot that doesn't make sense, resulting in a fragmented sentence and lost meaning. Choice *D* is unnecessarily repetitive and creates a run-on.

44. A: Choice *A* is correct because the sentence contains no errors. The comma after *bias* successfully links the two halves of the sentence, and the use of *it's* is correct as a contraction of *it is*. Choice *B* creates a sentence fragment, while Choice *C* creates a run-on. Choice *D* incorrectly changes *it's* to *its*.

45. D: Choice *D* correctly inserts a comma after *However* and fixes *over use* to *overuse*—in this usage, it is one word. Choice *A* is therefore incorrect, as is Choice *B*. Choice *C* is a good revision but does not fit well with the rest of the sentence.

46. B: Choice *B* is correct because it removes the apostrophe from *icon's*, since the noun *icon* is not possessing anything. This conveys the author's intent of setting *Frankenstein* apart from other icons of the romantic and science fiction genres. Choices *A* and *C* are therefore incorrect. Choice *D* is a good revision but alters the meaning of the sentence—*Frankenstein* is one of the icons, not the sole icon.

47 C: Choice *C* correctly adds a comma after *style*, successfully joining the dependent and the independent clauses as a single sentence. Choice *A* is incorrect because the dependent and independent clauses remain unsuccessfully combined without the comma. Choices *B* and *D* do nothing to fix this.

48. A: Choice *A* is correct, as the sentence doesn't require changes. Choice *B* incorrectly changes the noun *enlightenment* into the verb *enlighten*. Choices *C* and *D* alter the original meaning of the sentence.

49. B: Choice *B* is correct, fixing the incorrect split of *highlight*. This is a polyseme, a word combined from two unrelated words to make a new word. On their own, *high* and *light* make no sense for the sentence, making Choice *A* incorrect. Choice *C* incorrectly decapitalizes *Ancient*—since it modifies *Greece* and works with the noun to describe a civilization, *Ancient Greece* functions as a proper noun, which should be capitalized. Choice *D* uses *highlighting*, a gerund, but the present tense of *highlight* is what works with the rest of the sentence; to make this change, a comma would be needed after *Rome*.

50. A: Choice *A* is correct, as *not only* and *but also* are correlative pairs. In this sentence, *but* successfully transitions the first part into the second half, making punctuation unnecessary. Additionally, the use of *to* indicates that an idea or challenge is being presented to the reader. Choice *B*'s *with*, *C*'s *for*, and *D*'s *there before* are not as active, meaning these revisions weaken the sentence.

51. D: Choice *D* is correct, adding finer details to help the reader understand exactly what Prometheus did and his impact: fire came with knowledge and power. Choice *A* lacks a comma after *fire*. Choice *B* inserts unnecessary commas since *people* is not part of the list *knowledge and power*. Choice *C* is a strong revision but could be confusing, hinting that the fire was knowledge and power itself, as opposed to being symbolized by the fire.

52. C: Choice *C* reverses the order of the section, making the sentence more direct. Choice *A* lacks a comma after *gods*, and although Choice *B* adds this, the structure is too different from the first half of the sentence to flow correctly. Choice *D* is overly complicated and repetitious in its structure even though it doesn't need any punctuation.

53. B: Choice *B* fixes the two problems of the sentence, changing *faltered* to present tense in agreement with the rest of the passage, and correctly linking the two dependent clauses. Choice *A* is therefore incorrect. Choice *C* does not correct the past tense of *faltered*. Choice *D* correctly adds the conjunction *by*, but it lacks a comma after the conjunction *Yet*.

54. C: Choice *C* successfully applies a comma after *power*, distinguishing the causes of Frankenstein's suffering and maintaining parallel structure. Choice *A* is thus incorrect. Choice *B* lacks the necessary punctuation and unnecessarily changes *lack* to a gerund. Choice *D* adds unnecessary wording, making the sentence more cumbersome.

55. D: Choice *D* correctly inserts an apostrophe into the contraction *doesn't*. Choice *A* is incorrect because of this omission. Choices *B* and *C* are better than the original but do not fit well with the informal tone of the passage.

56. B: Choice *B* is correct, successfully combining the two independent clauses of this compound sentence by adding a comma before "and" to create the effective pause and transition between clauses. Choice *A* does not join the independent clauses correctly. Choices *C* and *D* offer alternate ways of joining these clauses, but since "and" is already part of the sentence, adding the comma is the most logical choice. This also keeps the informal tone set by the rest of the passage.

57. C: Choice *C* correctly fixes the homophone issue of *their* and *they're*. *Their* implies ownership, which is not needed here. The author intends *they're*, a contraction of *they are*. Thus, Choice *A* is incorrect, as is Choice *B*, using the homophone *there*. Choice *D* eliminates the homophone issue altogether, but the sentence becomes more clunky because of that.

58. B: Choice *B* correctly joins the two independent clauses with a comma before *but*. Choice *A* is incorrect because, without the comma, it is a run-on sentence. Choice *C* also lacks punctuation and uses *however*, which should be reserved for starting a new sentence or perhaps after a semicolon. Choice *D* is incorrect because the semicolon throws off the sentence structure and is incorrectly used; the correct revision would have also removed *but*.

59. A: Choice *A* is correct because the sentence does not require modification. Choice *B* is incorrect because it uses the faulty subject/verb agreement, "Physical proof are." Choice *C* is incorrect because a comma would need to follow *exists*. Choice *D* is incorrect because the comma after *science* is unnecessary.

60. D: Choice *D* correctly changes *this* to *the* and retains *validity*, making it the right choice. Choices *A* and *B* keep *this*, which is not as specific as "the." Choice *C* incorrectly pluralizes *validity*.

61. A: Choice *A* is correct because the sentence is fine without revisions. Choice *B* is incorrect, since removing *there is* is unnecessary and confusing. Choice *C* is incorrect since it inserts an unnecessary comma. Choice *D* introduces a homophone issue: *weather* refers to climatic states and atmospheric events, while *whether* expresses doubt, which is the author's intent.

62. C: Choice *C* correctly changes *continuing* to the present tense. Choice *A* is incorrect because of this out-of-place gerund use. Choice *B* not only does not fix this issue but also incorrectly changes *describe* into a gerund. While Choice *D* correctly uses *continue*, *describe* is incorrectly put in the past tense.

63. D: Choice *D* is correct, since it eliminates the unnecessary *as well* and adds a comma to separate the given example, making the sentence more direct. Choice *A* seems repetitive with *as well*, since it has *including*, and at the least needs punctuation. Choice *B* is poorly constructed, taking out the clearer *including*. Choice *C* also makes little sense.

64. B: Move the sentence so that it comes before the preceding sentence. For this question, place the underlined sentence in each prospective choice's position. To keep it as-is is incorrect because the father "going crazy" doesn't logically follow the fact that he was a "city slicker." Choice *C* is incorrect because the sentence in question is not a concluding sentence and does not transition smoothly into the second paragraph. Choice *D* is incorrect because the sentence doesn't necessarily need to be omitted since it logically follows the very first sentence in the passage.

65. D: Choice *D* is correct because "As it turns out" indicates a contrast from the previous sentiment, that the RV was a great purchase. Choice *A* is incorrect because the sentence needs an effective transition from the paragraph before. Choice *B* is incorrect because the text indicates it *is* surprising that the RV was a great purchase because the author was skeptical beforehand. Choice *C* is incorrect because the transition "Furthermore" does not indicate a contrast.

66. B: This sentence calls for parallel structure. Choice *B* is correct because the verbs "wake," "eat," and "break" are consistent in tense and parts of speech. Choice *A* is incorrect because the words "wake" and "eat" are present tense while the word "broke" is in past tense. Choice *C* is incorrect because this turns the sentence into a question, which doesn't make sense within the context. Choice *D* is incorrect because it breaks tense with the rest of the passage. "Waking," "eating," and "breaking" are all present participles, and the context around the sentence is in past tense.

67. C: Choice *C* is correct because it is clear, concise, and fits within the context of the passage. Choice *A* is incorrect because "We rejoiced as 'hackers'" does not give a reason why hacking was rejoiced. Choice *B* is incorrect because it does not mention a solution being found and is therefore not specific enough.

Choice *D* is incorrect because the meaning is eschewed by the helping verb "had to rejoice," and the sentence does not give enough detail as to what the problem entails.

68. A: The original sentence is correct because the verb tense as well as the order of the sentence makes sense in the given context. Choice *B* is incorrect because the order of the words makes the sentence more confusing than it otherwise would be. Choice *C* is incorrect because "We are even making" is in present tense. Choice *D* is incorrect because "We will make" is future tense. The surrounding text of the sentence is in past tense.

69. B: Choice *B* is correct because there is no punctuation needed if a dependent clause ("while traveling across America") is located behind the independent clause ("it allowed us to share adventures"). Choice *A* is incorrect because there are two dependent clauses connected and no independent clause, and a complete sentence requires at least one independent clause. Choice *C* is incorrect because of the same reason as Choice *A*. Semicolons have the same function as periods: there must be an independent clause on either side of the semicolon. Choice *D* is incorrect because the dash simply interrupts the complete sentence.

70. C: The rules for "me" and "I" is that one should use "I" when it is the subject pronoun of a sentence, and "me" when it is the object pronoun of the sentence. Break the sentence up to see if "I" or "me" should be used. To say "Those are memories that I have now shared" makes more sense than to say "Those are memories that me have now shared." Choice *D* is incorrect because "my siblings" should come before "I."

71. B: Choice *B* is correct because it adds an apostrophe to *ones*, which indicates *one's* possession of *survival*. Choice *A* doesn't do this, so it is incorrect. This is the same for Choice *C*, but that option also takes out the crucial comma after *Jiu-Jitsu*. Choice *D* is incorrect because it changes *play* to *plays*. This disagrees with the plural *Martial arts*, exemplified by having an example of its many forms, *Jiu-Jitsu*. Therefore, *play* is required.

72. C: Choice *C* is the best answer because it most clearly defines the point that the author is trying to make. The original sentence would need a comma after *however* in order to continue the sentence fluidly—but this option isn't available. Choice *B* is close, but this option changes the meaning of the sentence. Therefore, the best alternative is to begin the sentence with *However* and have a comma follow right after it in order to introduce a new idea. The original context is still maintained, but the flow of the language is more streamlined. Thus, Choice *A* is incorrect. Choice *D* would need a comma before and after *however*, so it is also incorrect.

73. A: Choice *A* is the best answer for several reasons. To begin, the section is grammatically correct in using a semicolon to connect the two independent clauses. This allows the two ideas to be connected without separating them. In this context, the semicolon makes more sense for the overall sentence structure and passage as a whole. Choice *B* is incorrect because it forms a run-on. Choice *C* applies a comma in incorrect positions. Choice *D* separates the sentence in a place that does not make sense for the context.

74. D: Choice *D* is the correct answer because it fixes two key issues. First, *their* is incorrectly used. *Their* is a possessive indefinite pronoun and also an antecedent—neither of these fit the context of the sentence, so Choices *A* and *B* are incorrect. What should be used instead is *they're*, which is the contraction of *they are*, emphasizing action or the result of action in this case. Choice *D* also corrects another contraction-related issue with *its*. Again, *its* indicates possession, while *it's* is the contraction of *it is*. The latter is what's needed for the sentence to make sense and be grammatically correct. Thus, Choice *C* is also incorrect.

75. A: Choice *A* is correct because the section contains no errors and clearly communicates the writer's point. Choice *B* is incorrect because it lacks a comma after *philosophy*, needed to link the first clause with the second. Choice *C* also has this issue but additionally alters *its* to *it's*; since *it is* does not make sense in this sentence, this is incorrect. Choice *D* is incorrect because *its* is already plural possessive and does not need an apostrophe on the end.

Practice Test #2

Reading Comprehension

Questions 1–10 are based on the following passage:

As long ago as 1860 it was the proper thing to be born at home. At present, so I am told, the high gods of medicine have decreed that the first cries of the young shall be uttered upon the anesthetic air of a hospital, preferably a fashionable one. So young Mr. and Mrs. Roger Button were fifty years ahead of style when they decided, one day in the summer of 1860, that their first baby should be born in a hospital. Whether this anachronism had any bearing upon the astonishing history I am about to set down will never be known.

I shall tell you what occurred, and let you judge for yourself.

The Roger Buttons held an enviable position, both social and financial, in ante-bellum Baltimore. They were related to the This Family and the That Family, which, as every Southerner knew, entitled them to membership in that enormous peerage which largely populated the Confederacy. This was their first experience with the charming old custom of having babies—Mr. Button was naturally nervous. He hoped it would be a boy so that he could be sent to Yale College in Connecticut, at which institution Mr. Button himself had been known for four years by the somewhat obvious nickname of "Cuff."

On the September morning <u>consecrated</u> to the enormous event he arose nervously at six o'clock, dressed himself, adjusted an impeccable stock, and hurried forth through the streets of Baltimore to the hospital, to determine whether the darkness of the night had borne in new life upon its bosom.

When he was approximately a hundred yards from the Maryland Private Hospital for Ladies and Gentlemen he saw Doctor Keene, the family physician, descending the front steps, rubbing his hands together with a washing movement—as all doctors are required to do by the unwritten ethics of their profession.

Mr. Roger Button, the president of Roger Button & Co., Wholesale Hardware, began to run toward Doctor Keene with much less dignity than was expected from a Southern gentleman of that picturesque period. "Doctor Keene!" he called. "Oh, Doctor Keene!"

The doctor heard him, faced around, and stood waiting, a curious expression settling on his harsh, medicinal face as Mr. Button drew near.

"What happened?" demanded Mr. Button, as he came up in a gasping rush. "What was it? How is she? A boy? Who is it? What—"

"Talk sense!" said Doctor Keene sharply. He appeared somewhat irritated.

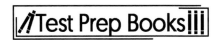

"Is the child born?" begged Mr. Button.

Doctor Keene frowned. "Why, yes, I suppose so—after a fashion." Again he threw a curious glance at Mr. Button.

From *The Curious Case of Benjamin Button* by F.S. Fitzgerald, 1922

1. According to the passage, what major event is about to happen in this story?
   a. Mr. Button is about to go to a funeral.
   b. Mr. Button's wife is about to have a baby.
   c. Mr. Button is getting ready to go to the doctor's office.
   d. Mr. Button is about to go shopping for new clothes.

2. What kind of tone does the above passage have?
   a. Nervous and Excited
   b. Sad and Angry
   c. Shameful and Confused
   d. Grateful and Joyous

3. As it is used in the fourth paragraph, the word *consecrated* most nearly means:
   a. Numbed
   b. Chained
   c. Dedicated
   d. Moved

4. What does the author mean to do by adding the following statement?

   "rubbing his hands together with a washing movement—as all doctors are required to do by the unwritten ethics of their profession."

   a. Suggesting that Mr. Button is tired of the doctor.
   b. Trying to explain the detail of the doctor's profession.
   c. Hinting to readers that the doctor is an unethical man.
   d. Giving readers a visual picture of what the doctor is doing.

5. Which of the following best describes the development of this passage?
   a. It starts in the middle of a narrative in order to transition smoothly to a conclusion.
   b. It is a chronological narrative from beginning to end.
   c. The sequence of events is backwards—we go from future events to past events.
   d. To introduce the setting of the story and its characters.

6. Which of the following is an example of an imperative sentence?
   a. "Oh, Doctor Keene!"
   b. "Talk sense!"
   c. "Is the child born?"
   d. "Why, yes, I suppose so—"

7. As it is used in the first paragraph, the word *anachronism* most nearly means:
   a. Comparison
   b. Misplacement

c. Aberration
d. Amelioration

8. This passage can best be described as what type of text?
a. Expository
b. Descriptive
c. Narrative
d. Persuasive

9. The main purpose of the first paragraph is:
a. To explain the setting of the narrative and give information about the story.
b. To present the thesis so that the audience can determine which points are valid later in the text.
c. To introduce a counterargument so that the author can refute it in the next paragraph.
d. To provide a description of the speaker's city and the building in which he works.

10. The end of the passage implies to the audience that:
a. There is bad weather coming.
b. The doctor thinks Mr. Button is annoying.
c. The baby and the mother did not make it through labor.
d. Something is unusual about the birth of the baby.

Questions 11–20 are based on the following passage:

I heartily accept the motto, "that government is best which governs least," and I should like to see it acted up to more rapidly and systematically. Carried out, it finally amounts to this, which also I believe—"that government is best which governs not at all," and when men are prepared for it, that will be the kind of government which they will have. Government is at best but an expedient; but most governments are usually, and all governments are sometimes, inexpedient. The objections which have been brought against a standing army, and they are many and weighty, and deserve to prevail, may also at last be brought against a standing government. The standing army is only an arm of the standing government. The government itself, which is only the mode which the people have chosen to execute their will, is equally liable to be abused and perverted before the people can act through it. Witness the present Mexican war, the work of comparatively a few individuals using the standing government as their tool; for, in the outset, the people would not have consented to this measure.

This American government—what is it but a tradition, though a recent one, endeavoring to transmit itself unimpaired to posterity, but each instant losing some of its integrity? It has not the vitality and force of a single living man; for a single man can bend it to his will. It is a sort of wooden gun to the people themselves. But it is not the less necessary for this; for the people must have some complicated machinery or other, and hear its din, to satisfy that idea of government which they have. Governments show thus how successfully men can be imposed on, even impose on themselves, for their own advantage. It is excellent, we must all allow. Yet this government never of itself furthered any enterprise, but by the alacrity with which it got out of its way. It does not keep the country free. It does not settle the West. It does not educate. The character inherent in the American people has done all that has been accomplished; and it would have done somewhat more, if the government had not sometimes got in its way. For government is an expedient by which men would fain succeed in letting one another alone; and, as has been said, when it is most expedient, the governed are most let alone by it. Trade and commerce, if they were not made of India-rubber, would never manage to bounce over the obstacles which legislators are continually putting in their way; and, if one were to judge these men wholly by the effects of their actions and not partly by their intentions, they would deserve to be classed and punished with those mischievous persons who put obstructions on the railroads.

But, to speak practically and as a citizen, unlike those who call themselves no-government men, I ask for, not at once no government, but at once a better government. Let every man make known what kind of government would command his respect, and that will be one step toward obtaining it.

Excerpt from *Civil Disobedience* by Henry David Thoreau

11. Which phrase best encapsulates Thoreau's use of the term *expedient* in the first paragraph?
    a. A dead end
    b. A state of order
    c. A means to an end
    d. Rushed construction

12. Which best describes Thoreau's view on the Mexican War?
    a. Government is inherently corrupt because it must wage war.
    b. Government can easily be manipulated by a few individuals for their own agenda.
    c. Government is a tool for the people, but it can also act against their interest.
    d. The Mexican War was a necessary action, but not all the people believed this.

13. What is Thoreau's purpose for writing?
    a. His goal is to illustrate how government can function if ideals are maintained.
    b. He wants to prove that true democracy is the best government, but it can be corrupted easily.
    c. Thoreau reflects on the stages of government abuses.
    d. He is seeking to prove that government is easily corruptible and inherently restrictive of individual freedoms that can simultaneously affect the whole state.

14. Which example best supports Thoreau's argument?
    a. A vote carries in the Senate to create a new road tax.
    b. The president vetoes the new FARM bill.
    c. Prohibition is passed to outlaw alcohol.
    d. Trade is opened between the United States and Iceland.

15. Which best summarizes this section from the following passage?

"This American government—what is it but a tradition, though a recent one, endeavoring to transmit itself unimpaired to posterity, but each instant losing some of its integrity? It has not the vitality and force of a single living man; for a single man can bend it to his will. It is a sort of wooden gun to the people themselves."

a. The government may be instituted to ensure the protections of freedoms, but this is weakened by the fact that it is easily manipulated by individuals.
b. Unlike an individual, government is uncaring.
c. Unlike an individual, government has no will, making it more prone to be used as a weapon against the people.
d. American government is modeled after other traditions but actually has greater potential to be used to control people.

16. According to Thoreau, what's the main reason why government eventually fails to achieve progress?
a. There are too many rules.
b. Legislation eventually becomes a hindrance to the lives and work of everyday people.
c. Trade and wealth eventually become the driving factor of those in government.
d. Government doesn't separate religion and state.

17. What type of passage is this?
a. Narrative
b. Descriptive
c. Persuasive
d. Expository

18. As it is used in the first paragraph, the word *liable* most nearly means:
a. Paramount
b. Inconceivable
c. Susceptible
d. Detrimental

19. According to the passage, which government is Thoreau talking about?
a. Mexican
b. American
c. Chinese
d. British

20. As it is used in the second paragraph, the word *posterity* most nearly means:
a. Persons of royal lineage.
b. All future generations of people.
c. A person involved in directing education.
d. A person who offers views on important life questions

Questions 21–30 are based on the following passage:

Four hundred years ago, in 1612, the north-west of England was the scene of England's biggest peacetime witch trial: the trial of the Lancashire witches. Twenty people, mostly from the Pendle area of Lancashire, were imprisoned in the castle as witches. Ten were hanged, one died in gaol, one was sentenced to stand in the pillory, and eight were acquitted. The 2012 anniversary sees a small flood of commemorative events, including works of fiction by Blake Morrison, Carol Ann Duffy, and Jeanette Winterson. How did this witch trial come about, and what accounts for its enduring fame?

We know so much about the Lancashire Witches because the trial was recorded in unique detail by the clerk of the court, Thomas Potts, who published his account soon afterwards as *The Wonderful Discovery of Witches in the County of Lancaster*. I have recently published a modern-English edition of this book, together with an essay piecing together what we know of the events of 1612. It has been a fascinating exercise, revealing how Potts carefully edited the evidence, and also how the case against the "witches" was constructed and manipulated to bring about a spectacular show trial. It all began in mid-March when a pedlar from Halifax named John Law had a frightening encounter with a poor young woman, Alizon Device, in a field near Colne. He refused her request for pins and there was a brief argument during which he was seized by a fit that left him with "his head ... drawn awry, his eyes and face deformed, his speech not well to be understood; his thighs and legs stark lame." We can now recognize this as a stroke, perhaps triggered by the stressful encounter. Alizon Device was sent for and surprised all by confessing to the bewitching of John Law and then begged for forgiveness.

When Alizon Device was unable to cure the pedlar, the local magistrate, Roger Nowell was called in. Characterized by Thomas Potts as "God's justice" he was alert to instances of witchcraft, which were regarded by the Lancashire's puritan-inclined authorities as part of the cultural rubble of "popery"—Roman Catholicism—long overdue to be swept away at the end of the country's very slow protestant reformation. "With weeping tears" Alizon explained that she had been led astray by her grandmother, "old Demdike," well-known in the district for her knowledge of old Catholic prayers, charms, cures, magic, and curses. Nowell quickly interviewed Alizon's grandmother and mother, as well as Demdike's supposed rival, "old Chattox" and her daughter Anne. Their panicky attempts to explain themselves and shift the blame to others eventually only ended up incriminating them, and the four were sent to Lancaster gaol in early April to await trial at the summer assizes. The initial picture revealed was of a couple of poor, marginal local families in the forest of Pendle with a longstanding reputation for magical powers, which they had occasionally used at the request of their wealthier neighbours. There had been disputes but none of these were part of ordinary village life. Not until 1612 did any of this come to the attention of the authorities.

The net was widened still further at the end of April when Alizon's younger brother James and younger sister Jennet, only nine years old, came up between them with a story about a "great meeting of witches" at their grandmother's house, known as Malkin Tower. This meeting was presumably to discuss the plight of those arrested and the threat of further arrests, but according to the evidence extracted from the children by the magistrates, a plot was hatched to blow up Lancaster castle with gunpowder, kill the gaoler, and rescue the imprisoned witches. It was, in short, a conspiracy against royal authority to rival the gunpowder plot of 1605—something to be expected in a county known for its particularly strong underground Roman Catholic presence.

Those present at the meeting were mostly family members and neighbours, but they also included Alice Nutter, described by Potts as "a rich woman [who] had a great estate, and children of good hope: in the common opinion of the world, of good temper, free from envy or malice." Her part in the affair remains mysterious, but she seems to have had Catholic family connections, and may have been one herself, providing an added motive for her to be prosecuted.

"The Lancashire Witches 1612–2012" by Robert Poole.

21. What's the point of this passage, and why did the author write it?
    a. The author is documenting a historic witchcraft trial while uncovering/investigating the role of suspicion and anti-Catholicism in the events.
    b. The author seeks long-overdue reparations for the ancestors of those accused and executed for witchcraft in Lancashire.
    c. The author is educating the reader about actual occult practices of the 1600s.
    d. The author argues that the Lancashire witch trials were more brutal than the infamous Salem trials.

22. Which term best captures the meaning of the author's use of *enduring* in the first paragraph?
    a. Un-original
    b. Popular
    c. Wicked
    d. Circumstantial

23. What textual information is present within the passage that most lends itself to the author's credibility?
    a. His prose is consistent with the time.
    b. This is a reflective passage; the author doesn't need to establish credibility.
    c. The author cites specific quotes.
    d. The author has published a modern account of the case and has written on the subject before.

24. What might the following excerpt suggest about the trial or, at the very least, Thomas Potts' account of the trial(s)?

> "It has been a fascinating exercise, revealing how Potts carefully edited the evidence, and also how the case against the 'witches' was constructed and manipulated to bring about a spectacular show trial."

    a. The events were so grand that the public was allowed access to such a spectacular set of cases.
    b. Sections may have been exaggerated or stretched to create notoriety on an extraordinary case.
    c. Evidence was faked, making the trial a total farce.
    d. The trial was corrupt from the beginning.

25. Which statement best describes the political atmosphere of the 1600s that influenced the Alizon Device witch trial/case?
    a. Fear of witches was prevalent during this period.
    b. Magistrates were seeking ways to cement their power during this period of unrest.
    c. In a highly superstitious culture, the Protestant church and government were highly motivated to root out any potential sources that could undermine the current regime.

d. Lancashire was originally a prominent area for pagan celebration, making the modern Protestants very weary of whispers of witchcraft and open to witch trials to resolve any potential threats to Christianity.

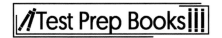

26. Which best describes the strongest "evidence" used in the case against Alizon and the witches?
   a. Knowledge of the occult and witchcraft
   b. "Spectral evidence"
   c. Popular rumors of witchcraft and Catholic association
   d. Self-incriminating speech

27. What type of passage is this?
   a. Persuasive
   b. Expository
   c. Narrative
   d. Descriptive

28. According to the passage, how many people were arrested as witches in the Lancashire trials?
   a. 10
   b. 20
   c. 30
   d. 40

29. As it is used in the first paragraph, the word *commemorative* most nearly means:
   a. Associated with being acquitted
   b. An act of disloyalty
   c. A circumstance to be disliked
   d. In honor of something

30. According to the passage, what is Malkin tower?
   a. The building where the trial of the Lancashire witches took place.
   b. The grandmother's house of the peddler who sought revenge on Alizon.
   c. Alizon's grandmother's house where a meeting of witches was held.
   d. The residence of a jury member who witnessed the cursing of the peddler.

Questions 31–40 are based upon the following passage:

> Insects as a whole are preeminently creatures of the land and the air. This is shown not only by the possession of wings by a vast majority of the class, but by the mode of breathing to which reference has already been made, a system of branching air-tubes carrying atmospheric air with its combustion-supporting oxygen to all the insect's tissues. The air gains access to these tubes through a number of paired air-holes or spiracles, arranged segmentally in series.
>
> It is of great interest to find that, nevertheless, a number of insects spend much of their time under water. This is true of not a few in the perfect winged state, as for example aquatic beetles and water-bugs ('boatmen' and 'scorpions') which have some way of protecting their spiracles when submerged, and, possessing usually the power of flight, can pass on occasion from pond or stream to upper air. But it is advisable in connection with our present subject to dwell especially on some insects that remain continually under water till they are ready to undergo their final moult and attain the winged state,

which they pass entirely in the air. The preparatory instars of such insects are aquatic; the adult instar is aerial. All may-flies, dragon-flies, and caddis-flies, many beetles and two-winged flies, and a few moths thus divide their life-story between the water and the air. For the present we confine attention to the Stone-flies, the May-flies, and the Dragon-flies, three well-known orders of insects respectively called by systematists the Plecoptera, the Ephemeroptera and the Odonata.

In the case of many insects that have aquatic larvae, the latter are provided with some arrangement for enabling them to reach atmospheric air through the surface-film of the water. But the larva of a stone-fly, a dragon-fly, or a may-fly is adapted more completely than these for aquatic life; it can, by means of gills of some kind, breathe the air dissolved in water.

This excerpt is from *The Life-Story of Insects* by Geo H. Carpenter

31. Which statement best details the central idea in this passage?
    a. It introduces certain insects that transition from water to air.
    b. It delves into entomology, especially where gills are concerned.
    c. It defines what constitutes as insects' breathing.
    d. It invites readers to have a hand in the preservation of insects.

32. Which definition most closely relates to the usage of the word *moult* in the passage?
    a. An adventure of sorts, especially underwater
    b. Mating act between two insects
    c. The act of shedding part or all of the outer shell
    d. Death of an organism that ends in a revival of life

33. What is the purpose of the first paragraph in relation to the second paragraph?
    a. The first paragraph serves as a cause, and the second paragraph serves as an effect.
    b. The first paragraph serves as a contrast to the second.
    c. The first paragraph is a description for the argument in the second paragraph.
    d. The first and second paragraphs are merely presented in a sequence.

34. What does the following sentence most nearly mean?

    "The preparatory instars of such insects are aquatic; the adult instar is aerial."

    a. The volume of water is necessary to prep the insect for transition rather than the volume of the air.
    b. The abdomen of the insect is designed like a star in the water as well as the air.
    c. The stage of preparation in between molting is acted out in the water, while the last stage is in the air.
    d. These insects breathe first in the water through gills yet continue to use the same organs to breathe in the air.

35. Which of the statements reflect information that one could reasonably infer based on the author's tone?

a. The author's tone is persuasive and attempts to call the audience to action.
b. The author's tone is passionate due to excitement over the subject and personal narrative.
c. The author's tone is informative and exhibits interest in the subject of the study.
d. The author's tone is somber, depicting some anger at the state of insect larvae.

36. Which statement best describes stoneflies, mayflies, and dragonflies?

a. They are creatures of the land and the air.
b. They have a way of protecting their spiracles when submerged.
c. Their larvae can breathe the air dissolved in water through gills of some kind.
d. The preparatory instars of these insects are aerial.

37. According to the passage, what is true of "boatmen" and "scorpions"?

a. They have no way of protecting their spiracles when submerged.
b. They have some way of protecting their spiracles when submerged.
c. They usually do not possess the power of flight.
d. They remain continually under water till they are ready to undergo their final moult.

38. The last paragraph indicates that the author believes

a. That the stonefly, dragonfly, and mayfly larvae are better prepared to live beneath the water because they have gills that allow them to do so.
b. That the stonefly is different from the mayfly because the stonefly can breathe underwater and the mayfly can only breathe above water.
c. That the dragonfly is a unique species in that its larvae lives mostly underwater for most of its young life.
d. That the stonefly larvae can breathe only by reaching the surface film of the water.

39. According to the passage, why are insects as a whole preeminently creatures of the land and the air?

a. Because insects are born on land but eventually end up adapting to life underwater for the rest of their adult lives.
b. Because most insects have legs made for walking on land and tube-like structures on their bellies for skimming the water.
c. Because a vast majority of insects have wings and also have the ability to breathe underwater.
d. Because most insects have a propulsion method specifically designed for underwater use, but they can only breathe on land.

40. As it is used in the first paragraph, the word *preeminently* most nearly means:

a. Unknowingly
b. Above all
c. Most truthfully
d. Not importantly

English Language

Questions 1–9 are based on the following passage:

The name "Thor" has always been associated with great power. (1) Arguably, Norse Mythologies most popular and powerful god is Thor of the Aesir. My first experience of Thor was not like most of today's generation. I grew up reading Norse mythology where (2) Thor wasn't a comic book superhero, but even mightier. There are stories of Thor destroying mountains, (3) defeating scores of giants and lifting up the world's largest creature the Midgard Serpent. But always, Thor was a protector.

Like in modern comics and movies, Thor was the god of thunder and wielded (4) the hammer Mjolnir however there are several differences between the ancient legend and modern hero. (5) For example, Loki, the god of mischief, isn't Thor's brother. Loki is actually Thor's servant, but this doesn't stop the trickster from causing chaos, chaos that Thor has to then quell. In all of his incarnations, Thor is a god that reestablishes order by tempering the chaos around him. (6) This is also symbolized in his prized weapon Mjolnir a magic hammer. A hammer is both a weapon and a (7) tool, but why would a god favor a seemingly everyday object?

A hammer is used to shape metal and create change. The hammer tempers raw iron, (8) ore that is in an chaotic state of impurities and shapelessness, to create an item of worth. Thus, a hammer is in many ways a tool that brings a kind of order to the world—like Thor. Hammers were also tools of everyday people, which further endeared Thor to the common man. Therefore, it's no surprise that Thor remains an iconic hero to this day.

I began thinking to myself, why is Thor so prominent in our culture today even though many people don't follow the old religion? (9) Well the truth is that every culture throughout time, including ours, needs heroes. People need figures in their lives that give them hope and make them aspire to be great. We need the peace of mind that chaos will eventually be brought to order and that good can conquer evil. Thor was a figure of hope and remains so to this day.

1. Which of the following would be the best choice for this sentence (reproduced below)?

(1) Arguably, Norse Mythologies most popular and powerful god is Thor of the Aesir.

a. NO CHANGE
b. Arguably Norse Mythologies most
c. Arguably, Norse mythology's most
d. Arguably, Norse Mythology's most

2. Which of the following would be the best choice for this sentence (reproduced below)?

I grew up reading Norse mythology where (2) Thor wasn't a comic book superhero, but even mightier.

a. NO CHANGE
b. Thor wasn't a comic book superhero. He was even mightier.
c. Thor wasn't a comic book superhero but even mightier.
d. Thor wasn't a comic book superhero, he was even mightier.

3. Which of the following would be the best choice for this sentence (reproduced below)?

There are stories of Thor destroying mountains, (3) defeating scores of giants and lifting up the world's largest creature the Midgard Serpent.

a. NO CHANGE
b. defeating scores of giants, and lifting up the world's largest creature, the Midgard Serpent.
c. defeating scores of giants, and lifting up the world's largest creature the Midgard Serpent.
d. defeating scores, of giants, and lifting up the world's largest creature the Midgard Serpent.

4. Which of the following would be the best choice for this sentence (reproduced below)?

Like in modern comics and movies, Thor was the god of thunder and wielded (4) the hammer Mjolnir however there are several differences between the ancient legend and modern hero.

a. NO CHANGE
b. the hammer Mjolnir, however there are several differences
c. the hammer Mjolnir. However there are several differences
d. the hammer Mjolnir. However, there are several differences

5. Which of the following would be the best choice for this sentence (reproduced below)?

(5) For example, Loki, the god of mischief, isn't Thor's brother.

a. NO CHANGE
b. For example, Loki the god of mischief isn't Thor's brother.
c. For example, Loki the god of mischief, isn't Thor's brother.
d. For example Loki, the god of mischief, isn't Thor's brother.

6. Which of the following would be the best choice for this sentence (reproduced below)?

(6) This is also symbolized in his prized weapon Mjolnir a magic hammer.

a. NO CHANGE
b. This is also symbolized in his prized weapon, Mjolnir a magic hammer.
c. This is also symbolized in his prized weapon, Mjolnir, a magic hammer.
d. This is also symbolized in his prized weapon Mjolnir, a magic hammer.

7. Which of the following would be the best choice for this sentence (reproduced below)?

A hammer is both a weapon and a (7) tool, but why would a god favor a seemingly everyday object?

a. NO CHANGE
b. tool; why would a god favor a seemingly everyday object?
c. tool, but, why would a god favor a seemingly everyday object?
d. tool, however, why would a god favor a seemingly everyday object?

8. Which of the following would be the best choice for this sentence (reproduced below)?

The hammer tempers raw iron, (8) ore that is in an chaotic state of impurities and shapelessness, to create an item of worth.

a. NO CHANGE
b. ore that is in a chaotic state of impurities and shapelessness,
c. ore that has the impurities and shapelessness of a chaotic state
d. ore that is in an chaotic state, of impurities and shapelessness,

9. Which of the following would be the best choice for this sentence (reproduced below)?

(9) Well the truth is that every culture throughout time, including ours, needs heroes.

a. NO CHANGE
b. Well, the truth is, every culture throughout time, including ours,
c. Well, every culture throughout time, including ours, in truth
d. Well, the truth is that every culture throughout time, including ours,

Questions 10–18 are based on the following passage:

In our essay and class discussion, (10) we came to talking about mirrors. It was an excellent class in which we focused on an article written by Salman Rushdie that compared the homeland to a mirror. (11) Essentially this mirror was an metaphor for us and our homeland. (12) When we look at our reflection we see the culture, our homeland staring back at us. An interesting analogy, but the conversation really began when we read that Rushdie himself stated that the cracked mirror is more valuable than a whole one. But why?

(13) After reflecting on the passage I found the answer to be simple. The analogy reflects the inherent nature of human individuality. The cracks in the mirror represent different aspects of our own being. Perhaps it is our personal views, our hobbies, or our differences with other people, but (14) whatever it is that makes us unique defines us, even while we are part of a big culture. (15) What this tells us is that we can have a homeland, but ultimately we ourselves are each different in it.

Just because one's (16) mirror is cracked, the individuals isn't disowned from the actual, physical homeland and culture within. It means that the homeland is uniquely perceived by the (17) individual beholding it and that there are in fact many aspects to culture itself. Like the various cracks, a culture has religion, language, and many other factors that form to make it whole. What this idea does is invite the viewer to accept their own view of their culture as a whole.

Like in Chandra's *Love and Longing in Bombay*, a single homeland has many stories to tell. Whether one is a cop or a retired war veteran, the individual will perceive the different aspects of the world with unduplicated eyes. (18) Rushdie, seems to be urging his readers to love their culture but to not be pressured by the common crowd. Again, the cracks represent differences which could easily be interpreted as views about the culture, so what this is saying is to accept the culture but accept oneself as well.

From the essay "Portals to Homeland: Mirrors"

10. Which of the following would be the best choice for this sentence (reproduced below)?

In our essay and class discussion, (10) we came to talking about mirrors.

a. NO CHANGE
b. we were talking about
c. we talked about
d. we came to talk about

11. Which of the following would be the best choice for this sentence (reproduced below)?

(11) Essentially this mirror is an metaphor for us and our homeland.

a. NO CHANGE
b. Essentially, this mirror is a metaphor for us and our homeland.
c. Essentially, this mirror is an metaphor for us and our homeland.
d. Essentially this mirror is an metaphor, for us and our homeland.

12. Which of the following would be the best choice for this sentence (reproduced below)?

(12) When we look at our reflection we see the culture, our homeland staring back at us.

a. NO CHANGE
b. When we look at our reflection we see our culture our homeland staring back at us.
c. When we look at our reflection we saw our culture, our homeland, staring back at us.
d. Looking at our reflection we see our culture as our homeland is staring back at us.

13. Which of the following would be the best choice for this sentence (reproduced below)?

(13) After reflecting on the passage I found the answer to be simple.

a. NO CHANGE
b. After reflecting on the passage; I found the answer to be simple.
c. After reflecting on the passage I finding the answer to be simple.
d. After reflecting on the passage, I found the answer to be simple.

14. Which of the following would be the best choice for this sentence (reproduced below)?

Perhaps it is our personal views, our hobbies, or our differences with other people, but (14) whatever it is that makes us unique defines us, even while we are part of a big culture.

a. NO CHANGE
b. whatever it is, that makes us unique, defines us, even while we are part of a big culture.
c. whatever it is that makes us unique also defines us, even while we are part of a bigger culture.
d. whatever it is that makes us unique defines us, even though we are part of a big culture.

15. Which of the following would be the best choice for this sentence (reproduced below)?

(15) <u>What this tells us is that we can have a homeland, but ultimately we ourselves are each different in it.</u>

a. NO CHANGE
b. What this tells us is that we can have a homeland, but ultimately, we ourselves are each different in it.
c. What this tells us is that we can have a homeland, however, ultimately, we ourselves are each different in it.
d. What this tells us is that we can have a homeland, ultimately we ourselves are each different in it.

16. Which of the following would be the best choice for this sentence (reproduced below)?

Just because one's (16) <u>mirror is cracked, the individuals isn't disowned</u> from the actual, physical homeland and culture within.

a. NO CHANGE
b. mirror is cracked, the individuals will not be disowned
c. mirror is cracked, the individuals aren't disowned
d. mirror is cracked, the individual isn't disowned

17. Which of the following would be the best choice for this sentence (reproduced below)?

It means that the homeland is uniquely perceived by the (17) <u>individual beholding it and that there are, in fact, many aspects</u> of culture itself.

a. NO CHANGE
b. individual beholding it; and that there are in fact many aspects
c. individual beholding it and that there is, in fact, many aspects
d. individual beholding it and there's in fact, many aspects

18. Which of the following would be the best choice for this sentence (reproduced below)?

(18) <u>Rushdie, seems to be urging his readers</u> to love their culture but to not be pressured by the common crowd.

a. NO CHANGE
b. Rushdie seemed to be urging his readers
c. Rushdie, seeming to urge his readers,
d. Rushdie seems to be urging his readers

Questions 19–27 are based on the following passage:

> *The Odyssey* reading performed by Odds Bodkin (19) was an especially rewarding experience. Myths continue to help us (20) understood ancient cultures while still helping us connect to real-world lessons through narrative. (21) While myths were not read exactly the way Bodkin performed *The Odyssey*, his performance truly combined ancient and modern artistic styles.
>
> (22) Originally, myths were not written down instead, stories like The Odyssey were transferred to written form thousands of years after they were originally told. *Told* is a (23) key term here: myths were passing on to generations orally. They were sung, or at least accompanied by music. Of course, we no longer gather in halls to hear (24) myths; we read it, or perhaps listen to audio versions. The Odds Bodkin reading was unique in that it offered a traditional glimpse into what it might have been like to receive a myth in its original form of delivery.
>
> What I thought was especially interesting, was that Bodkin used his guitar to build an atmosphere or tempo around the story. In points of action, like when the wooden horse was being moved into Troy, or when Odysseus leads his men in search of the missing crew (lotus episode), he played a signature tune. (25) This creates a kind of soundtrack for the story, providing a unique feeling for the scene. While (26) there is no visual stimuli like in motion picture, one is moved by the guitar's playing. Accompanied by his dramatic reading, the music reflects the action of the plot and even emotions/insights of the characters. Interestingly, Bodkin also used physical gestures to tell the story as well. He occasionally acted out scenes with his hands and sometimes with sound effects.
>
> The best scene was when Bodkin played the Cyclops, Polyphemus, grabbing and gorging himself on Odysseus' men. (27) In addition from bringing a kind of animation to the presentation, it linked the story to the physical world too. He wasn't just reading, he was acting. It gave this a three-dimensional aspect of the telling of *The Odyssey* that I thought was especially great.

19. Which of the following would be the best choice for this sentence (reproduced below)?

    The Odyssey reading performed by Odds Bodkin (19) was an especially rewarding experience.

    a. NO CHANGE
    b. was, an especially, rewarding experience.
    c. was a especially rewarding experience.
    d. was an especially rewarded experience.

20. Which of the following would be the best choice for this sentence (reproduced below)?

    Myths continue to help us (20) understood ancient cultures while still helping us connect to real-world lessons through narrative.

    a. NO CHANGE
    b. understand ancient cultures
    c. understood ancient cultures,
    d. understanding ancient cultures

21. Which of the following would be the best choice for this sentence (reproduced below)?

(21) While myths were not read exactly the way Bodkin performed The Odyssey, his performance truly combined ancient and modern artistic styles.

a. NO CHANGE
b. While myths were not exactly the way Bodkin read/performed *The Odyssey*,
c. While myths were not read, exactly, the way Bodkin performed *The Odyssey*,
d. While myths were not read exactly the way Bodkin performed *The Odyssey*.

22. Which of the following would be the best choice for this sentence (reproduced below)?

(22) Originally, myths were not written down instead, stories like The Odyssey were transferred to written form thousands of years after they were originally told.

a. NO CHANGE
b. Myths, originally, were not written down instead, stories like *The Odyssey*
c. Originally myths were not written down; instead stories like *The Odyssey*
d. Originally, myths were not written down. Instead, stories like *The Odyssey*

23. Which of the following would be the best choice for this sentence (reproduced below)?

Told is a (23) key term here: myths were passing on to generations orally.

a. NO CHANGE
b. key term here: myths were passed on to generations orally.
c. key term here: myths passed on to generations orally.
d. key term here: myths pass on to generations orally.

24. Which of the following would be the best choice for this sentence (reproduced below)?

Of course, we no longer gather in halls to hear (24) myths, we read it, or perhaps listen to audio versions.

a. NO CHANGE
b. myths; we read it or
c. myths; they are read, or
d. myths; we read them, or

25. Which of the following would be the best choice for this sentence (reproduced below)?

(25) This creates a kind of soundtrack for the story, providing a unique feeling for the scene.

a. NO CHANGE
b. This creates a kind of soundtrack for the story;
c. This creates, a kind of soundtrack, for the story,
d. This creates a kinds of soundtrack for the story,

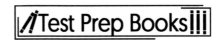

26. Which of the following would be the best choice for this sentence (reproduced below)?

While (26) there is no visual stimuli like in motion picture, one is moved by the guitar's playing.

a. NO CHANGE
b. there is no visual stimuli, like in motion picture,
c. there are no visual stimuli, like in motion pictures,
d. there are no visual stimuli like in motion picture,

27. Which of the following would be the best choice for this sentence (reproduced below)?

(27) In addition from bringing a kind of animation to the presentation, it linked the story to the physical world too.

a. NO CHANGE
b. In addition to bringing a kind of animation
c. In addition too bringing, a kind of animation,
d. In addition for bringing a kind of animation

Questions 28–36 are based on the following passage:

Quantum mechanics, which describes how the universe works on its smallest scale, is inherently weird. Even the founders of the field (28) including Max Planck, Werner Heisenberg, and Wolfgang Pauli unsettled by the new theory's implications. (29) Instead of a deterministic world where everything can be predicted by equations, events at the quantum scale are purely probabilistic. (30) Every outcome exist simultaneously, while the actual act of observation forces nature to choose one path.

In our everyday lives, (31) this concept of determinism, is actually expressed in the thought experiment of Schrödinger's cat. Devised by Erwin Schrödinger, one of the founders of quantum mechanics, (32) it's purpose is to show how truly strange the framework is. Picture a box containing a cat, a radioactive element, and a vial of poison. (33) If the radioactive element decays, it will release the poison and kill the cat. The box is closed, so there is no way for anyone outside to know what is happening inside. Since the cat's status—alive and dead—are mutually exclusive, only one state can exist. (34) What quantum mechanics says however is that the cat is simultaneously alive and dead, existing in both states until the box's lid is removed and one outcome is chosen.

(35) Further confounding our sense of reality, Louis de Broglie proposed that, on the smallest scales, particles and waves are indistinguishable. This builds on Albert Einstein's famous theory that matter and energy are interchangeable. Although there isn't apparent evidence for this in our daily lives, various experiments have shown the validity of quantum mechanics. One of the most famous experiments is the double-slit experiment, which initially proved the wave nature of light. When shone through parallel slits onto a screen, (36) light creates a interference pattern of alternating bands of light and dark. But when electrons were fired at the slits, the act of observation changed the outcome. If observers monitored which slit the electrons travelled through, only one band was seen on the screen. This is expected, since we know electrons act as particles. However, when they monitored the screen only, an interference pattern is created—implying that the electrons behaved as waves!

28. Which of the following would be the best choice for this sentence (reproduced below)?

(28) Even the founders of the field including Max Planck, Werner Heisenberg, and Wolfgang Pauli unsettled by the new theory's implications.

a. NO CHANGE
b. including Max Planck, Werner Heisenberg, and Wolfgang Pauli; unsettled by the new theory's implications.
c. including Max Planck, Werner Heisenberg, and Wolfgang Pauli were unsettled by the new theories' implications.
d. including Max Planck, Werner Heisenberg, and Wolfgang Pauli were unsettled by the new theory's implications.

29. Which of the following would be the best choice for this sentence (reproduced below)?

(29) Instead of a deterministic world where everything can be predicted by equations, events at the quantum scale are purely probabilistic.

a. NO CHANGE
b. Instead, of a deterministic world where everything can be predicted by equations,
c. Instead of a deterministic world where everything can be predicting by equations,
d. Instead of a deterministic world, where everything can be predicted by equations,

30. Which of the following would be the best choice for this sentence (reproduced below)?

(30) Every outcome exist simultaneously, while the actual act of observation forces nature to choose one path.

a. NO CHANGE
b. Each of these outcome exist simultaneously,
c. Every outcome, existing simultaneously,
d. Every outcome exists simultaneously,

31. Which of the following would be the best choice for this sentence (reproduced below)?

In our everyday lives, (31) this concept of determinism, is actually expressed in the thought experiment of Schrödinger's cat.

a. NO CHANGE
b. this concept of determinism is actually expressed
c. this, concept of determinism, is actually expressed
d. this concept of determinism, is expressed actually

32. Which of the following would be the best choice for this sentence (reproduced below)?

Devised by Erwin Schrödinger, one of the founders of quantum mechanics, (32) it's purpose is to show how truly strange the framework is.

a. NO CHANGE
B. its purposes is to show how truly strange
c. its purpose is to show how truly strange
d. it's purpose, showing how truly strange

33. Which of the following would be the best choice for this sentence (reproduced below)?

(33) If the radioactive element decays, it will release the poison and kill the cat.

a. NO CHANGE
b. If, the radioactive element decays, it will release the poison and kill the cat.
c. If the radioactive element decays. It will release the poison and kill the cat.
d. If the radioactive element decays, releasing the poison and kill the cat.

34. Which of the following would be the best choice for this sentence (reproduced below)?

(34) What quantum mechanics says however is that the cat is simultaneously alive and dead, existing in both states until the box's lid is removed and one outcome is chosen.

a. NO CHANGE
b. What quantum mechanics says however, is
c. What quantum mechanics says. However, is
d. What quantum mechanics says, however, is

35. Which of the following would be the best choice for this sentence (reproduced below)?

(35) Further confounding our sense of reality, Louis de Broglie proposed that, on the smallest scales, particles and waves are indistinguishable.

a. NO CHANGE
b. Further confounding our sense of reality Louis de Broglie proposed that on the smallest scales, particles and waves are indistinguishable.
c. Further confounding our sense of reality, Louis de Broglie proposed that on the smallest scales, particles and waves are indistinguishable.
d. Further, confounding our sense of reality, Louis de Broglie proposed that, on the smallest scales, particles and waves are indistinguishable.

36. Which of the following would be the best choice for this sentence (reproduced below)?

> When shone through parallel slits onto a screen, (36) light creates a interference pattern of alternating bands of light and dark.

a. NO CHANGE
b. light created an interference
c. lights create a interference
d. light, creating an interference,

Questions 37–45 are based on the following passage:

> (37) As the adage goes knowledge is power. Those who are smart and understand the world as it is are the most fit to lead. Intelligence (38) doesn't necessarily require a deep understanding of complex scientific principles. Rather, having the basic knowledge of how the world works, particularly how people go about gaining what they need to survive and thrive, (39) are more important.
>
> Any leadership position, whether on the job or informally, tends to be fraught with politics. (40) Smart leaders will engage in critical thinking allowing them to discern ulterior motives and identify propaganda. Besides catching negative intentions, (41) these practice will serve to highlight the positives in group interactions. Gaining insights into different viewpoints will make leaders more (42) receptive to constructive criticism and ideas from unexpected sources. As with many aspects of being a good and well-rounded person, the seeds for this trait are sown in pre-school. Besides facts and figures, students need to be taught critical thinking skills to survive in a world flooded with subliminal messages and scams. (43) Sadly our current society is plagued by many inconvenient truths that are attacked as lies. Wise leaders should recognize when someone is trying to save the world or merely push a political agenda.
>
> Just as important as the knowledge of how the world works (44) is understood of how humanity operates. Leaders should be able to tactfully make friends and influence people using the doctrines of psychology. People who say whatever comes into their heads without thinking demonstrate a lack of basic diplomatic understanding, not to mention a deficiency of self-control and lack of respect. Breaches of courtesy, whether intentional or otherwise, strain relations and can ruin potential alliances.
> While the best leaders are tolerant of other (45) cultural practices and diverse perspectives, those who exhibit disregard and unwarranted contempt for others shouldn't be expected to find favor. Knowledge extends past textbook learning to practical awareness, encompassing skills for a successful life as a decent human being all around. These skills include risk management and creative solutions. Someone who fails to hone these abilities—or neglects to apply their knowledge—will likely be overthrown by those they are supposed to lead.

37. Which of the following would be the best choice for this sentence (reproduced below)?

(37) As the adage goes knowledge is power.

a. NO CHANGE
b. Knowledge is power as the adage goes.
c. As the adage goes, "knowledge is power."
d. As, the adage goes, knowledge is power.

38. Which of the following would be the best choice for this sentence (reproduced below)?

Intelligence (38) doesn't necessarily require a deep understanding of complex scientific principles.

a. NO CHANGE
b. doesn't, necessarily, require
c. doesn't require necessarily
d. aren't necessarily require

39. Which of the following would be the best choice for this sentence (reproduced below)?

Rather, having the basic knowledge of how the world works, particularly how people go about gaining what they need to survive and thrive, (39) are more important.

a. NO CHANGE
b. is more important.
c. are the most important.
d. is most important.

40. Which of the following would be the best choice for this sentence (reproduced below)?

(40) Smart leaders will engage in critical thinking allowing them to discern ulterior motives and identify propaganda.

a. NO CHANGE
b. Smart leaders will engage in critical thinking allowing them to discern ulterior motives, and identify propaganda.
c. Smart leaders will engage in critical thinking, allowing them to discern ulterior motives and identify propaganda.
d. Smart leaders will engage in critical thinking allows them to discern ulterior motives and identify propaganda.

41. Which of the following would be the best choice for this sentence (reproduced below)?

Besides catching negative intentions, (41) these practice will serve to highlight the positives in group interactions.

a. NO CHANGE
b. this practices will serve to highlight
c. these practice serve to highlight
d. this practice will serve to highlight

42. Which of the following would be the best choice for this sentence (reproduced below)?

Gaining insights into different viewpoints will make leaders more (42) receptive to constructive criticism and ideas from unexpected sources.

a. NO CHANGE
b. receptive for constructive criticism and ideas from unexpected sources.
c. receptive from unexpected sources to construct criticism and ideas.
d. receptive, to constructive criticism and ideas, from unexpected sources.

43. Which of the following would be the best choice for this sentence (reproduced below)?

(43) Sadly our current society is plagued by many inconvenient truths that are attacked as lies.

a. NO CHANGE
b. Sadly, our current society is plagued by many inconvenient truths that are attacked as lies.
c. Sadly our current society is plagued by many inconvenient truths, that are attacked as lies.
d. Sadly our current society is plaguing by many inconvenient truths that are attacking as lies.

44. Which of the following would be the best choice for this sentence (reproduced below)?

Just as important as the knowledge of how the world works (44) is understood of how humanity operates.

a. NO CHANGE
b. is to understand of how humanity operates.
c. is understanding of how humanity operates.
d. is an understanding of how humanity operates.

45. Which of the following would be the best choice for this sentence (reproduced below)?

While the best leaders are tolerant of other (45) cultural practices and diverse perspectives, those who exhibit disregard and unwarranted contempt for others shouldn't be expected to find favor.

a. NO CHANGE
b. cultural practices and diverse perspectives. Those who exhibit disregard
c. cultural practices, and diverse perspectives, those who exhibit disregard
d. cultural practices and diverse perspectives, those whom exhibit disregard

Questions 46–54 are based on the following passage:

While the various tales do take on the individual perspectives, (46) Chaucer's internal character retain a unique presence throughout the text. *The Canterbury Tales* provides the ultimate example of a story (47) about stories also being a story containing multiple stories. (48) Chaucer does these by compiling embedded narratives from multiple sources while delivering them through a single, primary voice. From the (49) beginning, it's clear that Chaucer is the source of the text. Yet, Chaucer is more than just a storyteller; he's an honest storyteller. Chaucer provides bold character descriptions of (50) these individual, including their faults. This can be seen when Chaucer sheds light on the nature of the Prioress. He describes that, (51) while her supposed to be a pious nun, she is actually a walking façade. The prioress is noted for counterfeiting courtly behavior so that people think highly of her.

With Chaucer providing such detailed observations, the readers have a more complete picture of what is going on and who the other characters really are. Another example of this is (52) the sarcastic and brutal honest description of the miller: "The millere, that for drunken was al pale." This description of the (53) miller's drunkenness shed's light on why he seems so crazy. It's because he's a drunk. Thus, Chaucer's own narrative gives readers a reliable perspective amongst a host of questionable storytellers. He also provides information on the characters that can help the reader grasp their tales more fully.

One of the signature methods of Chaucer's storytelling is that he doesn't just tell a story, his characters do as well. As a writer, Chaucer actually immerses himself into the collective character discussions. In many ways, Chaucer is a vehicle for the characters to tell their individual stories. Chaucer actually takes on the styles and voice of the characters. A good, eloquent tale like the *Knight's Tale* is written that way because that's how the knight would have told it. (54) Likewise, it's also why several tales are poorly written, have crass delivery, or lack a driven plotline. The *Miller's Tale* is rather crazy and crass because he is drunk while telling it. Chaucer seeks to tell the story in the way his drunken character would have.

46. Which of the following would be the best choice for this sentence (reproduced below)?

While the various tales do take on the individual perspectives, (46) Chaucer's internal character retain a unique presence throughout the text.

a. NO CHANGE
b. Chaucer's internal character retains a unique presence throughout the text.
c. Chaucer's internal character retaining a unique presence throughout the text.
d. Chaucer's internal character retained a unique presence throughout the text.

47. Which of the following would be the best choice for this sentence (reproduced below)?

The Canterbury Tales provides the ultimate example of a story (47) about stories also being a story containing multiple stories.

a. NO CHANGE
b. about stories; not to mention stories within a single story.
c. about stories, also being a story containing multiple stories.
d. about stories, as well as being a story containing multiple stories.

48. Which of the following would be the best choice for this sentence (reproduced below)?

(48) Chaucer does these by compiling embedded narratives from multiple sources while delivering them through a single, primary voice.

a. NO CHANGE
b. Chaucer does this, compiling embedded narratives
c. Chaucer does this by compiling embedded narratives
d. Chaucer does these through compiling embedded narratives

49. Which of the following would be the best choice for this sentence (reproduced below)?

From the (49) beginning, it's clear that Chaucer is the source of the text.

a. NO CHANGE
b. beginning. It's clear that Chaucer
c. beginning, Chaucer clearly
d. beginning, it's clear, that Chaucer

50. Which of the following would be the best choice for this sentence (reproduced below)?

Chaucer provides bold character descriptions of (50) these individual, including their faults.

a. NO CHANGE
b. these individuals, including their faults
c. these individual including their faults
d. these individuals; including their faults

51. Which of the following would be the best choice for this sentence (reproduced below)?

He describes that, (51) while her supposed to be a pious nun, she is actually a walking façade.

a. NO CHANGE
b. her supposed nun's piety,
c. while her is supposed to be a pious nun,
d. while she's supposed to be a pious nun,

52. Which of the following would be the best choice for this sentence (reproduced below)?

Another example of this is (52) the sarcastic and brutal honest description of the miller: "The millere, that for drunken was al pale."

a. NO CHANGE
b. the sarcastic, and brutal, honest description of
c. the sarcastic and brutally honest description of
d. the sarcastic, brutal honest description of

53. Which of the following would be the best choice for this sentence (reproduced below)?

This description of the (53) miller's drunkenness shed's light on why he seems so crazy.

a. NO CHANGE
b. miller's drunkenness sheds light on
c. miller's drunk, which sheds light on
d. miller's drunkenness, shed's light on

54. Which of the following would be the best choice for this sentence (reproduced below)?

<u>Likewise, it's also why several tales are poorly written,</u> have crass delivery, or lack a driven plotline.

a. NO CHANGE
b. Likewise it's also why several tales are poorly written,
c. Likewise it's also why several tales are, poorly written,
d. Likewise, it's also why several tales are, poorly written,

Questions 55–58 are based on the following passage:

(55) <u>Practitioner of Ju-jitsu, and other martial arts, strive away</u> from the act of total violence. We tend not to be violent individuals in the first place because of our training. From the first day on the mat, physical restraint is emphasized. The moves we learn are inherently harmful, (56) <u>so them should used sparingly</u> and not to advance our own satisfaction. The lessons taught in Ju-juitsu urge people to be mindful of their capabilities while also being decisive when defense is required. Having grace, even in the face of danger, is a central theme within martial arts studies.

Everything we do, whether striking a blow or undertaking a certain task, carries responsibility. One must be motivated by pure intention because action cannot be taken back. Life is precious, and its preservation must be top priority. Even when defending against someone who seeks to end your own life, a true Ju-jitsu practitioner should strive to defend themselves while not ending the opponent's life. To abuse this power would only stain the soul and demine the art. (57) <u>Having restraint is testament to how one values life and the possibilities within.</u> Life is about growth, like the study of Ju-jitsu. Ju-jitsu is all about a process of learning and relearning, dedication, struggle, and then understanding. The study (58) <u>of Ju-jitsu, like any trial throughout one's life,</u> is a test of faith and willpower. The end result benefits others as well as oneself.

From the essay "Morality and the Warrior's Path"

55. Which of the following would be the best choice for this sentence (reproduced below)?

(55) <u>Practitioner of Ju-jitsu, and other martial arts, strive away</u> from the act of total violence.

a. NO CHANGE
b. Practitioners of Ju-jitsu, and other martial arts, strive away
c. Practitioners of Ju-jitsu, and other martial arts strive away
d. Practitioner of Ju-jitsu, and other martial arts, strives away

56. Which of the following would be the best choice for this sentence (reproduced below)?

The moves we learn are inherently harmful, (56) <u>so them should used sparingly</u> and not to advance our own satisfaction.

a. NO CHANGE
b. so them should be used sparingly
c. so they should used sparingly
d. so they should be used sparingly

57. Which of the following would be the best choice for this sentence (reproduced below)?

(57) Having restraint is testament to how one values life and the possibilities within.

a. NO CHANGE
b. Having restraint is an testament to how one values life and the possibilities within.
c. Having restraint is a testament to how one values life and the possibilities within.
d. Having restraint is testament to how one values life and the possibilities, within.

58. Which of the following would be the best choice for this sentence (reproduced below)?

The study (58) of Ju-jitsu, like any trial throughout one's life is a test of faith and willpower.

a. NO CHANGE
b. of Ju-jitsu like any trial throughout one's life
c. of Ju-jitsu, like, any trial throughout one's life
d. of Ju-jitsu, like any trial throughout one's life,

Questions 59–67 are based on the following passage:

Our modern society (59) would actually look down on some of Plato's ideas in *The Republic.* But why? (60) Certainly his ideas could help create a more orderly and fair system, but at what cost? The simple truth is that in many of his examples, we see that Plato has taken the individual completely out of the equation. Plato's ideal society is one that places human (61) desire aside to focuses on what will benefit the entire community. To enforce these ideas, Plato seeks to use government to regulate and mandate these rules. This may seem to (62) equalize the population, its possible that this is actually the greatest breech of freedom.

Today, people would think Plato's (63) suggestion to confiscate citizens children and place them in different homes is utterly barbaric. We cannot imagine the pain of losing one's own child to be raised by others. In a modern trial, the judge and (64) jury would see these as kidnapping and ultimately condemn the philosopher. (65) As parents and emotional beings, this seems like cruelty. However, the reason Plato makes this suggestion is to benefit both society and the individual. The reason for this confiscation and placement is for the child to grow to the best of their potential. If the child is brilliant and placed with a (66) similar family than the child will have access to more opportunities. Prosperous or intellectual parents could help develop the child's talents. The child would be placed in an (67) environment that encourage growth. This brilliant child—developed through this different upbringing—would then grow to be a positive presence in the community, a force that would benefit everyone. Thus, in this scenario, Plato *is* thinking of the individual, but resorting to extreme means to *help* them fully develop talents for the good of all the republic.

While our modern views may oppose this idea, we have to acknowledge that this isn't an evil idea. Rather, this is a suggestion to help society through the sacrifice of a few individual liberties. However, one must question how much sacrifice is needed to attain true freedom.

59. Which of the following would be the best choice for this sentence (reproduced below)?

Our modern society (59) would actually look down on some of Plato's ideas in *The Republic.*

a. NO CHANGE
b. would actually look down upon some
c. would actually be looking down on some
d. would actually look down on something

60. Which of the following would be the best choice for this sentence (reproduced below)?

(60) Certainly his ideas could help create a more orderly and fair system, but at what cost?

a. NO CHANGE
b. Certainly, his ideas could help create a more orderly and fair system, at what cost?
c. Certainly, his ideas could help create a more orderly and fair system, but at what cost?
d. Certainly his ideas could help create a more orderly and fair system, at what cost?

61. Which of the following would be the best choice for this sentence (reproduced below)?

Plato's ideal society is one that places human (61) desire aside to focuses on what will benefit the entire community.

a. NO CHANGE
b. desire aside to focus on
c. desire aside focusing on
d. desire aside, focuses on

62. Which of the following would be the best choice for this sentence (reproduced below)?

This may seem to (62) equalize the population, its possible that this is actually the greatest breech of freedom.

a. NO CHANGE
b. equalize the population it's possible that this is
c. equalize the population, but it's possible that this is
d. equalize the population, however possible that this is

63. Which of the following would be the best choice for this sentence (reproduced below)?

Today, people would think Plato's (63) suggestion to confiscate citizens children and place them in different homes is utterly barbaric.

a. NO CHANGE
b. suggestion for confiscating citizens children
c. suggestion for confiscating citizen's children
d. suggestion to confiscate citizens' children

64. Which of the following would be the best choice for this sentence (reproduced below)?

In a modern trial, the judge and (64) jury would see these as kidnapping and ultimately condemn the philosopher.

a. NO CHANGE
b. jury would see this as kidnapping and
c. jury would see these kidnappings
d. jury would see those as kidnapping and

65. Which of the following would be the best choice for this sentence (reproduced below)?

(65) As parents and emotional beings, this seems like cruelty.

a. NO CHANGE
b. As parents and emotional beings this seems like cruelty.
c. As parents and emotional beings; this seems like cruelty.
d. As parents and emotional beings those seems like cruelty.

66. Which of the following would be the best choice for this sentence (reproduced below)?

If the child is brilliant and placed with a (66) similar family than he will have access to more opportunities.

a. NO CHANGE
b. similar family, than the child will have access to
c. similar family then the child will access to
d. similar family, the child will have access to

67. Which of the following would be the best choice for this sentence (reproduced below)?

The child would be placed in an (67) environment that encourage growth.

a. NO CHANGE
b. environment encouraging growth.
c. environment that encourages growth.
d. environment which encourage growth.

Questions 68–75 are based on the following passage:

Early in my career, (68) a master's teacher shared this thought with me "Education is the last bastion of civility." While I did not completely understand the scope of those words at the time, I have since come to realize the depth, breadth, truth, and significance of what he said. (69) Education provides society with a vehicle for (70) raising it's children to be civil, decent, human beings with something valuable to contribute to the world. It is really what makes us human and what (71) distinguishes us as civilised creatures.

Being "civilized" humans means being "whole" humans. Education must address the mind, body, and soul of students. (72) It would be detrimental to society, only meeting the needs of the mind, if our schools were myopic in their focus. As humans, we are multi-dimensional, multifaceted beings who need more than head knowledge to survive. (73) The human heart and psyche have to be fed in order for the mind to develop properly, and the body must be maintained and exercised to help fuel the working of the brain. Education is a basic human right, and it allows us to sustain a democratic society in which participation is fundamental to its success. It should inspire students to seek better solutions to world problems and to dream of a more equitable society. Education should never discriminate on any basis, and it should create individuals who are self-sufficient, patriotic, and tolerant of (74) others' ideas.

(75) All children can learn. Although not all children learn in the same manner. All children learn best, however, when their basic physical needs are met, and they feel safe, secure, and loved. Students are much more responsive to a teacher who values them and shows them respect as individual people. Teachers must model at all times the way they expect students to treat them and their peers. If teachers set high expectations for their students, the students will rise to that high level. Teachers must make the well-being of students their primary focus and must not be afraid to let students learn from their own mistakes.

From the essay "Education is Essential to Civilization"

68. Which is the best version of the underlined portion of this sentence (reproduced below)?

Early in my career, (68) a master's teacher shared this thought with me "Education is the last bastion of civility."

a. NO CHANGE
b. a master's teacher shared this thought with me: "Education is the last bastion of civility."
c. a master's teacher shared this thought with me: "Education is the last bastion of civility".
d. a master's teacher shared this thought with me. "Education is the last bastion of civility."

69. Which is the best version of the underlined portion of this sentence (reproduced below)?

(69) Education provides society with a vehicle for raising it's children to be civil, decent, human beings with something valuable to contribute to the world.

a. NO CHANGE
b. Education provide
c. Education will provide
d. Education providing

70. Which is the best version of the underlined portion of this sentence (reproduced below)?

Education provides society with a vehicle for (70) raising it's children to be civil, decent, human beings with something valuable to contribute to the world.

a. NO CHANGE
b. raises its children to be
c. raising its' children to be
d. raising its children to be

71. Which of these, if any, is misspelled?

It is really what makes us human and what (71) distinguishes us as civilised creatures.

a. NO CHANGE
b. distinguishes
c. civilised
d. creatures

72. Which is the best version of the underlined portion of this sentence (reproduced below)?

(72) It would be detrimental to society, only meeting the needs of the mind, if our schools were myopic in their focus.

a. NO CHANGE
b. It would be detrimental to society if our schools were myopic in their focus, only meeting the needs of the mind.
c. Only meeting the needs of our mind, our schools were myopic in their focus, detrimental to society.
d. Myopic is the focus of our schools, being detrimental to society for only meeting the needs of the mind.

73. Which of these sentences, if any, should begin a new paragraph?

(73) The human heart and psyche have to be fed in order for the mind to develop properly, and the body must be maintained and exercised to help fuel the working of the brain. Education is a basic human right, and it allows us to sustain a democratic society in which participation is fundamental to its success. It should inspire students to seek better solutions to world problems and to dream of a more equitable society.

a. NO CHANGE
b. The human heart and psyche have to be fed in order for the mind to develop properly, and the body must be maintained and exercised to help fuel the working of the brain.
c. Education is a basic human right, and it allows us to sustain a democratic society in which participation is fundamental to its success.
d. It should inspire students to seek better solutions to world problems and to dream of a more equitable society.

74. Which is the best version of the underlined portion of this sentence (reproduced below)?

Education should never discriminate on any basis, and it should create individuals who are self-sufficient, patriotic, and tolerant of others' ideas.

a. NO CHANGE
b. other's ideas
c. others ideas
d. others's ideas

75. Which is the best version of the underlined portion of this sentence (reproduced below)?

> (75) <u>All children can learn. Although not all children learn in the same manner.</u>

a. NO CHANGE
b. All children can learn although not all children learn in the same manner.
c. All children can learn although, not all children learn in the same manner.
d. All children can learn, although not all children learn in the same manner.

Writing

Please read the prompt below and answer in an essay format.

> Coaches of kids' sports teams are increasingly concerned about the behavior of parents at games. Parents are screaming and cursing at coaches, officials, players, and other parents. Physical fights have even broken out at games. Parents need to be reminded that coaches are volunteers, giving up their time and energy to help kids develop in their chosen sport. The goal of kids' sports teams is to learn and develop skills, but it's also to have fun. When parents are out of control at games and practices, it takes the fun out of the sport.

1. Analyze and evaluate the passage given.

2. State and develop your own perspective.

3. Explain the relationship between your perspective and the one given.

Answer Explanations #2

Reading Comprehension

1. B: Mr. Button's wife is about to have a baby. The passage begins by giving the reader information about traditional birthing situations. Then, we are told that Mr. and Mrs. Button decide to go against tradition to have their baby in a hospital. The next few passages are dedicated to letting the reader know how Mr. Button dresses and goes to the hospital to welcome his new baby. There is a doctor in this excerpt, as Choice *C* indicates, and Mr. Button does put on clothes, as Choice *D* indicates. However, Mr. Button is not going to the doctor's office nor is he about to go shopping for new clothes.

2. A: The tone of the above passage is nervous and excited. We are told in the fourth paragraph that Mr. Button "arose nervously." We also see him running without caution to the doctor to find out about his wife and baby—this indicates his excitement. We also see him stuttering in a nervous yet excited fashion as he asks the doctor if it's a boy or girl. Though the doctor may seem a bit abrupt at the end, indicating a bit of anger or shame, neither of these choices is the overwhelming tone of the entire passage. Despite the circumstances, joy and gratitude are not the main tone in the passage.

3. C: Dedicated. Mr. Button is dedicated to the task before him. Choice *A*, *numbed*, Choice *B*, *chained*, and Choice *D*, *moved*, all could grammatically fit in the sentence. However, they are not synonyms with *consecrated* like Choice *C* is.

4. D: Giving readers a visual picture of what the doctor is doing. The author describes a visual image—the doctor rubbing his hands together—first and foremost. The author may be trying to make a comment about the profession; however, the author does not "explain the detail of the doctor's profession" as Choice *B* suggests.

5. D: To introduce the setting of the story and its characters. We know we are being introduced to the setting because we are given the year in the very first paragraph along with the season: "one day in the summer of 1860." This is a classic structure of an introduction of the setting. We are also getting a long explanation of Mr. Button, what his work is, who is related to him, and what his life is like in the third paragraph.

6. B: "Talk sense!" is an example of an imperative sentence. An imperative sentence gives a command. The doctor is commanding Mr. Button to talk sense. Choice *A* is an example of an exclamatory sentence, which expresses excitement. Choice *C* is an example of an interrogative sentence—these types of sentences ask questions. Choice *D* is an example of a declarative sentence. This means that the character is simply making a statement.

7. B: The word *anachronism* most nearly means misplacement. Choice *A*, *comparison*, is an analogy or similarity to something. Choice *C*, *aberration*, means abnormality. Choice *D*, *amelioration*, means improvement.

8. C: This passage can best be described as a narrative, which is a type of passage that tells a story. Choice *A*, expository, is a text organized logically to investigate a problem. Choice *B*, descriptive, is a text that mostly goes about describing something or someone in detail. Choice *D*, persuasive, is a text that is organized as an argument and meant to persuade the audience to do something.

9. A: To explain the setting of the narrative and give information about the story. The setting of a narrative is the time and place. We see from the first paragraph that the year is 1860. We also can discern that it is summer, and Mr. and Mrs. Button are about to have a baby. This tells us both the setting and information about the story.

10. D: Something is unusual about the birth of the baby. The word "curious" is thrown in at the end twice, which tells us the doctor is suspicious about something having to do with the birth of the baby, since that is the most recent event to happen. Mr. Button is acting like a father who is expecting a baby, and the doctor seems confused about something.

11. C: This is a tricky question, but it can be solved through careful context analysis and vocabulary knowledge. One can infer that the use of "expedient," while not necessarily very positive, isn't inherently bad in this context either. Note how in the next line, he says, "but most governments are usually, and all governments are sometimes, inexpedient." This use of "inexpedient" indicates that a government becomes a hindrance rather than a solution; it slows progress rather than helps facilitate progress. Thus, Choice *A* and Choice *D* can be ruled out because these are more of the result of government, not the intention or initial design. Choice *B* makes no logical sense. Therefore, Choice *C* is the best description of *expedient.* Essentially, Thoreau is saying that government is constructed as a way of developing order and people's rights, but the rigidness of government soon inhibits justice and human rights.

12. B: While Choice *D* is the only answer that mentions the Mexican War directly, Thoreau clearly thinks the war is unnecessary because the people generally didn't consent to the war. Choices *A*, *B*, and *C* are all correct to a degree, but the answer asks for the best description. Therefore, Choice *B* is the most accurate representation of Thoreau's views. Essentially, Thoreau brings to light the fact that the few people in power can twist government and policy for their own needs.

13. D: Choices *A* and *B* are completely incorrect. Thoreau is not defending government in any way. His views are set against government. As mentioned in the text, he appreciates little government but favors having no government structure at all. The text is reflective by nature but not reflective on the stages of government abuses as Choice *C* suggests. Choice *D* is the more appropriate answer because of the presence of evidence in the text. Thoreau cites current events and uses them to illustrate the point he's trying to make.

14. C: One of Thoreau's biggest criticisms of government is its capacity to impose on the people's freedoms and liberties, enacting rules that the people don't want and removing power from the individual. None of the scenarios directly impose specific regulations or restrictions on the people, except Prohibition. Prohibition removed the choice to consume alcohol in favor of abstinence, which was favored by the religious conservatives of the time. Thus, Thoreau would point out that this is a clear violation of free choice and an example of government meddling.

15. A: Choice *B* is totally irrelevant. Choice *C* is also incorrect; Thoreau never personifies government. Also, this doesn't coincide with his wooden gun analogy. Choice *D* is compelling because of its language but doesn't define the statement. Choice *A* is the most accurate summary of the main point of Thoreau's statement.

16. B: Thoreau specifically cites that legislators "are continually putting in their way." This reflects his suspicion and concern of government intervention. Recall that Thoreau continually mentions that government, while meant as a way to establish freedom, is easily used to suppress freedom, piling on regulations and rules that inhibit progress. Choice *B* is the answer that most directly states how Thoreau sees government getting in the way of freedom.

17. D: This passage is an expository essay, which means that an idea is investigated and then expanded upon. Thoreau is investigating the idea of government here and how the U.S. government works in relation to the people.

18. C: The word *liable* most nearly means susceptible. The text says, "The government itself, which is only the mode which the people have chosen to execute their will, is equally liable to be abused and perverted before the people can act through it." Thoreau is saying here that the government is vulnerable enough to be abused. Choice *A*, *paramount*, means having importance. Choice *B*, *inconceivable*, means unbelievable. Choice *D*, *detrimental*, means damaging.

19. B: Thoreau is talking about the American government. We see this information in the beginning of the second paragraph. The passage mentions the Mexican War, but the passage itself does not relay the vulnerabilities of the Mexican government. The other two countries are not mentioned in the passage.

20. B: Posterity means all future generations of people. The sentence would say, "The American government—what is it but a tradition, though a recent one, endeavoring to transmit itself unimpaired to all future generations of people . . ." Choice *A* would be the definition of *royalty.* Choice *C* would be the definition of an *educator*. Choice *D* would be the definition of a *philosopher*.

21. A: Choice *D* can be eliminated because the Salem witch trials aren't mentioned. While sympathetic to the plight of the accused, the author doesn't demand or urge the reader to demand reparations to the descendants; therefore, Choice *B* can also be ruled out. It's clear that the author's main goal is to educate the reader and shed light on the facts and hidden details behind the case. However, his focus isn't on the occult, but the specific Lancashire case itself. He goes into detail about suspects' histories and ties to Catholicism, revealing how the fears of the English people at the time sealed the fate of the accused witches. Choice *A* is correct.

22. B: It's important to note that these terms may not be an exact analog for *enduring*. However, through knowledge of the definition of *enduring*, as well as the context in which it's used, an appropriate synonym can be found. Plugging "circumstantial" into the passage in place of "enduring" doesn't make sense. Nor does "un-original" work, since this particular case of witchcraft stands out in history. "Wicked" is very descriptive, but this is an attribute applied to people, not events; therefore, this is an inappropriate choice as well. *Enduring* literally means long lasting, referring to the continued interest in this particular case of witchcraft. Therefore, it's a popular topic of 1600s witch trials, making "popular," Choice *B*, the best choice.

23. D: Choices *A* and *B* are irrelevant and incorrect. The use of quotes lends credibility to the author. However, the presence of quotes alone doesn't necessarily mean that the author has a qualified perspective. What establishes the writer as a reliable voice is that the author's previous writing on the subject has been published before. This qualification greatly establishes the author's credentials as a historical writer, making Choice *D* the correct answer.

24. B: Choice *B* is the best answer because it ultimately encompasses the potentiality of Choices *C* and *D*. Choice *A* is incorrect because it takes the statement literally. For Choice *C,* it's possible that evidence was tampered with or even falsified, but this statement doesn't refer to this. While the author alludes that there may have been evidence tampering and potentially corruption (Choice *D*), what the writer is directly saying is that the documentation of the court indicates an elaborate trial.

25. C: Several of these answers could have contributed to the fear and political motivations around the Lancashire witch trials. What this answer's looking for is very specific: political motivations and issues that played a major role in the case. Choice *C* clearly outlines the public fears of the time. It also describes how the government can use this fear to weed out and eliminate traces of Catholicism (and witchcraft too). Catholicism and witchcraft were seen as dangerous and undermining to English Protestantism and governance. Choice *D* can be eliminated; while this information may have some truth and is certainly consistent with the general fear of witchcraft, the details about Lancashire's ancient history aren't mentioned in the text. Choice *A* is true but not necessarily political in nature. Choice *B* is very promising, though not outright mentioned.

26. D: The best evidence comes from Alizon herself. The text mentions that she confessed to bewitching John Law, thinking that she did him harm. From here she names her grandmother, who she believes corrupted her. Choice *B* can be ruled out; spectral evidence isn't mentioned. The case draws on knowledge of superstition of witchcraft, but this in itself can't be considered evidence, so Choice *A* is incorrect. Choice *C* isn't evidence in a modern sense; rumors have no weight in court and therefore are not evidence. While this is used as evidence to some degree, this still isn't the *best* evidence against Alizon and the witches.

27. B: This type of passage would be considered expository, which is an informative passage. Choice *A*, persuasive, means to take a side of an argument, and this essay is merely divulging information. Choice *C*, narrative, means to tell a story. Although a story is being told indirectly, the essay doesn't follow a traditional narrative. Choice *D*, descriptive, means a detailed description of a person or place.

28. B: According to the passage, 20 people were arrested as witches in the Lancashire trials. The essay tells us that "ten were hanged, one died in goal (jail), one was sentenced to death in the pillory, and eight were acquitted."

29. D: The word *commemorative* means in honor of something. The context clue here includes the "works of fiction" by the authors Blake Morrison, Ann Duffy, and Jeanette Winterson, no doubt to celebrate the preserved history of the famous trial.

30. C: Malkin tower is the house of Alizon's grandmother. It is also a place where a meeting of witches was said to be held in the passage. The passage says, "The net was widened still further at the end of April when Alizon's younger brother James and younger sister Jennet, only nine years old, came up between them with a story about a "great meeting of witches" at their grandmother's house, known as Malkin Tower."

31. A: It introduces certain insects that transition from water to air. Choice *B* is incorrect because although the passage talks about gills, it is not the central idea of the passage. Choices *C* and *D* are incorrect because the passage does not "define" or "invite," but only serves as an introduction to stoneflies, dragonflies, and mayflies and their transition from water to air.

32. C: The act of shedding part or all of the outer shell. Choices *A*, *B*, and *D* are incorrect. The word in the passage is mentioned here: "But it is advisable in connection with our present subject to dwell especially on some insects that remain continually under water till they are ready to undergo their final moult and attain the winged state, which they pass entirely in the air."

33. B: The first paragraph serves as a contrast to the second. Notice how the first paragraph goes into detail describing how insects are able to breathe air. The second paragraph acts as a contrast to the first by stating "[i]t is of great interest to find that, nevertheless, a number of insects spend much of their time under water." Watch for transition words such as "nevertheless" to help find what type of passage you're dealing with.

34: C: The stage of preparation in between molting is acted out in the water, while the last stage is in the air. Choices *A, B,* and *D* are all incorrect. *Instars* is the phase between two periods of molting, and the text explains when these transitions occur.

35. C: The author's tone is informative and exhibits interest in the subject of the study. Overall, the author presents us with information on the subject. One moment where personal interest is depicted is when the author states, "It is of great interest to find that, nevertheless, a number of insects spend much of their time under water."

36. C: Their larva can breathe the air dissolved in water through gills of some kind. This is stated in the last paragraph. Choice *A* is incorrect because the text mentions this in a general way at the beginning of the passage concerning "insects as a whole." Choice *B* is incorrect because this is stated of beetles and water-bugs, and not the insects in question. Choice *D* is incorrect because this is the opposite of what the text says of instars.

37. B: According to the passage, boatmen and scorpions have some way of protecting their spiracles when submerged. We see this in the second paragraph, which says "(boatmen and scorpions) which have some way of protecting their spiracles when submerged."

38. A: The best answer Choice is *A*: the author believes that the stonefly, dragonfly, and mayfly larvae are better prepared to live beneath the water because they have gills that allow them to do so. We see this when the author says "But the larva of a stone-fly, a dragon-fly, or a may-fly is adapted more completely than these for aquatic life; it can, by means of gills of some kind, breathe the air dissolved in water."

39. C: Because a vast majority of insects have wings and also have the ability to breathe underwater. The entire first paragraph talks of how insects have wings, and how insects also have "a system of branching air-tubes" that carries oxygen to the insect's tissues.

40. B: The word *preeminently* most nearly means *above all* or *in particular*. The author is saying that above all, insects are creatures of both land and water.

English Language

1. C: Choice *C* is correct, changing *Mythologies* to *mythology's*. Since one myth system is being referred to—and one particular component of it—the possessive is needed. Additionally, *Mythology's* does not need to be capitalized, since only the culture represents a proper noun. Choice *A* therefore is incorrect, with Choice *B* failing to fix the plural and Choice *D* having extraneous capitalization.

2. A: Choice *A* is incorrect because the sentence has no issues. While Choice *B* separates the sentence correctly, it makes more sense in this context of a direct comparison to keep the sentence intact. Choice *C* is incorrect because the sentence needs a comma after *superhero*. Choice *D* is unnecessarily long and lacks the *but* that helps the author differentiate ideas.

3. B: Choice *B* is correct because it adds the two commas needed to clarify key subjects individually and establish a better flow to the sentence. Since *destroying mountains*, *defeating scores of giants*, and *lifting up the world's largest creature* are separate feats, commas are needed to separate them. Also, because *the world's largest creature* can stand alone in the sentence, a comma needs to proceed its name; *the Midgard Serpent* is not necessary to the sentence but rather provides extra information as an aside. Choice *A* is unclear and thus incorrect. Choice *C* is still missing a comma, while Choice *D* put an extraneous one in an incorrect place.

4. D: Choice *D* is correct since the sentence is lengthy as originally presented and should be split into two. Additionally, *however*, being a conjunction, needs a comma afterwards. Choice *A* is therefore incorrect due to missing punctuation. Choice *B* is an improvement but could separate the sentence's ideas better and more clearly. Choice *C* lacks the necessary comma after *However*.

5. A: Choice *A* is correct because this sentence has no issues with punctuation, content, or sentence construction. While there are three commas used, they serve to appropriately introduce an idea, an individual person, and transition into another line of thinking. Choices *B* and *C* miss commas needed to offset Loki's title as *the god of mischief*, while Choice *D* misses the comma needed to introduce the example.

6. C: Choice *C* is correct because the sentence needs two commas to emphasize the proper name of Mjolnir. Since Mjolnir is being talked about, directly addressed, and then explained, it must be flanked by commas to signify its role in the sentence. Choice *A* lacks necessary punctuation and is confusing. Choices *B* and *D* miss commas on either side of *Mjolnir*.

7. A: Choice *A* is correct, as this is an example of a compound sentence written correctly. Because of the conjunction *but* and the proceeding comma, the two independent clauses are able to form a single sentence coherently. While Choice *B* makes the question more direct, it doesn't go well with the remainder of the sentence. Choice *C* applies a comma after *but*, which is incorrect and confusing. Choice *D* inserts *however*, which is out of place and makes the sentence awkward.

8. B: Choice *B* correctly changes *an* to *a*, since *an* is only required when *a* precedes a word that begins with a vowel. Choice *A* therefore uses the incorrect form of *a*. Choice *C* fixes the issue but unnecessarily reverses the structure of the sentence, making it less direct and more confusing. Choice *D* does not fix the error and adds extraneous commas.

9. D: Choice *D* is correct, simply applying a comma after *Well* to introduce an idea. Choice *A* is therefore incorrect. Choice *B* introduces too many commas, resulting in a fractured sentence structure. Choice *C* applies a comma after *Well*, which is correct, but interrupts the flow of the sentence by switching the structure of the sentence. This makes the sentence lack fluidity and serves to confuse the reader.

10. C: Choice C is simple and straightforward, describing the event clearly for the reader to follow; talked is past tense, which is consistent with the rest of the passage. Choice A is incorrect, since we came to talking about confuses the tense of the sentence and the verb talk. Choices B and D are wordy and not as straightforward as Choice C.

11. B: Choice *B* is the correct answer because it adds a comma after *Essentially* and changes *an* to *a*. This is called the indefinite article, when an unspecified thing or quantity is referred to. However, *an* doesn't agree with *metaphor*, since *an* should only be used when the next word starts with a vowel. Choice *A* uses the article *an* and lacks the crucial comma after *Essentially*. Choice *C* is incorrect because it only provides the comma after *Essentially*, neglecting the indefinite article disagreement. Choice *D* is incorrect because neither issue is fixed and an unnecessary comma is introduced.

12. A: Choice *A* is correct because there are no errors present in the sentence. Choice *B* is a run on, because the clauses are not broken up by commas. Choice *C* has a verbal disagreement: *look* and *saw* are different tenses. Choice *D* changes the structure of the sentence but fails to add a transition to make this correct.

13. D: Choice *D* is correct because it uses a comma after the word *passage*, successfully connecting the dependent clause with its independent clause to form a complete thought/sentence. Choice *A* is therefore incorrect. Choice *B* uses a semicolon unwisely. The two clauses need to be connected to each other in order to make sense, otherwise they are just two fragments improperly combined. Choice *C* does not have the required comma and changes *found* to *finding*, an inappropriate tense for the verb in this sentence.

14. C: Choice *C* is correct because it fixes two major flaws in the original portion of the sentence. First, it inserts the adverb *also* to show the connection between *whatever it is that makes us unique* and *defines us*. Without this adverb, the sentence lacks clarity, and the connection is lost. Second, *big* is incorrect in this context. The sentence needs the superlative *bigger* in order to communicate the scope and scale of the author's assessment of how people relate to others on a grand scale. Choice *A* is therefore incorrect, Choice *B* inserts unnecessary commas, and Choice *D* subtly alters the original meaning.

15. B: Choice *B* is correct because a comma is correctly inserted after *ultimately*. This serves to express a side thought that helps transition into the rest of the sentence without having to break it apart. Choice *A* is incorrect because it lacks the comma after *ultimately*. Choice *C* uses too many commas and is overly complicated. Choice *D* lacks the necessary conjunction after the comma (*but)* before *ultimately*, making it a run-on sentence. It also lacks the important comma after *ultimately*.

16. D: Choice *D* corrects the subject-verb disagreement. *One's* is the possessive form of *one*, a single individual, not the plural *individuals. Isn't* is the singular contraction of *is not*, which conflicts with *individuals*. To correct this, either *isn't* must change to *aren't* or *individuals* should become the singular *individual*. The latter is correct because of the context of the sentence. Choice *A* is incorrect because of the subject-verb disagreement. Choice *B* uses the future tense, while Choice *C*'s *aren't* conflicts with *one's*, which is possessive singular.

17. A: Choice *A* contains no grammatical errors and communicates the writer's message clearly. Choice *B* inserts an unnecessary semicolon. Choice *C* uses *is*, which disagrees with the plural *aspects. Are* must be used because it is plural. This is the same for Choice *D*, which uses *there's* (*there is*).

18. D: Choice *D* is the correct answer because it removes the comma after *Rushdie*. Adding a comma after the proper name in this case is incorrect because *Rushdie* is not being addressed directly. Rather, the writer is talking about Rushdie. Therefore, Choices *A* disrupts the construction of the sentence. Choice *B* is incorrect because *seemed*, in this context, should be present tense. The author is talking about a theme and idea that *Rushdie* had but that is still relevant and being actively studied. Choice *C* fails to remove the comma after Rushdie and applies the gerund *seeming* incorrectly.

19. A: Choice *A* is the correct answer. The sentence requires no punctuation and clearly communicates the author's idea. Choice *B* is incorrect because it misuses multiple commas. Choice *C* is incorrect because it uses *a* instead of *an*, which is necessary because the next word (*essentially*) begins with a vowel. Choice *D* changes *rewarding* to *rewarded*, which clashes with the earlier use of *was*, indicating past tense, making it incorrect.

20. B: Choice *B* is correct because it uses the present tense of *understand* instead of the past tense *understood*. *Continues* emphasizes something ongoing. Therefore, the present tense of *understand* is needed. Choice *A* therefore has tense disagreement. Choice *C* uses an extraneous comma. While Choice *D's* use of the gerund is a better option, *in* would need to be added before *understanding* for correctness.

21. A: Choice *A* is correct; the dependent and independent clauses are successfully combined to form a sentence. Choice *A* is also the most concise and straightforward option, presenting the information appropriately so as not to be confusing. Choice *B* can then be eliminated. Choice *C* unnecessarily flanks *exactly* with commas. Choice *D* is incorrect because a period after the underlined phrase would result in two incomplete sentences.

22. D: Choice *D* is correct because of how it successfully connects the two sentences. By starting a new sentence with *instead*, the two ideas are clearly and correctly presented. Choice *A* is a run-on. Choice *B* is incorrect because the commas used are misplaced and confusing. Choice *C* is incorrect because there needs to be a comma after *originally*.

23. B: Choice *B* correctly uses the word *passed* instead of *passing*. The word *were* is being used as a past tense modifier; therefore, it disagrees with the *passing* participle. Combining the helping verb *were* with the past tense *passed* creates the correct past tense compound verb, *were passed*, which is needed to be grammatically consistent with the rest of the sentence. Choices *A*, *C*, and *D* thus have incongruent tenses.

24. D: Choice *D* is correct because it corrects the subject-verb disagreement between the plural *myths* and the singular *it*. This is done by changing *it* to *them*, reflecting that more than one type of *myths* are being talked about. Because of the subject-verb disagreement, Choice *A* is incorrect. Choice *B* does not correct this at all. Choice *C* addresses this disagreement, but at the cost of maintaining parallel structure within the sentence.

25. A: Choice *A* is correct because this sentence contains no grammatical errors, unlike the others. Choice *B* uses the semicolon when only a comma is required. Choice *C* uses commas to unnecessarily isolate *a kind of soundtrack* from its connected phrase. Choice *D* is incorrect because the plural *kinds* disagrees with the singular pronoun *This*.

26. C: Choice *C* is the correct answer because the plural *are* and *motion pictures* agree with the subject *stimuli* (the plural form of *stimulus*). All verbs and nouns in the sentence should be in agreement with each other in tense and number. Choices *A*, *B*, and *D* all violate this number agreement.

27. B: Choice *B* correctly replaces the preposition *from* with the correct proposition *to*. *To* is used to emphasize an action or idea being presented rather than received. This is why Choice *A* is incorrect. Choice *C* is incorrect because it uses the adverb *too*, which emphasizes a higher level of something or the addition of something in a sentence; this isn't relevant here. Choice *D* uses the preposition *for* instead of *to*.

28. D: Choice *D* is correct because it adds the helping verb *were* to modify *unsettled*. This allows the sentence to reflect that the founders were unsettled by the implications. Without *were* to connect *the founders* to *unsettled*, the sentence doesn't make sense. Choice *A* lacks the crucial helping verb, making it incorrect. Choice *B* is incorrect because of its unnecessary semicolon. Choice *C* changes *theory's*, which is singular possessive, to *theories'* (plural possessive), which isn't consistent with the sentence's context.

29. A: Choice *A* is correct because it contains no errors and requires no additional punctuation to form a coherent sentence. The single comma, used successfully, unites the two clauses and enables a solid grammatical structure. Choice *B* incorrectly places a comma after *Instead*, Choice *C* incorrectly changes *predicted* to *predicting*, and Choice *D* incorrectly separates *where everything can be predicted by equations* from the rest of the sentence.

30. D: Choice *D* is correct because it fixes the subject-verb disagreement with *Every outcome* and *exist*. *Exists* is third person present but also appropriate to reflect multiple outcomes, as indicated by *every outcome*. Choices *A* and *B* use *exist*, not *exists*, which makes them both incorrect. Choice *C* is fine on its own but does not fit with the rest of the sentence.

31. B: Choice *B* is correct because the comma after *determinism* isn't needed. Adding a comma in the selected area actually breaks up the independent clause of the sentence, thus compromising the overall structure of the sentence. Choices *A*, *C*, and *D* are therefore incorrect.

32. C: Choice *C* is the correct answer because it removes the contraction of *it is*, *it's*. Choice *A*, which is incorrect, originally used *it's*—note the apostrophe before *s*. *It's* simply means *it is*, while *its* (no apostrophe) shows possession. In this sentence, *its* is referring to the idea devised by Schrödinger, giving ownership of the purpose to the idea. Choice *B* is incorrect because *purpose* should remain singular. Choice *D* is incorrect because it uses *it's*.

33. A: Choice *A* is correct because the sentence is well-formed and grammatically correct. Choice *B* is incorrect because it adds an unnecessary comma after *if*. Choice *C* breaks the sentence apart, creating a sentence fragment. Choice *D* is incorrect because it changes *release* to a gerund and fails to make a coherent sentence, leaving only two dependent clauses.

34. D: Choice *D* is the correct answer. This is a tricky question, but Choice *D* is correct because, in the context of this sentence, it's important to have *however* flanked by commas. This is because the use of *however* is basically an aside to the reader, addressing an idea and then redirecting the reader to an alternative outcome or line of reasoning. Choice *A* is therefore confusing, with *however* floating in the sentence aimlessly. Choice *B* only uses one comma, which is incorrect. Choice *C* creates two incomplete sentences.

35. A: Choice *A* is correct. The sentence uses a lot of commas, but these are used effectively to highlight key points while continuing to focus on a central idea. Choice *B* is incorrect because the commas after *reality* and *that* are required. Choice *C* is incorrect because there should be a comma after *that* because *on the smallest scales* elaborates on the idea itself but not necessarily what Broglie said. Choice *D* puts a comma after *further*, which is unnecessary in this context.

36. B: Choice *B* correctly uses *an* instead of *a* to modify *interference*. The indefinite article *an* must be used before words that start with a vowel sound. The verb *created* is also in agreement with the tense of the story. Choice *C* incorrectly changes *creates* to *create* and pluralizes *light*, which is inconsistent with the rest of the sentence. Choice *D* modifies *creates* inappropriately and adds an incorrect comma after *light*.

37. C: Choice *C* is correct because it applies the single comma needed to combine the independent clause with the dependent clause, forming a functional sentence. It also includes quotes. Choice *A* is an awkward, disjointed sentence because it lacks a comma after *goes*. The other answers result in oddly constructed sentences (Choice *B*), and a misused comma after *As* (Choice *D*).

38. A: Choice *A* is the correct answer because the proper contraction for does not (doesn't) is used. There is also no need for commas or punctuation here as well, making Choices *B* and *C* incorrect. Choice *D* needlessly changes *doesn't* to *aren't*.

39. B: Choice *B* is correct because it fixes the subject-verb disagreement between the subject *the basic knowledge* and the verb *are*. Because *knowledge* is singular, the verb *are*, which is plural, is incorrect. Instead, the singular *is* must be used in place of *are*. This makes Choices *A* and *C* incorrect. Choice *D* is incorrect because it changes the meaning of the sentence.

40. C: Choice *C* is the correct answer because it employs a comma to effectively combine the independent clause with the dependent clause to form a complete sentence. Choice *A* lacks the comma after *thinking* needed to unite the two parts of the sentence. The independent clause is *Smart leaders will engage in critical thinking*, while the independent clause is *allowing them to discern ulterior motives and identify propaganda*. Choice *B* incorrectly adds a comma after *motives*. Choice *D* is incorrect because it still lacks connective punctuation and incorrectly alters the gerund *allowing* to *allows*; this would be fine if a comma and *which* were added before *allows* to effectively combine the clauses.

41. D: Choice *D* is the best answer because it changes *these* to *this*, making it properly modify the singular *practice*. Choice *A* is incorrect because of this lack of numerical agreement. Choice *B* is incorrect for the same reason—*this* is singular while *practices* is plural. Choice *C* is also incorrect because it doesn't fix *these* and takes out *will*, which is important for the tense of the overall sentence.

42. A: Choice *A* is correct because the sentence is fine as it is. Commas are not necessary here. Choices *B* and *C* replace *to* with *for* and *from*, respectively, which don't work in the context of the sentence: if leaders are *receptive*, they are receiving something, so *to* is appropriate. Choice *D* introduces unnecessary commas.

43. B: Choice *B* is the correct answer because it appropriately applies a comma after the opening word *Sadly*. This is because the author is introducing an idea or feeling, then transitioning into an elaborative explanation. *Sadly* is an aside, so there must be a comma afterwards to transition between thoughts and avoid a long-winded sentence. Choice *A* lacks the comma, so it is incorrect. Choice *C* incorrectly separates *that are attacked as lies* from the rest of the sentence, breaking its flow. Choice *D* still lacks the comma and incorrectly changes the two past tense verbs, *plagued* and *attacked*, into gerunds.

44. D: Choice *D* is the correct answer because the tense of *understanding* best applies to the context of the sentence. *Understanding* is also preceded by the modifier *an*. The combined *an understanding* forms a compound noun that is the direct object and focus of the sentence. Choices *A* and *B* use *understand* as a verb, which doesn't complement the sentence. Choice *C* lacks the modifying *an.*

45. A: Choice *A* is the best option. There are no errors in the original sentence, as both parts of the sentence (dependent and independent clauses) are combined through the central comma. Choice *B* creates two new sentences, the first of which is not complete with *While* still present. Choice *C* introduces an unnecessary comma after *practices*. Choice *D* uses *whom* instead of *who*, which is the correct form for this sentence.

46. B: Choice *B* is the correct answer because it corrects the subject-verb disagreement between *character* and *retain* by using *retains* instead. *Retain* is plural, which clashes with the singular *character*, making Choice *A* incorrect. *Retains* is the correct form because it is third person singular, meaning that Choice *C* is also incorrect. Choice *D* is possible as a revision but does not agree with the tense of *do take on* earlier in the sentence.

47. D: Choice *D* is the correct answer because it uses a comma to link the two halves of the sentence and adds the phrase *as well as* to help transition into the dependent clause. *As well as* is also used to communicate that *The Canterbury Tales* shares other qualities besides being *a story about stories*. Choice *A* is incorrect because it is a run on. In particular, *stories also being a story* is very unclear, necessitating the swap of *also* for *as well as*. Choice *B* has an awkward construction and uses the semicolon unwisely; this is certainly not the best option. Choice *C* uses the correct comma but lacks the phrase *as well as*.

48. C: Choice *C* is the correct answer because *these* is the incorrect pronoun for this particular section of the sentence; instead, the singular pronoun *this* should be used. Therefore, Choice *A* is incorrect. While Choice *B* correctly uses *this*, it also inserts a comma afterwards, which disrupts the flow of the sentence. Choice *D* is incorrect because it uses *these* and incorrectly uses *through* instead of *by*.

49. A: Choice *A* is correct. The original sentence has no issues and the author's thoughts are communicated clearly. Choice *B* incorrectly separates the sentence into two sentences, which creates a sentence fragment. Choice *C* rearranges the section in a way that clashes with the rest of the sentence. Choice *D* is incorrect because of the comma inserted after *clear,* breaking up the sentence unnecessarily.

50. B: Choice *B* is the correct answer because it corrects the subject-verb disagreement within the underlined portion. *These* is plural, so it must modify a plural noun. Thus, the plural *individuals* is required. Another clue for this is the fact that *descriptions* is also plural. Choice *A* is therefore incorrect. Choice *C* removes the necessary comma, while Choice *D* inserts an unnecessary semicolon.

51. D: Choice *D* is correct for two reasons. The incorrect pronoun *her* is replaced with the appropriate pronoun *she*. More specifically, Choice *D* uses *she's*, the contraction of *she is*. This emphasizes that the subject, *she,* is acting in a certain way or doing something. Clearly, the author is describing the nun's actions or characteristics. Choice *A* is incorrect because *her* is an inappropriate pronoun in this context, and there is no form of *is* to express what the nun is doing. Choices *B* and *C* still use *her*, so they are incorrect, with the former also altering the sentence completely.

52. C: Choice *C* is the answer, correctly changing the adjective *brutal* to the adverb *brutally* so it can properly modify the adjective *honest*. Without this change, the sentence makes no sense because it presents a stream of adjectives that don't cleanly fit together. Thus, Choice *A* is incorrect. Choice *B* introduces too many commas and remains incoherent, while Choice *D* fails to modify *brutal*.

53. B: Choice *B* is the correct choice because it fixes the confusion of *shed's*. In this context, *shed* is not used as a noun but as a verb, and a verb cannot be possessive. What the sentence should have is *sheds*, the third-person simple singular present form of the verb to complete the phrase: *sheds light on*. This means Choice *A* is incorrect. Choice *C* alters the section in a way that clashes with the whole sentence. Choice *D* fails to correct *shed's* and introduces an unnecessary comma.

54. A: Choice *A* is the correct answer because there are no issues with this section of the sentence. The whole sentence is clear and uses proper punctuation. Choice *B* lacks an introductory comma after *likewise*, which is incorrect. Choices *C* and *D* add unnecessary commas.

55. B: Choice *B* is correct because it makes *Practitioners* plural, enabling it to agree with the verb *strive*. Making *Practitioners* plural also matches the context of the sentence. Therefore, Choice *A* is incorrect. Choice *C* is incorrect because it takes away a necessary comma. Choice *D* makes *Practitioner* and *strives* both singular, but without a modifier like *A* or *The* in front of *practitioner*, the sentence is not correct.

56. D: Choice *D* is the best answer because it corrects the two key errors in the section. *Them* is not the proper pronoun to use in this sentence. *They*, the third-person plural personal pronoun, should be used instead. Choices *A* and *B* are thus incorrect. Choice *D* also adds *be* to modify the main verb *used*, forming the appropriate compound verb. Choice *C* is missing this essential component.

57. C: Choice *C* is correct because the sentence requires the presence of *a* to introduce and modify the noun *testament*. *Testament* is a noun meaning evidence of quality or belief; it's not a verb, which is how Choice *A* uses it. This makes Choice *A* incorrect. Choice *B* uses *an* instead of *a*, which is not necessary because *testament* begins with a consonant. Choice *D* adds an unneeded comma after *possibilities*.

58. D: Choice *D* is the answer because it applies the two commas needed around *like any trial throughout one's life* in order to introduce a side thought in the sentence clearly, without breaking up the flow. The direct object is *test*. Therefore, the commas implemented before and after the phrase are required. Choice *A* doesn't contain the comma after *life*. Choice *B* lacks both the needed commas. Choice *C* applies the second comma incorrectly after *like*, which disrupts the construction of the sentence.

59. A: Choice *A* is correct because it contains no errors that mar the grammar or flow of the sentence. Choice *B* is incorrect because *upon* is incorrectly used to replace *on*. *Upon* refers specifically to a surface, which is not appropriate for this sentence. The preposition *on* is needed here. Choice *C* alters the sentence unnecessarily, confusing the tense and focus of the sentence by using *looking* instead of *look*. Choice *D* changes *some* to *something*, which makes no sense for the rest of the sentence.

60. C: Choice *C* is the correct answer because it adds a comma after *Certainly*. This is important because the author is addressing the audience before moving on to explore *his ideas*. Choice *A* is incorrect because the lack of a comma makes this sentence a run-on. Choices *B* and *D* are incorrect because, while the former applies the comma after *Certainly*, they both take away the *but* that modifies *at what costs*.

61. B: Choice *B* corrects the verb tense of *focuses*. The phrase *to focuses* is not an appropriate infinitive; the best replacement is *to focus*. The sentence is not providing the reason why *Plato's ideal society is one that places human desire*, so Choice *A* is incorrect. Using *focus* allows the prepositional phrase *to focus on* to fluidly transition into the second half of the sentence. Choice *C* is not a bad option, but it lacks the comma needed to transition into *focusing on*. Choice *D* incorrectly eliminates *to*.

62. C: Choice *C* is the correct answer because it replaces the possessive *its* with the contraction *it's* and adds a transition to an alternate viewpoint. *But* should be added as a conjunction after the comma, linking the dependent clause and independent clause. Choices *A* and *B* are therefore incorrect. Choice *D* adds a transition but incorrectly removes *its*, rendering the sentence incoherent.

63. D: Choice *D* is the correct answer because it adds an apostrophe to *citizens*, making it *citizens'*. This gives ownership to *citizens*, which clearly indicates the idea of many citizens having their children confiscated. Choices *A*, *B*, and *C* are all incorrect because they don't give ownership to citizens: the latter adds the apostrophe in a place that indicates only one citizen is impacted.

64. B: Choice *B* is correct because it changes the plural *these* to the singular *this* in order to agree with the singular noun *kidnapping*. Choice *A* is incorrect because of this number disagreement. Choice *C* would be a good alternative, but it lacks the adverb *as* to clarify the use of *kidnappings* and eliminates *and*, which serves as the connection to the rest of the sentence. Choice *D* is incorrect because *those* is plural while *kidnapping* remains singular.

65. A: Choice *A* is correct because the sentence lacks grammatical errors and successfully joins the dependent clause with the independent clause by inserting a single comma after *beings*. Choice *B* is incorrect because it needs a comma to connect the dependent clause and independent clause. Choice *C* uses a semicolon instead of a simple comma. Choice *D* is incorrect because the plural *those* replaces *this*. *This* is singular to describe a single event, which agrees with *seems*.

66. D: Choice *D* is the correct choice because it fixes two issues with the underlined section that cause confusion for the whole sentence. First, *than* is incorrectly used in the original section. *Than* is a conjunction used to make a comparison, while *then* (acting as an adverb) serves to express a result of something, like a sequence of events. Therefore, Choices *A* and *B* are incorrect. However, therein lies the trickiness of the question because none of the answer choices use *then* without altering the meaning of the sentence (Choice *C*). Choice *D* compensates for this by replacing *than/then* with a simple comma to link the two clauses and transition from the central idea to the potential outcome of the idea (the child having more opportunities).

67. C: Choice *C* corrects the only flaw in this sentence by fixing the tense of *encourage*. *Encourages* is the third person present form of the original verb and as such fits much better because the sentence is written in the third person. Choice *A* is incorrect because the tense of *encourage* doesn't sync with the rest of the sentence. Choice *B* is incorrect; the gerund form of *encourage* is unnecessary. Choice *D* uses the conjunction *which* instead *that*, which is incorrect, in addition to not fixing the tense of *encourage*.

68. B: Choice *B* is correct. Here, a colon is used to introduce an explanation. Colons either introduce explanations or lists. Additionally, the quote ends with the punctuation inside the quotes, unlike Choice *C*.

69. A: The verb tense in this passage is predominantly in the present tense, so Choice *A* is the correct answer. Choice *B* is incorrect because the subject and verb do not agree. It should be *Education provides,* not *Education provide*. Choice *C* is incorrect because the passage is in present tense, and *Education will provide* is future tense. Choice *D* doesn't make sense when placed in the sentence.

70. D: The possessive form of the word *it* is *its*. The contraction *it's* denotes *it is*. Thus, Choice *A* is incorrect. The word *raises* in Choice *B* makes the sentence grammatically incorrect. Choice *C* adds an apostrophe at the end of *its*. While adding an apostrophe to most words would indicate possession, adding *'s* to the word *it* indicates a contraction.

71. C: The word *civilised* should be spelled *civilized.* The words *distinguishes* and *creatures* are both spelled correctly.

72. B: Choice *B* is correct because it provides clarity by describing what *myopic* means right after the word itself. Choice *A* is incorrect because the explanation of *myopic* comes before the word; thus, the meaning is skewed. It's possible that Choice *C* makes sense within context. However, it's not the *best* way to say this. Choice *D* is confusingly worded. Using *myopic focus* is not detrimental to society; however, the way *D* is worded makes it seem so.

73. C: Again, we see where the second paragraph can be divided into two parts due to separate topics. The first section's main focus is education addressing the mind, body, and soul. The first section, then, could end with the concluding sentence, "The human heart and psyche . . ." The next sentence to start a new paragraph would be "Education is a basic human right." The rest of this paragraph talks about what education is and some of its characteristics.

74. A: Choice *A* is correct because the phrase *others' ideas* is both plural and indicates possession. Choice *B* is incorrect because *other's* indicates only one *other* that's in possession of *ideas*, which is incorrect. Choice *C* is incorrect because no possession is indicated. Choice *D* is incorrect because the word *other* does not end in *s*. *Others's* is not a correct form of the word in any situation.

75. D: This sentence must have a comma before *although* because the word *although* is connecting two independent clauses. Thus, Choices *B* and *C* are incorrect. Choice *A* is incorrect because the second sentence in the underlined section is a fragment.

Practice Test #3

Reading Comprehension

Questions 1–10 are based on the following passage:

"Mademoiselle Eugénie is pretty—I think I remember that to be her name."

"Very pretty, or rather, very beautiful," replied Albert, "but of that style of beauty which I don't appreciate; I am an ungrateful fellow."

"Really," said Monte Cristo, lowering his voice, "you don't appear to me to be very enthusiastic on the subject of this marriage."

"Mademoiselle Danglars is too rich for me," replied Morcerf, "and that frightens me."

"Bah," exclaimed Monte Cristo, "that's a fine reason to give. Are you not rich yourself?"

"My father's income is about 50,000 francs per annum; and he will give me, perhaps, ten or twelve thousand when I marry."

"That, perhaps, might not be considered a large sum, in Paris especially," said the count; "but everything doesn't depend on wealth, and it's a fine thing to have a good name, and to occupy a high station in society. Your name is celebrated, your position magnificent; and then the Comte de Morcerf is a soldier, and it's pleasing to see the integrity of a Bayard united to the poverty of a Duguesclin; disinterestedness is the brightest ray in which a noble sword can shine. As for me, I consider the union with Mademoiselle Danglars a most suitable one; she will enrich you, and you will ennoble her."

Albert shook his head, and looked thoughtful. "There is still something else," said he.

"I confess," observed Monte Cristo, "that I have some difficulty in comprehending your objection to a young lady who is both rich and beautiful."

"Oh," said Morcerf, "this repugnance, if repugnance it may be called, isn't all on my side."

"Whence can it arise, then? for you told me your father desired the marriage."

"It's my mother who dissents; she has a clear and penetrating judgment, and doesn't smile on the proposed union. I cannot account for it, but she seems to entertain some prejudice against the Danglars."

"Ah," said the count, in a somewhat forced tone, "that may be easily explained; the Comtesse de Morcerf, who is aristocracy and refinement itself, doesn't relish the idea of being allied by your marriage with one of ignoble birth; that is natural enough."

Excerpt from the Count of Monte Cristo by Alexandre Dumas

1. The meaning of the word *repugnance* is closest to:
   a. Strong resemblance
   b. Strong dislike
   c. Extreme shyness
   d. Extreme dissimilarity

2. What can be inferred about Albert's family?
   a. Their finances are uncertain.
   b. Albert is the only son in his family.
   c. Their name is more respected than the Danglars'.
   d. Albert's mother and father both agree on their decisions.

3. What is Albert's attitude towards his impending marriage?
   a. Pragmatic
   b. Romantic
   c. Indifferent
   d. Apprehensive

4. What is the best description of the Count's relationship with Albert?
   a. He's like a strict parent, criticizing Albert's choices.
   b. He's like a wise uncle, giving practical advice to Albert.
   c. He's like a close friend, supporting all of Albert's opinions.
   d. He's like a suspicious investigator, asking many probing questions.

5. Which sentence is true of Albert's mother?
   a. She belongs to a noble family.
   b. She often makes poor choices.
   c. She is primarily occupied with money.
   d. She is unconcerned about her son's future.

6. Based on this passage, what is probably NOT true about French society in the 1800s?
   a. Children often received money from their parents.
   b. Marriages were sometimes arranged between families.
   c. The richest people in society were also the most respected.
   d. People were often expected to marry within their same social class.

7. Why is the Count puzzled by Albert's attitude toward his marriage?
   a. He seems reluctant to marry Eugénie, despite her wealth and beauty.
   b. He is marrying against his father's wishes, despite usually following his advice.
   c. He appears excited to marry someone he doesn't love, despite being a hopeless romantic.
   d. He expresses reverence towards Eugénie, despite being from a higher social class than her.

8. The passage is made up mostly of what kind of text?
   a. Narration
   b. Dialogue
   c. Description
   d. Explanation

9. What does the word *ennoble* mean in the middle of the passage?
   a. To create beauty in another person
   b. To endow someone with wealth
   c. To make someone chaste again
   d. To give someone a noble rank or title

10. Why is the count said to have a "forced tone" in the last paragraph?
   a. Because he is in love with Mademoiselle Eugénie and is trying to keep it a secret.
   b. Because he finally agrees with Albert's point of view but still doesn't understand it.
   c. Because he finally understands Albert's point of view but still doesn't agree with it.
   d. Because he is only pretending that Albert is his friend to get information out of him.

Questions 11–20 are based upon the following passage:

> "MANKIND being originally equals in the order of creation, the equality could only be destroyed by some subsequent circumstance; the distinctions of rich, and poor, may in a great measure be accounted for, and that without having recourse to the harsh ill sounding names of oppression and avarice. Oppression is often the consequence, but seldom or never the means of riches; and though avarice will preserve a man from being necessitously poor, it generally makes him too timorous to be wealthy.
>
> But there is another and greater distinction for which no truly natural or religious reason can be assigned, and that is, the distinction of men into KINGS and SUBJECTS. Male and female are the distinctions of nature, good and bad the distinctions of heaven; but how a race of men came into the world so exalted above the rest, and distinguished like some new species, is worth enquiring into, and whether they are the means of happiness or of misery to mankind.
>
> In the early ages of the world, according to the scripture chronology, there were no kings; the consequence of which was there were no wars; it is the pride of kings which throw mankind into confusion. Holland without a king hath enjoyed more peace for this last century than any of the monarchical governments in Europe. Antiquity favors the same remark; for the quiet and rural lives of the first patriarchs hath a happy something in them, which vanishes away when we come to the history of Jewish royalty.
>
> Government by kings was first introduced into the world by the Heathens, from whom the children of Israel copied the custom. It was the most prosperous invention the Devil ever set on foot for the promotion of idolatry. The Heathens paid divine honors to their deceased kings, and the Christian world hath improved on the plan by doing the same to their living ones. How impious is the title of sacred majesty applied to a worm, who in the midst of his splendor is crumbling into dust!
>
> As the exalting one man so greatly above the rest cannot be justified on the equal rights of nature, so neither can it be defended on the authority of scripture; for the will of the Almighty, as declared by Gideon and the prophet Samuel, expressly disapproves of government by kings. All anti-monarchical parts of scripture have been very smoothly glossed over in monarchical governments, but they undoubtedly merit the attention of countries, which have their governments yet to form. "Render unto Caesar the things which are Caesar's" is the scripture doctrine of courts, yet it is no support of

monarchical government, for the Jews at that time were without a king, and in a state of vassalage to the Romans.

Near three thousand years passed away from the Mosaic account of the creation, till the Jews under a national delusion requested a king. Till then their form of government (except in extraordinary cases, where the Almighty interposed) was a kind of republic administered by a judge and the elders of the tribes. Kings they had none, and it was held sinful to acknowledge any being under that title but the Lord of Hosts. And when a man seriously reflects on the idolatrous homage which is paid to the persons of Kings, he need not wonder, that the Almighty ever jealous of his honor, should disapprove of a form of government which so impiously invades the prerogative of heaven.

Excerpt from "Common Sense" by Thomas Paine

11. According to passage, what role does avarice, or greed, play in poverty?
    a. It can make a man very wealthy
    b. It is the consequence of wealth
    c. Avarice can prevent a man from being poor, but too fearful to be very wealthy
    d. Avarice is what drives a person to be very wealthy

12. Of these distinctions, which does the author believe to be beyond natural or religious reason?
    a. Good and bad
    b. Male and female
    c. Human and animal
    d. King and subjects

13. According to the passage, what are the Heathens responsible for?
    a. Government by kings
    b. Quiet and rural lives of patriarchs
    c. Paying divine honors to their living kings
    d. Equal rights of nature

14. Which of the following best states Paine's rationale for the denouncement of monarchy?
    a. It is against the laws of nature
    b. It is against the equal rights of nature and is denounced in scripture
    c. Despite scripture, a monarchal government is unlawful
    d. Neither the law nor scripture denounce monarchy

15. Based on the passage, what is the best definition of the word *idolatrous*?
    a. Worshipping heroes
    b. Being deceitful
    c. Sinfulness
    d. Engaging in illegal activities

16. What is the essential meaning of lines 41–44?

> And when a man seriously reflects on the idolatrous homage which is paid to the persons of Kings, he need not wonder, that the Almighty ever jealous of his honor, should disapprove of a form of government which so impiously invades the prerogative of heaven.

a. God would disapprove of the irreverence of a monarchical government.
b. With careful reflection, men should realize that heaven is not promised.
c. God will punish those that follow a monarchical government.
d. Belief in a monarchical government cannot coexist with belief in God.

17. Based on the passage, what is the best definition of the word *timorous* in the first paragraph?
a. Being full of fear
b. A characteristic of shyness
c. Being able to see through someone
d. Being full of anger and hatred

18. The author's attitude toward the subject can best be described as:
a. Indifferent and fatigued
b. Impassioned and critical
c. Awed and enchanted
d. Enraged and sulky

19. The main purpose of the fourth paragraph is:
a. To persuade the audience that heathens were more advanced than Christians.
b. To explain how monarchs came into existence and how Christians adopted the same system.
c. To describe the divination of English monarchs and how it is their birthright to be revered.
d. To counteract the preceding paragraph by giving proof of the damage monarchs can cause.

20. In the last paragraph, what does the author mean by the "Mosaic account of creation"?
a. The author means that creation is based on individuals composed of cells of two genetically different types.
b. The author implies that the work of God is like a mosaic painting due to the various formations of creation.
c. The author means that the kings of the past developed a system in which to maintain accounts of creation.
d. The author implies that the recorded history of creation is a collection, collage, or pattern taken from various accounts of cultures.

Questions 21–30 are based on the following two passages:

Passage 1

People who argue that William Shakespeare is not responsible for the plays attributed to his name are known as anti-Stratfordians (from the name of Shakespeare's birthplace, Stratford-upon-Avon). The most common anti-Stratfordian claim is that William Shakespeare simply was not educated enough or from a high enough social class to have written plays overflowing with references to such a wide range of subjects like history, the classics, religion, and international culture. William Shakespeare was the son of a glove-maker, he only had a basic grade school education, and he never set foot outside of England—so how could he have produced plays of such sophistication and imagination? How could he have written in such detail about historical figures and events, or about different cultures and locations around Europe? According to anti-Stratfordians, the depth of knowledge contained in Shakespeare's plays suggests a well-traveled writer from a wealthy background with a university education, not a countryside writer like Shakespeare. But in fact, there is not much substance to such speculation, and most anti-Stratfordian arguments can be refuted with a little background about Shakespeare's time and upbringing.

First of all, those who doubt Shakespeare's authorship often point to his common birth and brief education as stumbling blocks to his writerly genius. Although it is true that Shakespeare did not come from a noble class, his father was a very *successful* glove-maker and his mother was from a very wealthy land-owning family—so while Shakespeare may have had a country upbringing, he was certainly from a well-off family and would have been educated accordingly. Also, even though he did not attend university, grade school education in Shakespeare's time was actually quite rigorous and exposed students to classic drama through writers like Seneca and Ovid. It is not unreasonable to believe that Shakespeare received a very solid foundation in poetry and literature from his early schooling.

Next, anti-Stratfordians tend to question how Shakespeare could write so extensively about countries and cultures he had never visited before (for instance, several of his most famous works like *Romeo and Juliet* and *The Merchant of Venice* were set in Italy, on the opposite side of Europe!). But again, this criticism does not hold up under scrutiny. For one thing, Shakespeare was living in London, a bustling metropolis of international trade, the most populous city in England, and a political and cultural hub of Europe. In the daily crowds of people, Shakespeare would certainly have been able to meet travelers from other countries and hear firsthand accounts of life in their home country. And, in addition to the influx of information from world travelers, this was also the age of the printing press, a jump in technology that made it possible to print and circulate books much more easily than in the past. This also allowed for a freer flow of information across different countries, allowing people to read about life and ideas from throughout Europe. One needn't travel the continent in order to learn and write about its culture.

Passage 2

Now there is very good authority for saying, and I think the truth is so, that at least two of the plays published among the works of Shakespeare are not his at all; that at least three others contain very little, if any, of his writing; and that of the remainder, many contain long passages that are non-Shakespearean. But when we have submitted them all the crucible of criticism we have a magnificent residuum of the purest gold. Here is the true Shakespeare; here is the great magician who, by a wave of his wand, could transmute brass into gold, or make dry bones live and move and have immortal being. Who was this great magician—this mighty dramatist who was "not of an age, but for all time"? Who was the writer of *Venus* and *Lucrece* and the *Sonnets* and *Lear* and *Hamlet*? Was it William Shakespeare of Stratford, the Player? So it is generally believed, and that hypothesis I had accepted in unquestioning faith till my love of the works naturally led me to an examination of the life of the supposed author of them. Then I found that as I read my faith melted away "into thin air." It was not, certainly, that I had (nor have I now) any wish to disbelieve. I was, and I am, altogether willing to accept the Player as the immortal poet if only my reason would allow me to do so. Why not? . . . But the question of authorship is, nevertheless, a most fascinating one. If it be true, as the Rev. Leonard Bacon wrote that "The great world does not care sixpence who wrote *Hamlet*," the great world must, at the same time, be a very small world, and many of us must be content to be outside it. Having given, then, the best attention I was able to give to the question, and more time, I fear, than I ought to have devoted to it, I was brought to the conclusion, as many others have been, that the man who is, truly enough, designated by Messrs. Garnett and Gosse as a "Stratford rustic" is not the true Shakespeare. . .

That Shakespeare the "Stratford rustic and London actor" should have acquired this learning, this culture, and this polish; that *he* should have travelled into foreign lands, studied the life and topography of foreign cities, and the manners and customs of all sorts and conditions of men; that *he* should have written some half-dozen dramas . . . besides qualifying himself as a professional actor; that *he* should have done all this and a good deal more between 1587 and 1592 is a supposition so wild that it can only be entertained by those who are prepared to accept it as a miracle. "And miracles do not happen!"

The following passage is from *The Shakespeare Problem Restated* by G.G. Greenwood

21. Which sentence contains the author's thesis in the first passage?
    a. People who argue that William Shakespeare is not responsible for the plays attributed to his name are known as anti-Stratfordians.
    b. But in fact, there is not much substance to such speculation, and most anti-Stratfordian arguments can be refuted with a little background about Shakespeare's time and upbringing.
    c. It is not unreasonable to believe that Shakespeare received a very solid foundation in poetry and literature from his early schooling.
    d. Next, anti-Stratfordians tend to question how Shakespeare could write so extensively about countries and cultures he had never visited before.

22. In the first paragraph in Passage 1, "How could he have written in such detail about historical figures and events, or about different cultures and locations around Europe?" is an example of which of the following?
    a. Hyperbole
    b. Onomatopoeia
    c. Rhetorical question
    d. Appeal to authority

23. In Passage 1, how does the author respond to the claim that Shakespeare was not well-educated because he did not attend university?
    a. By insisting upon Shakespeare's natural genius.
    b. By explaining grade school curriculum in Shakespeare's time.
    c. By comparing Shakespeare with other uneducated writers of his time.
    d. By pointing out that Shakespeare's wealthy parents probably paid for private tutors.

24. In Passage 1, the word *bustling* in the third paragraph most nearly means which of the following?
    a. Busy
    b. Foreign
    c. Expensive
    d. Undeveloped

25. In passage 2, the following sentence is an example of what?

Here is the true Shakespeare; here is the great magician who, by a wave of his wand, could transmute brass into gold, or make dry bones live and move and have immortal being.

a. Personification
b. Metaphor
c. Simile
d. Allusion

26. In passage 2, the author's attitude toward Stratfordians can be described as which of the following?
a. Accepting and forgiving
b. Uncaring and neutral
c. Uplifting and admiring
d. Disbelieving and critical

27. What is the relationship between these two sentences from Passage 2?

Sentence 1: So it is generally believed, and that hypothesis I had accepted in unquestioning faith till my love of the works naturally led me to an examination of the life of the supposed author of them.

Sentence 2: Then I found that as I read my faith melted away "into thin air."

a. Sentence 2 explains the main idea in Sentence 1.
b. Sentence 2 continues the definition begun in Sentence 1.
c. Sentence 2 analyzes the comment in Sentence 1.
d. Sentence 2 is a contrast to the idea in Sentence 1.

28. The writing style of Passage 1 could be best described as what?
a. Expository
b. Persuasive
c. Narrative
d. Descriptive

29. In passage 2, the word *topography* in the second paragraph most nearly means which of the following?
a. Climate features of an area.
b. Agriculture specific to place.
c. Shape and features of the Earth.
d. Aspects of humans within society.

30. The authors of the passages differ in their opinion of Shakespeare in that the author of Passage 2
a. Believes that Shakespeare the actor did not write the plays.
b. Believes that Shakespeare the playwright did not in act in the plays.
c. Believes that Shakespeare was both the actor and the playwright.
d. Believes that Shakespeare was neither the actor nor the playwright.

Questions 31–40 are based on the following passage:

In the quest to understand existence, modern philosophers must question if humans can fully comprehend the world. Classical western approaches to philosophy tend to hold that one can understand something, be it an event or object, by standing outside of the phenomena and observing it. It is then by unbiased observation that one can grasp the details of the world. This seems to hold true for many things. Scientists conduct experiments and record their findings, and thus many natural phenomena become comprehendible. However, several of these observations were possible because humans used tools in order to make these discoveries.

This may seem like an extraneous matter. After all, people invented things like microscopes and telescopes in order to enhance their capacity to view cells or the movement of stars. While humans are still capable of seeing things, the question remains if human beings have the capacity to fully observe and see the world in order to understand it. It would not be an impossible stretch to argue that what humans see through a microscope is not the exact thing itself, but a human interpretation of it.

This would seem to be the case in the "Business of the Holes" experiment conducted by Richard Feynman. To study the way electrons behave, Feynman set up a barrier with two holes and a plate. The plate was there to indicate how many times the electrons would pass through the hole(s). Rather than casually observe the electrons acting under normal circumstances, Feynman discovered that electrons behave in two totally different ways depending on whether or not they are observed. The electrons that were observed had passed through either one of the holes or were caught on the plate as particles. However, electrons that weren't observed acted as waves instead of particles and passed through both holes. This indicated that electrons have a dual nature. Electrons seen by the human eye act like particles, while unseen electrons act like waves of energy.

This dual nature of the electrons presents a conundrum. While humans now have a better understanding of electrons, the fact remains that people cannot entirely perceive how electrons behave without the use of instruments. We can only observe one of the mentioned behaviors, which only provides a partial understanding of the entire function of electrons. Therefore, we're forced to ask ourselves whether the world we observe is objective or if it is subjectively perceived by humans. Or, an alternative question: can man understand the world only through machines that will allow them to observe natural phenomena?

Both questions humble man's capacity to grasp the world. However, those ideas don't consider that many phenomena have been proven by human beings without the use of machines, such as the discovery of gravity. Like all philosophical questions, whether man's reason and observation alone can understand the universe can be approached from many angles.

31. The word *extraneous* in paragraph 2 can be best interpreted as referring to which one of the following?
   a. Indispensable
   b. Bewildering
   c. Superfluous
   d. Exuberant

32. What is the author's motivation for writing the passage?
   a. To bring to light an alternative view on human perception by examining the role of technology in human understanding.
   b. To educate the reader on the latest astroparticle physics discovery and offer terms that may be unfamiliar to the reader.
   c. To argue that humans are totally blind to the realities of the world by presenting an experiment that proves that electrons are not what they seem on the surface.
   d. To reflect on opposing views of human understanding.

33. Which of the following most closely resembles the way in which paragraph four is structured?
   a. It offers one solution, questions the solution, and then ends with an alternative solution.
   b. It presents an inquiry, explains the details of that inquiry, and then offers a solution.
   c. It presents a problem, explains the details of that problem, and then ends with more inquiry.
   d. It gives a definition, offers an explanation, and then ends with an inquiry.

34. For the classical approach to understanding to hold true, which of the following must be required?
   a. A telescope
   b. A recording device
   c. Multiple witnesses present
   d. The person observing must be unbiased

35. Which best describes how the electrons in the experiment behaved like waves?
   a. The electrons moved up and down like actual waves.
   b. The electrons passed through both holes and then onto the plate.
   c. The electrons converted to photons upon touching the plate.
   d. Electrons were seen passing through one hole or the other.

36. The author mentions "gravity" in the last paragraph in order to do what?
   a. To show that different natural phenomena test man's ability to grasp the world.
   b. To prove that since man has not measured it with the use of tools or machines, humans cannot know the true nature of gravity.
   c. To demonstrate an example of natural phenomena humans discovered and understood without the use of tools or machines.
   d. To show an alternative solution to the nature of electrons that humans have not thought of yet.

37. Which situation best parallels the revelation of the dual nature of electrons discovered in Feynman's experiment?
    a. A man is born color-blind and grows up observing everything in lighter or darker shades. With the invention of special goggles he puts on, he discovers that there are other colors in addition to different shades.
    b. The coelacanth was thought to be extinct, but a live specimen was just recently discovered. There are now two living species of coelacanth known to man, and both are believed to be endangered.
    c. In the Middle Ages, blacksmiths added carbon to iron, thus inventing steel. The consequences of this important discovery would have its biggest effects during the industrial revolution.
    d. In order to better examine and treat broken bones, the x-ray machine was invented and put to use in hospitals and medical centers.

38. Which statement about technology would the author likely disagree with?
    a. Technology can help expand the field of human vision.
    b. Technology renders human observation irrelevant.
    c. Developing tools used in observation and research indicates growing understanding of our world itself.
    d. Studying certain phenomena necessitates the use of tools and machines.

39. As it is used in paragraph 4, the word *conundrum* most nearly means:
    a. Platitude
    b. Enigma
    c. Solution
    d. Hypothesis

40. What is the author's purpose in paragraph 3?
    a. To prove to the audience the thesis of the passage by providing evidence suggesting that electrons behave differently when observed by the human eye.
    b. To propose that the experiment conducted was not ethically done and to provide evidence that a new experiment should be conducted in order to reach the truth.
    c. To introduce the topic to the audience in a manner that puts it into a practical as well as historical understanding.
    d. To pose a question relating to the topic about whether humans fully observe phenomena in an objective or subjective sense.

English Language

Questions 1–15 are based on the following passage:

> The knowledge of an aircraft engineer is acquired through years of education, and special (1) <u>licenses are required</u>. Ideally, an individual will begin his or her preparation for the profession in high school (2) <u>by taking chemistry physics trigonometry and calculus.</u> Such curricula will aid in (3) <u>one's pursuit of a bachelor's degree</u> in aircraft engineering, which requires several physical and life sciences, mathematics, and design courses.
>
> (4) <u>Some of universities provide internship or apprentice opportunities</u> for the students enrolled in aircraft engineer programs. A bachelor's in aircraft engineering is commonly accompanied by a master's degree in advanced engineering or business administration.

Such advanced degrees enable an individual to position himself or herself for executive, faculty, and/or research opportunities. (5) These advanced offices oftentimes require a Professional Engineering (PE) license which can be obtained through additional college courses, professional experience, and acceptable scores on the Fundamentals of Engineering (FE) and Professional Engineering (PE) standardized assessments.

(6) Once the job begins, this lines of work requires critical thinking, business skills, problem solving, and creativity. This level of (7) expertise (8) allows aircraft engineers to (9) apply mathematical equation and scientific processes to aeronautical and aerospace issues or inventions. (10) For example, aircraft engineers may test, design, and construct flying vessels such as airplanes, space shuttles, and missile weapons. As a result, aircraft engineers are compensated with generous salaries. In fact, in May 2014, the lowest 10 percent of all American aircraft engineers earned less than $60,110 while the highest paid ten-percent of all American aircraft engineers earned $155,240. (11) In May 2015, the United States Bureau of Labor Statistics (BLS) reported that the median annual salary of aircraft engineers was $107,830. (12) Conversely, (13) employment opportunities for aircraft engineers are projected to decrease by 2 percent by 2024. This decrease may be the result of a decline in the manufacturing industry. (14) Nevertheless aircraft engineers who know how to utilize modeling and simulation programs, fluid dynamic software, and robotic engineering tools (15) is projected to remain the most employable.

1. Which of the following would be the best choice for this sentence (reproduced below)?

The knowledge of an aircraft engineer is acquired through years of education, and special (1) licenses are required.

a. NO CHANGE
b. licenses will be required
c. licenses may be required
d. licenses should be required

2. Which of the following would be the best choice for this sentence (reproduced below)?

Ideally, an individual will begin his or her preparation for the profession in high school (2) by taking chemistry physics trigonometry and calculus.

a. NO CHANGE
b. by taking chemistry; physics; trigonometry; and calculus.
c. by taking chemistry, physics, trigonometry, and calculus.
d. by taking chemistry, physics, trigonometry, calculus.

3. Which of the following would be the best choice for this sentence (reproduced below)?

Such curricula will aid in (3) one's pursuit of a bachelor's degree in aircraft engineering, which requires several physical and life sciences, mathematics, and design courses.

a. NO CHANGE
b. ones pursuit of a bachelors degree
c. one's pursuit of a bachelors degree
d. ones pursuit of a bachelor's degree

4. Which of the following would be the best choice for this sentence (reproduced below)?

(4) Some of universities provide internship or apprentice opportunities for the students enrolled in aircraft engineer programs.

a. NO CHANGE
b. Some of universities provided internship or apprentice opportunities
c. Some of universities provide internship or apprenticeship opportunities
d. Some universities provide internship or apprenticeship opportunities

5. Which of the following would be the best choice for this sentence (reproduced below)?

(5) These advanced offices oftentimes require a Professional Engineering (PE) license which can be obtained through additional college courses, professional experience, and acceptable scores on the Fundamentals of Engineering (FE) and Professional Engineering (PE) standardized assessments.

a. NO CHANGE
b. These advanced positions oftentimes require acceptable scores on the Fundamentals of Engineering (FE) and Professional Engineering (PE) standardized assessments in order to achieve a Professional Engineering (PE) license. Additional college courses and professional experience help.
c. These advanced offices oftentimes require acceptable scores on the Fundamentals of Engineering (FE) and Professional Engineering (PE) standardized assessments to gain the Professional Engineering (PE) license which can be obtained through additional college courses, professional experience.
d. These advanced positions oftentimes require a Professional Engineering (PE) license which is obtained by acceptable scores on the Fundamentals of Engineering (FE) and Professional Engineering (PE) standardized assessments. Further education and professional experience can help prepare for the assessments.

6. Which of the following would be the best choice for this sentence (reproduced below)?

(6) Once the job begins, this lines of work requires critical thinking, business skills, problem solving, and creativity.

a. NO CHANGE
b. Once the job begins, this line of work
c. Once the job begins, these line of work
d. Once the job begin, this line of work

7. Which of the following would be the best choice for this sentence (reproduced below)?

This level of (7) expertise allows aircraft engineers to apply mathematical equation and scientific processes to aeronautical and aerospace issues or inventions.

a. NO CHANGE
b. expertis
c. expirtise
d. excpertise

8. Which of the following would be the best choice for this sentence (reproduced below)?

This level of expertise (8) allows aircraft engineers to apply mathematical equation and scientific processes to aeronautical and aerospace issues or inventions.

a. NO CHANGE
b. Inhibits
c. Requires
d. Should

9. Which of the following would be the best choice for this sentence (reproduced below)?

This level of expertise allows aircraft engineers to (9) apply mathematical equation and scientific processes to aeronautical and aerospace issues or inventions.

a. NO CHANGE
b. apply mathematical equations and scientific process
c. apply mathematical equation and scientific process
d. apply mathematical equations and scientific processes

10. Which of the following would be the best choice for this sentence (reproduced below)?

(10) For example, aircraft engineers may test, design, and construct flying vessels such as airplanes, space shuttles, and missile weapons.

a. NO CHANGE
b. Therefore,
c. However,
d. Furthermore,

11. Which of the following would be the best choice for this sentence (reproduced below)?

(11) In May 2015, the United States Bureau of Labor Statistics (BLS) reported that the median annual salary of aircraft engineers was $107,830.

a. NO CHANGE
b. May of 2015, the United States Bureau of Labor Statistics (BLS) reported that the median annual salary of aircraft engineers was $107,830.
c. In May of 2015 the United States Bureau of Labor Statistics (BLS) reported that the median annual salary of aircraft engineers was $107,830.
d. In May, 2015, the United States Bureau of Labor Statistics (BLS) reported that the median annual salary of aircraft engineers was $107,830.

12. Which of the following would be the best choice for this sentence (reproduced below)?

(12) Conversely, employment opportunities for aircraft engineers are projected to decrease by 2 percent by 2024.

a. NO CHANGE
b. Similarly,
c. In other words,
d. Accordingly,

13. Which of the following would be the best choice for this sentence (reproduced below)?

Conversely, (13) employment opportunities for aircraft engineers are projected to decrease by 2 percent by 2024.

a. NO CHANGE
b. employment opportunities for aircraft engineers will be projected to decrease by 2 percent in 2024.
c. employment opportunities for aircraft engineers is projected to decrease by 2 percent in 2024.
d. employment opportunities for aircraft engineers were projected to decrease by 2 percent in 2024.

14. Which of the following would be the best choice for this sentence (reproduced below)?

(14) Nevertheless aircraft engineers who know how to utilize modeling and simulation programs, fluid dynamic software, and robotic engineering tools is projected to remain the most employable.

a. NO CHANGE
b. Nevertheless; aircraft engineers who know how to utilize
c. Nevertheless, aircraft engineers who know how to utilize
d. Nevertheless—aircraft engineers who know how to utilize

15. Which of the following would be the best choice for this sentence (reproduced below)?

Nevertheless aircraft engineers who know how to utilize modeling and simulation programs, fluid dynamic software, and robotic engineering tools (15) is projected to remain the most employable.

a. NO CHANGE
b. am projected to remain
c. was projected to remain
d. are projected to remain

Questions 16–30 are based on the following passage:

On September 11th, 2001, a group of terrorists hijacked four American airplanes. The terrorists crashed the planes into the World Trade Center in New York City, the Pentagon in Washington D.C., and a field in Pennsylvania. Nearly 3,000 people died during the attacks, which propelled the United States into a (16) "War on Terror".

About the Terrorists

(17) Terrorists commonly uses fear and violence to achieve political goals. The nineteen terrorists who orchestrated and implemented the attacks of September 11th were militants associated with al-Qaeda, an Islamic extremist group founded by Osama bin Landen, Abdullah Azzam, and others in the late 1980s. (18) Bin Laden orchestrated the attacks as a response to what he felt was American injustice against Islam and hatred towards Muslims. In his words, "Terrorism against America deserves to be praised."

Islam is the religion of Muslims, (19) who live mainly in south and southwest Asia and Sub-Saharan Africa. The majority of Muslims practice Islam peacefully. However, fractures in Islam have led to the growth of Islamic extremists who strictly oppose Western influences. They seek to institute stringent Islamic law and destroy those who violate Islamic code.

In November 2002, bin Laden provided the explicit motives for the 9/11 terror attacks. According to this list, (20) Americas support of Israel, military presence in Saudi Arabia, and other anti-Muslim actions were the causes.

The Timeline of the Attacks

The morning of September 11 began like any other for most Americans. Then, at 8:45 a.m., a Boeing 767 plane (21) crashed into the north tower of the World Trade Center in New York City. Hundreds were instantly killed. Others were trapped on higher floors. The crash was initially thought to be a freak accident. When a second plane flew directly into the south tower eighteen minutes later, it was determined that America was under attack.

At 9:45 a.m., (22) slamming into the Pentagon was a third plane, America's military headquarters in Washington D.C. The jet fuel of this plane caused a major fire and partial building collapse that resulted in nearly 200 deaths. By 10:00 a.m., the south tower of the World Trade Center collapsed. Thirty minutes later, the north tower followed suit.

While this was happening, a fourth plane that departed from New Jersey, United Flight 93, was hijacked. The passengers learned of the attacks that occurred in New York and Washington D.C. and realized that they faced the same fate as the other planes that crashed. The passengers were determined to overpower the terrorists in an effort to prevent the deaths of additional innocent American citizens. Although the passengers were successful in (23) diverging the plane, it crashed in a western Pennsylvania field and killed everyone on board. The plane's final target remains uncertain, (24) but believed by many people was the fact that United Flight 93 was heading for the White House.

Heroes and Rescuers

(25) Close to 3,000 people died in the World Trade Center attacks. This figure includes 343 New York City firefighters and paramedics, 23 New York City police officers, and 37 Port Authority officers. Nevertheless, thousands of men and women in service worked (26) valiantly to evacuate the buildings, save trapped workers, extinguish infernos, uncover victims trapped in fallen rubble, and tend to nearly 10,000 injured individuals.

About 300 rescue dogs played a major role in the after-attack salvages. Working twelve-hour shifts, the dogs scoured the rubble and alerted paramedics when they found signs of life. While doing so, the dogs served as a source of comfort and therapy for the rescue teams.

Initial Impacts on America

The attacks of September 11, 2001 resulted in the immediate suspension of all air travel. No flights could take off from or land on American soil. (27) American airports and airspace closed to all national and international flights. Therefore, over five hundred flights had to turn back or be redirected to other countries. Canada alone received 226 flights and thousands of stranded passengers. (28) Needless to say, as cancelled flights are rescheduled, air travel became backed up and chaotic for quite some time.

At the time of the attacks, George W. Bush was the president of the United States. President Bush announced that "We will make no distinction between the terrorists who committed these acts and those who harbor them." The rate of hate crimes against American Muslims spiked, despite President Bush's call for the country to treat them with respect.

Additionally, relief funds were quickly arranged. The funds were used to support families of the victims, orphaned children, and those with major injuries. In this way, the tragic event brought the citizens together through acts of service towards those directly impacted by the attack.

Long-Term Effects of the Attacks

Over the past fifteen years, the attacks of September 11th have transformed the United States' government, travel safety protocols, and international relations. Anti-terrorism legislation became a priority for many countries as law enforcement and intelligence agencies teamed up to find and defeat alleged terrorists.

Present George W. Bush announced a War on Terror. He (29) desired to bring bin Laden and al-Qaeda to justice and prevent future terrorist networks from gaining strength. The War in Afghanistan began in October of 2001 when the United States and British forces bombed al-Qaeda camps. (30) The Taliban, a group of fundamental Muslims who protected Osama bin Laden, was overthrown on December 9, 2001. However, the war continued in order to defeat insurgency campaigns in neighboring countries. Ten years later, the United State Navy SEALS killed Osama bin Laden in Pakistan. During 2014, the United States declared the end of its involvement in the War on Terror in Afghanistan.

Museums and memorials have since been erected to honor and remember the thousands of people who died during the September 11th attacks, including the brave rescue workers who gave their lives in the effort to help others.

16. Which of the following would be the best choice for this sentence (reproduced below)?

Nearly 3,000 people died during the attacks, which propelled the United States into a (16) "War on Terror".

a. NO CHANGE
b. "war on terror".
c. "war on terror."
d. "War on Terror."

17. Which of the following would be the best choice for this sentence (reproduced below)?

(17) Terrorists commonly uses fear and violence to achieve political goals.

a. NO CHANGE
b. Terrorist's commonly use fear and violence to achieve political goals.
c. Terrorists commonly use fear and violence to achieve political goals.
d. Terrorists commonly use fear and violence to achieves political goals.

18. Which of the following would be the best choice for this sentence (reproduced below)?

(18) Bin Laden orchestrated the attacks as a response to what he felt was American injustice against Islam and hatred towards Muslims.

a. NO CHANGE
b. Bin Laden orchestrated the attacks as a response to what he felt was American injustice against Islam, and hatred towards Muslims.
c. Bin Laden orchestrated the attacks, as a response to what he felt was American injustice against Islam and hatred towards Muslims.
d. Bin Laden orchestrated the attacks as responding to what he felt was American injustice against Islam and hatred towards Muslims.

19. Which of the following would be the best choice for this sentence (reproduced below)?

    Islam is the religion of Muslims, (19) who live mainly in south and southwest Asia and Sub-Saharan Africa.

    a. NO CHANGE
    b. who live mainly in the South and Southwest Asia
    c. who live mainly in the south and Southwest Asia
    d. who live mainly in the south and southwest asia

20. Which of the following would be the best choice for this sentence (reproduced below)?

    According to this list, (20) Americas support of Israel, military presence in Saudi Arabia, and other anti-Muslim actions were the causes.

    a. NO CHANGE
    b. America's support of israel,
    c. Americas support of Israel
    d. America's support of Israel,

21. Which of the following would be the best choice for this sentence (reproduced below)?

    Then, at 8:45 a.m., a Boeing 767 plane (21) crashed into the north tower of the World Trade Center in New York City.

    a. NO CHANGE
    b. crashes into the north tower of the World Trade Center
    c. crashing into the north tower of the World Trade Center
    d. crash into the north tower of the World Trade Center

22. Which of the following would be the best choice for this sentence (reproduced below)?

    At 9:45 a.m., (22) slamming into the Pentagon was a third plane, America's military headquarters in Washington D.C.

    a. NO CHANGE
    b. into the Pentagon slammed a third plane,
    c. a third plane slammed into the Pentagon,
    d. the Pentagon was slamming by a third plane,

23. Which of the following would be the best choice for this sentence (reproduced below)?

    Although the passengers were successful in (23) diverging the plane, it crashed in a western Pennsylvania field and killed everyone on board.

    a. NO CHANGE
    b. Diverting
    c. Converging
    d. Distracting

24. Which of the following would be the best choice for this sentence (reproduced below)?

The plane's final target remains uncertain, (24) but believed by many people was the fact that United Flight 93 was heading for the White House.

a. NO CHANGE
b. but many believe that United Flight 93 was heading for the White House.
c. also heading for the white house United Flight 93 was believed to be.
d. then many believe that United Flight 93 was heading for the White House.

25. Which of the following would be the best choice for this sentence (reproduced below)?

(25) Close to 3,000 people died in the World Trade Center attacks.

a. NO CHANGE
b. 3,000 people in the World Trade Center attacks died.
c. Dying in the World Trade Center attacks were around 3,000 people.
d. In the World Trade Center attacks were around 3,000 people dying.

26. Which of the following would be the best choice for this sentence (reproduced below)?

Nevertheless, thousands of men and women in service worked (26) valiantly to evacuate the buildings, save trapped workers, extinguish infernos, uncover victims trapped in fallen rubble, and tend to nearly 10,000 injured individuals.

a. NO CHANGE
b. valiently
c. valently
d. vanlyantly

27. Which of the following would be the best choice for this sentence (reproduced below)?

(27) American airports and airspace closed to all national and international flights.

a. NO CHANGE
b. American airports and airspace close to all national and international flights.
c. American airports and airspaces closed to all national and international flights.
d. American airspace and airports were closed to all national and international flights.

28. Which of the following would be the best choice for this sentence (reproduced below)?

(28) Needless to say, as cancelled flights are rescheduled, air travel became backed up and chaotic for quite some time.

a. NO CHANGE
b. As cancelled flights are rescheduled, air travel became backed up and chaotic for quite some time.
c. Needless to say, as cancelled flights were rescheduled, air travel became backed up and chaotic for quite some time.
d. Needless to say, as cancelled flights are rescheduled, air travel became backed up and chaotic over a period of time.

29. Which of the following would be the best choice for this sentence (reproduced below)?

He (29) desired to bring bin Laden and al-Qaeda to justice and prevent future terrorist networks from gaining strength.

a. NO CHANGE
b. Perceived
c. Intended
d. Assimilated

30. Which of the following would be the best choice for this sentence (reproduced below)?

(30) The Taliban, a group of fundamental Muslims who protected Osama bin Laden, was overthrown on December 9, 2001. However, the war continued in order to defeat insurgency campaigns in neighboring countries.

a. NO CHANGE
b. The Taliban was overthrown on December 9, 2001. They were a group of fundamental Muslims who protected Osama bin Laden. However, the war continued in order to defeat insurgency campaigns in neighboring countries.
c. The Taliban, a group of fundamental Muslims who protected Osama bin Laden, on December 9, 2001 was overthrown. However, the war continued in order to defeat insurgency campaigns in neighboring countries.
d. Osama bin Laden's fundamental Muslims who protected him were called the Taliban and overthrown on December 9, 2001. Yet the war continued in order to defeat the insurgency campaigns in neighboring countries.

Questions 31–46 are based on the following passage:

(31) Seeing a lasting social change for African American people Fred Hampton desired to see through nonviolent means and community recognition. (32) As a result, he became an African American activist during the American Civil Rights Movement and led the Chicago chapter of the Black Panther Party.

Hampton's Education

(33) Born and raised in Maywood of Chicago, Illinois in 1948 was Hampton. (34) He was gifted academically and a natural athlete, he became a stellar baseball player in high school. (35) After graduating from Proviso East High School in 1966, he later went on to study law at Triton Junior College.

While studying at Triton, Hampton joined and became a leader of the National Association for the Advancement of Colored People (NAACP). (36) The NAACP gained more than 500 members resulting from his membership. Hampton worked relentlessly to acquire recreational facilities in the neighborhood and improve the educational resources provided to the impoverished black community of Maywood.

The Black Panthers

The Black Panther Party (BPP) was another activist group that formed around the same time as the NAACP. Hampton was quickly attracted to the Black Panther's approach to the fight for equal rights for African Americans. (37) Hampton eventually joined the chapter, and relocated to downtown Chicago to be closer to its headquarters.

His charismatic personality, organizational abilities, sheer determination, and rhetorical skills enabled him to (38) quickly risen through the chapter's ranks. (39) Hampton soon became the leader of the Chicago chapter of the BPP where he organized rallies, taught political education classes, and established a free medical clinic. He also took part in the community police supervision project and played an instrumental role in the BPP breakfast program for impoverished African American children.

(40) Leading the BPP Hampton's greatest achievement may be his fight against street gang violence in Chicago. In 1969, (41) Hampton was held by a press conference where he made the gangs agree to a nonaggression pact known as the Rainbow Coalition. As a result of the pact, a multiracial alliance between blacks, Puerto Ricans, and poor youth was developed.

Assassination

As the Black Panther Party's popularity and influence grew, the Federal Bureau of Investigation (FBI) placed the group under constant surveillance. In an attempt to (42) neutralize the party, the FBI launched several harassment campaigns against the BPP, raided its headquarters in Chicago three times, and arrested over one hundred of the group's members. (43) During such a raid that occurred Hampton was shot on the morning of December 4th 1969.

In 1976, seven years after the event, it was revealed that William O'Neal, Hampton's trusted bodyguard, was an undercover FBI agent. (44) O'Neal providing the FBI with detailed floor plans of the BPP's headquarters, identifying the exact location of Hampton's bed. (45) It was because of these floor plans that the police were able to target and kill Hampton.

The assassination of Hampton fueled outrage amongst the African American community. It was not until years after the assassination that the police admitted wrongdoing. The Chicago City Council now (46) commemorates December 4th as Fred Hampton Day.

31. Which of the following would be the best choice for this sentence (reproduced below)?

    (31) Seeing a lasting social change for African American people Fred Hampton desired to see through nonviolent means and community recognition.

    a. NO CHANGE
    b. Desiring to see a lasting social change for African American people, Fred Hampton
    c. Fred Hampton desired to see lasting social change for African American people
    d. Fred Hampton desiring to see last social change for African American people

32. Which of the following would be the best choice for this sentence (reproduced below)?

(32) As a result, he became an African American activist during the American Civil Rights Movement and led the Chicago chapter of the Black Panther Party.

a. NO CHANGE
b. As a result he became an African American activist
c. As a result: he became an African American activist
d. As a result of, he became an African American activist

33. Which of the following would be the best choice for this sentence (reproduced below)?

(33) Born and raised in Maywood of Chicago, Illinois in 1948 was Hampton.

a. NO CHANGE
b. Hampton was born and raised in Maywood of Chicago, Illinois in 1948.
c. Hampton is born and raised in Maywood of Chicago, Illinois in 1948.
d. Hampton was born and raised in Maywood of Chicago Illinois in 1948.

34. Which of the following would be the best choice for this sentence (reproduced below)?

(34) He was gifted academically and a natural athlete, he became a stellar baseball player in high school.

a. NO CHANGE
b. A natural athlete and gifted though he was,
c. A natural athlete, and gifted,
d. Gifted academically and a natural athlete,

35. Which of the following would be the best choice for this sentence (reproduced below)?

(35) After graduating from Proviso East High School in 1966, he later went on to study law at Triton Junior College.

a. NO CHANGE
b. He later went on to study law at Triton Junior College graduating from Proviso East High School in 1966.
c. Graduating from Proviso East High School and Triton Junior College went to study.
d. Later at Triton Junior College, studying law, from Proviso East High School in 1966.

36. Which of the following would be the best choice for this sentence (reproduced below)?

(36) The NAACP gained more than 500 members resulting from his membership.

a. NO CHANGE
b. A gain of 500 members happened to the NAACP due to his membership.
c. As a result of his leadership, the NAACP gained more than 500 members.
d. 500 members were gained due to his NAACP membership.

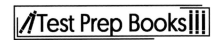

37. Which of the following would be the best choice for this sentence (reproduced below)?

(37) Hampton eventually joined the chapter, and relocated to downtown Chicago to be closer to its headquarters.

a. NO CHANGE
b. Hampton eventually joined the chapter; and relocated to downtown Chicago to be closer to its headquarters.
c. Hampton eventually joined the chapter relocated to downtown Chicago to be closer to its headquarters.
d. Hampton eventually joined the chapter and relocated to downtown Chicago to be closer to its headquarters.

38. Which of the following would be the best choice for this sentence (reproduced below)?

His charismatic personality, organizational abilities, sheer determination, and rhetorical skills enabled him to (38) quickly risen through the chapter's ranks.

a. NO CHANGE
b. quickly rise
c. quickly rose
d. quickly rosed

39. Which of the following would be the best choice for this sentence (reproduced below)?

(39) Hampton soon became the leader of the Chicago chapter of the BPP where he organized rallies, taught political education classes, and established a free medical clinic.

a. NO CHANGE
b. As the leader of the BPP, Hampton: organized rallies, taught political education classes, and established a free medical clinic.
c. As the leader of the BPP, Hampton; organized rallies, taught political education classes, and established a free medical clinic.
d. As the leader of the BPP, Hampton—organized rallies, taught political education classes, and established a medical free clinic.

40. Which of the following would be the best choice for this sentence (reproduced below)?

(40) Leading the BPP Hampton's greatest achievement may be his fight against street gang violence in Chicago.

a. NO CHANGE
b. Greatest achievement of Hampton leading the BPP
c. Hampton's greatest achievement as the leader of the BPP
d. Leader of the BPP Hampton and greatest achievement

41. Which of the following would be the best choice for this sentence (reproduced below)?

In 1969, (41) Hampton was held by a press conference where he made the gangs agree to a nonaggression pact known as the Rainbow Coalition.

a. NO CHANGE
b. a press conference held Hampton
c. held by a press conference was Hampton
d. Hampton held a press conference

42. Which of the following would be the best choice for this sentence (reproduced below)?

In an attempt to (42) neutralize the party, the FBI launched several harassment campaigns against the BPP, raided its headquarters in Chicago three times, and arrested over one hundred of the group's members.

a. NO CHANGE
b. Accommodate
c. Assuage
d. Praise

43. Which of the following would be the best choice for this sentence (reproduced below)?

(43) During such a raid that occurred Hampton was shot on the morning of December 4th 1969.

a. NO CHANGE
b. A raid, occurring because Hampton was shot
c. Hampton was shot during such a raid that occurred
d. Such a raid that occurred, Hampton was shot at

44. Which of the following would be the best choice for this sentence (reproduced below)?

(44) O'Neal providing the FBI with detailed floor plans of the BPP's headquarters, identifying the exact location of Hampton's bed.

a. NO CHANGE
b. O'Neal is providing
c. O'Neal provides
d. O'Neal provided

45. Which of the following would be the best choice for this sentence (reproduced below)?

(45) It was because of these floor plans that the police were able to target and kill Hampton.

a. NO CHANGE
b. These floor plans made it possible for the police to target and kill Hampton.
c. For the police to target and kill Hampton, these floor plans made it possible.
d. These floor plans make it possible for the police to target and kill Hampton.

46. Which of the following would be the best choice for this sentence (reproduced below)?

The Chicago City Council now (46) commemorates December 4th as Fred Hampton Day.

a. NO CHANGE
b. disparages
c. exculpates
d. brandishes

Questions 47–60 are based on the following passage:

A flood occurs when an area of land that is normally dry becomes submerged with water. Floods have affected Earth since the (47) beginning of time, and are caused by many different factors. Flooding can occur slowly or within seconds and can submerge small regions or extend over vast areas of land. Their impact on society and the environment can be harmful or helpful.

What Causes Flooding?

Floods may be caused by natural phenomenon, induced by the activities of humans and other animals, or the failure of an infrastructure. (48) Areas located near bodies of water are prone to flooding as are low-lying regions.

Global warming is the result of air pollution (49) that prevents the suns radiation from being emitted back into space. Instead, the radiation is trapped in Earth and results in global warming. The warming of the Earth has resulted in climate changes. As a result, floods have been occurring with increasing regularity. Some claim that the increased temperatures on Earth may cause the icebergs to melt. They fear that the melting of icebergs will cause the (50) oceans levels to rise and flood coastal regions.

Most commonly, flooding is caused by excessive rain. The ground is not able to absorb all the water produced by a sudden heavy rainfall or rainfall that occurs over a prolonged period of time. Such rainfall (51) may cause to overflow the water in rivers and other bodies of water. The excess water can cause dams to break. Such events can cause flooding of the surrounding riverbanks or coastal regions.

Flash flooding can occur without warning and without rainfall. Flash floods may be caused by a river being blocked by (52) a glacier; avalanche; landslide; logjam; a beaver's obstruction; construction; or dam. Water builds behind such a blockage. Eventually, the mass and force of the built-up water become so extreme that it causes the obstruction to break. Thus, enormous amounts of water rush out towards the surrounding areas.

Areal or urban flooding occurs because the land has become hardened. The hardening of land may result from urbanization or drought. Either way, the hardened land prevents water from seeping into the ground. Instead, the water resides on top of the land.

(53) Finally, flooding may result after severe hurricanes, tsunamis, then tropical cyclones. Local defenses and infrastructures are no matches for the tidal surges and waves caused by these natural phenomena. Such events are bound to result in the flooding of nearby coastal regions or estuaries.

A Flood's After-Effects

Flooding can result in severe devastation of nearby areas. Flash floods and tsunamis can result in sweeping waters that travel at destructive speeds. Fast-moving water has the power to demolish all obstacles in its path such as homes, trees, bridges, and buildings. Animals, plants, and humans may all lose their lives during a flood.

Floods can also cause pollution and infection. Sewage may seep from drains or septic tanks and contaminate drinking water or surrounding lands. Similarly, toxins, fuels, debris from annihilated buildings, and other hazardous materials can leave water unusable for consumption. (54) As the water begins to drain, mold may begin to grow. As a result, residents of flooded areas may be left without power, drinkable water, or be exposed to toxins and other diseases.

(55) Although often associated with devastation, not all flooding results in adverse circumstances. (56) For thousands of years, people have inhabited floodplains of rivers. (57) Examples include the Mississippi Valley of the United States, the Nile River in Egypt, and the Tigris River of the Middle East. The flooding of such rivers (58) caused nutrient-rich silts to be deposited on the floodplains. Thus, after the floods recede, an extremely fertile soil is left behind. This soil is conducive to the agriculture of bountiful crops and has sustained the diets of humans for millennium.

Proactive Measures Against Flooding

Technologies now allow scientists to predict where and when flooding is likely to occur. Such technologies can also be used (59) to project the severity of an anticipated flood. In this way, local inhabitants can be warned and take preventative measures such as boarding up their homes, gathering necessary provisions, and moving themselves and possessions to higher grounds.

The picturesque views of coastal regions and rivers have long enticed people to build near such locations. Due to the costs associated with the repairs needed after the flooding of such residencies, many governments now require inhabitants of flood-prone areas to purchase flood insurance and build flood-resistant structures. Pictures of all items within a building or home should be taken so that proper reimbursement for losses can be made in the event that a flood does occur.

Staying Safe During a Flood

If a forecasted flood does occur, (60) so people should retreat to higher ground such as a mountain, attic, or roof. Flooded waters may be contaminated, contain hidden debris, or travel at high speeds. Therefore, people should not attempt to walk or drive through a flooded area. To prevent electrocution, electrical outlets and downed power lines need to be avoided.

The Flood Dries Up

Regardless of the type or cause of a flood, floods can result in detrimental alterations to nearby lands and serious injuries to nearby inhabitants. By understanding flood cycles, civilizations can learn to take advantage of flood seasons. By taking the proper precautionary measures, people can stay safe when floods occur. Thus, proper knowledge can lead to safety and prosperity during such an adverse natural phenomenon.

47. Which of the following would be the best choice for this sentence (reproduced below)?

Floods have affected Earth since the (47) beginning of time, and are caused by many different factors.

a. NO CHANGE
b. beginning of time and are causing
c. beginning of time so to cause
d. beginning of time and are caused

48. Which of the following would be the best choice for this sentence (reproduced below)?

(48) Areas located near bodies of water are prone to flooding as are low-lying regions.

a. NO CHANGE
b. Low-lying regions are prone to flooding, areas located near bodies of water are prone to flooding.
c. Areas located near bodies of water are prone to flooding, as are low-lying regions.
d. Near bodies of water are areas that are prone to flooding and areas near low-lying regions are prone to flooding.

49. Which of the following would be the best choice for this sentence (reproduced below)?

Global warming is the result of air pollution (49) that prevents the suns radiation from being emitted back into space.

a. NO CHANGE
b. that which prevents the sun's radiation
c. the sun's radiation being prevented
d. that prevents the sun's radiation

50. Which of the following would be the best choice for this sentence (reproduced below)?

They fear that the melting of icebergs will cause the (50) oceans levels to rise and flood coastal regions.

a. NO CHANGE
b. ocean levels
c. ocean's levels
d. levels of the oceans

51. Which of the following would be the best choice for this sentence (reproduced below)?

Such rainfall (51) may cause to overflow the water in rivers and other bodies of water.

a. NO CHANGE
b. may been causing the rivers and other bodies of water to overflow.
c. may cause the rivers and other bodies of water to overflow.
d. may cause other bodies of water and water in rivers to overflow.

52. Which of the following would be the best choice for this sentence (reproduced below)?

Flash floods may be caused by a river being blocked by (52) a glacier; avalanche; landslide; logjam; a beaver's obstruction; construction; or dam.

a. NO CHANGE
b. a glacier avalanche landslide logjam a beaver's obstruction construction or dam.
c. a glacier, avalanche, landslide, logjam, a beavers obstruction, construction, or dam.
d. a glacier, avalanche, landslide, logjam, a beaver's obstruction, construction, or dam.

53. Which of the following would be the best choice for this sentence (reproduced below)?

(53) Finally, flooding may result after severe hurricanes, tsunamis, then tropical cyclones.

a. NO CHANGE
b. Finally, flooding may result after severe hurricanes, tsunamis, or tropical cyclones.
c. Finally, flooding may result after severe hurricanes, tsunamis, so tropical cyclones.
d. Finally, flooding may result after severe hurricanes, tsunamis, but tropical cyclones.

54. Which of the following would be the best choice for this sentence (reproduced below)?

(54) As the water begins to drain, mold may begin to grow.

a. NO CHANGE
b. As the waters begins to drain, mold may begin to grow.
c. Mold may begin grow as the water begins to drain.
d. The water will begin to drain and mold will begin to grow.

55. Which of the following would be the best choice for this sentence (reproduced below)?

(55) Although often associated with devastation, not all flooding results in adverse circumstances.

a. NO CHANGE
b. Although often associated with devastation not all flooding results
c. Although often associated with devastation. Not all flooding results
d. While often associated with devastation, not all flooding results

56. Which of the following would be the best choice for this sentence (reproduced below)?

(56) For thousands of years, people have inhabited floodplains of rivers.

a. NO CHANGE
b. For thousands of years, people have inhabited river floodplains.
c. For thousands of years people have inhabited river floodplains.
d. For thousand's of years, people have inhabited floodplains of rivers.

57. Which of the following would be the best choice for this sentence (reproduced below)?

(57) Examples include the Mississippi Valley of the United States, the Nile River in Egypt, and the Tigris River of the Middle East.

a. NO CHANGE
b. Examples of floodplains include the Mississippi Valley of the United States, the Nile River in Egypt, and the Tigris River of the Middle East.
c. Examples include the Mississippi Valley of the United States . . . the Nile River in Egypt . . . and the Tigris River of the Middle East.
d. Examples of floodplains include the Mississippi Valley of the United States the Nile River in Egypt and the Tigris River of the Middle East.

58. Which of the following would be the best choice for this sentence (reproduced below)?

The flooding of such rivers (58) caused nutrient-rich silts to be deposited on the floodplains.

a. NO CHANGE
b. Cause
c. Causing
d. Causes

59. Which of the following would be the best choice for this sentence (reproduced below)?

Such technologies can also be used (59) to project the severity of an anticipated flood.

a. NO CHANGE
b. Projecting
c. Project
d. Projected

60. Which of the following would be the best choice for this sentence (reproduced below)?

If a forecasted flood does occur, (60) so people should retreat to higher ground such as a mountain, attic, or roof.

a. NO CHANGE
b. then people
c. and people
d. for people

Questions 61–75 are based on the following passage:

In (61) "The Odyssey," Odysseus develops out of his experiences and the people he meets along his journey home. Many of his encounters involve female characters, some of whom offer Odysseus aid in his journey. (62) However, several of these characters deceive and even pose great danger to the hero. (63) This makes his journey home harder, it forces Odysseus himself to change and adapt in order to deal with the challenges. (64) For the time Odysseus reaches home, he has become notably distrustful of women and even those who have true intentions. It is this sense of caution that ultimately serves Odysseus in successfully defeating the suitors of Penelope upon his return home.

Odysseus would not have been able to defeat the suitors without stealth and deception. He had (65) to conceal himself in order to achieve revenge. This is something we see earlier in Odysseus' encounter with Polyphemus the Cyclops. While not female, Polyphemus displayed feminine qualities characterized by his "womb-like cave." (66) Entering into the dwelling Odysseus directly demanded hospitality Polyphemus instead butchered his men in spite of custom. In order to survive the encounter, Odysseus (67) relinquishes his true identity by telling Polyphemus his name is "Nobody." After the carnage of his men, he does not entrust the Cyclops with his true name. Rather, Odysseus uses disguise and cunning to trick Polyphemus into reopening the cave. When he emerges, he is then reborn again as "Odysseus."

This pattern is echoed again when Odysseus reaches Ithaca: "I look for endless ground to be spattered by the blood and brains of the suitors, these men who are eating all your substance away. But come now, let me make you so that no mortal can recognize you." Here, Athena reveals her plan to disguise Odysseus as he makes his move against the suitors. Why would Odysseus embrace the idea? With Polyphemus, Odysseus entered the cave trusting he would be received as a welcomed guest, but he wasn't. (68) Clearly, Odysseus isn't making the same mistake twice in trusting people to automatically abide by custom. Using a disguise allows Odysseus to apply strategy in a similar manner he had with Polyphemus. (69) This passage specifically described the suitors as eating away at Odysseus' substance, seeming to further the parallel with Polyphemus who devoured Odysseus' men. (70) Also like with Polyphemus, Odysseus only reveals his true identity when he knows his plan has succeeded. The disguise concept presents a strategic role, but it also sheds further light on the impact of Odysseus' travels. To conceal (71) ones identity is to withhold trust.

The Circe episode matches Odysseus against someone he already knows to be untrustworthy. It is known that Circe welcomes all men who (72) enter upon her island with food and drink, but this is a deception meant to ensnare them. This xenia, or hospitality, that Odysseus would have been accustomed to, turns out to be farce. She violates the trust of her guests by turning them into swine, thus making her a deceitful host and a woman Odysseus cannot trust. In order to (73) assure his and the crew's safety, Odysseus must look past her empty courtesy and deceive her in a way that will remedy the situation. With the knowledge of Circe's dark intentions (and Hermes' instructions), Odysseus attempts to out-maneuver Circe by making her think he will kill her. By doing this, he is taking on deceitful qualities so as to ensure he can bend her to proper behavior, which works. Still untrusting of Circe's submission, Odysseus makes her swear a formal oath: "I would not be willing to go to bed with you unless you can bring yourself, O goddess, to swear me a great oath that there is no other evil hurt you devise against me" (10:342-344). Even though Odysseus tames Circe, he is still distrustful. The oath becomes a final assurance that she is sincere. Until he knows for certain that no more treachery can befall him (the oath), he does not partake in showing any form of trust.

In the Land of the Dead, Odysseus encounters Agamemnon, who describes his own murder at the hand of his wife, Klytaimestra. Not only is this an example of a wife's betrayal, but a betrayal that appears close to Odysseus' own situation. Like Agamemnon, Odysseus (74) is returning home to his wife. However, Agamemnon didn't realize his wife had foul intentions, he trusted her to receive him with open arms:

> See, I had been thinking that I would be welcome to my children and thralls of my household when I came home, but she with thoughts surpassing grisly splashed the shame on herself and on the rest of her sex, on women still to come, even on the one whose acts are virtuous.

Clearly this is a cautionary story for Odysseus. After telling Odysseus of Klytaimestra's betrayal, Agamemnon warns Odysseus that all women are inherently distrustful. By this time, Odysseus has already been deceived and nearly killed by female/female-like characters. Agamemnon's logic seems to back up what he already experienced. (75) As the text progresses, Odysseus encounters the Sirens and Calypso, who seem to corroborate the idea that women are bad news. However, what is most impressionable on Odysseus is Agamemnon's distrust of even virtuous women, "even on the one whose acts are virtuous." Who is to say that they cannot turn against him like Klytaimestra did against Agamemnon. This seems to cement in Odysseus a fear of betrayal.

61. Which of the following would be the best choice for this sentence (reproduced below)?

In (61) "The Odyssey," Odysseus develops out of his experiences and the people he meets along his journey home.

a. NO CHANGE
b. 'The Odyssey'
c. *The Odyssey*
d. The Odyssey

62. Which of the following would be the best choice for this sentence (reproduced below)?

(62) However, several of these characters deceive and even pose great danger to the hero.

a. NO CHANGE
b. However these
c. However several of these
d. Several of these

63. Which of the following would be the best choice for this sentence (reproduced below)?

(63) This makes his journey home harder, it forces Odysseus himself to change and adapt in order to deal with the challenges.

a. NO CHANGE
b. This makes his journey home harder it forces Odysseus himself to change and adapt
c. This makes his journey home harder which forces Odysseus himself to change and adapt
d. This makes his journey home harder, forcing Odysseus to change and adapt

64. Which of the following would be the best choice for this sentence (reproduced below)?

(64) For the time Odysseus reaches home, he has become notably distrustful of women and even those who have true intentions.

a. NO CHANGE
b. When the time Odysseus reaches home,
c. By the time Odysseus reaches home,
d. At the time Odysseus reaches home,

65. Which of the following would be the best choice for this sentence (reproduced below)?

He had (65) to conceal himself in order to achieve revenge.

a. NO CHANGE
b. To be concealed
c. Conceals
d. Concealing

66. Which of the following would be the best choice for this sentence (reproduced below)?

(66) Entering into the dwelling Odysseus directly demanded hospitality Polyphemus instead butchered his men in spite of custom.

a. NO CHANGE
b. Entering into the dwelling, Odysseus directly demanded hospitality. Polyphemus instead butchered his men in spite of custom.
c. Entering into the dwelling, Odysseus directly demanded hospitality, Polyphemus instead butchered his men in spite of custom.
d. Entering into the dwelling; Odysseus directly demanded hospitality; Polyphemus instead butchered his men in spite of custom.

67. Which of the following would be the best choice for this sentence (reproduced below)?

In order to survive the encounter, Odysseus (67) relinquishes his true identity by telling Polyphemus his name is "Nobody."

a. NO CHANGE
b. Conceals
c. Withholds
d. Surrenders

68. Which of the following would be the best choice for this sentence (reproduced below)?

(68) Clearly, Odysseus isn't making the same mistake twice in trusting people to automatically abide by custom.

a. NO CHANGE
b. Clearly Odysseus isn't making the same mistake twice in trusting people to automatically abide by custom.
c. Clearly, Odysseus isn't making the same mistake twice; trusting people to automatically abide by custom.
d. Odysseus isn't making the same mistake twice in trusting people, clearly, to automatically abide by custom.

69. Which of the following would be the best choice for this sentence (reproduced below)?

(69) This passage specifically described the suitors as eating away at Odysseus' substance, seeming to further the parallel with Polyphemus who devoured Odysseus' men.

a. NO CHANGE
b. This passages specifically describes
c. This passage specifically describes
d. These passage specifically describes

70. Which of the following would be the best choice for this sentence (reproduced below)?

(70) Also like with Polyphemus, Odysseus only reveals his true identity when he knows his plan has succeeded.

a. NO CHANGE
b. As he did with Polyphemus
c. As he did before
d. With the exact method as he had with Polyphemus

71. Which of the following would be the best choice for this sentence (reproduced below)?

To conceal (71) ones identity is to withhold trust.

a. NO CHANGE
b. one's
c. someone's
d. oneself

72. Which of the following would be the best choice for this sentence (reproduced below)?

It is known that Circe welcomes all men who (72) enter upon her island with food and drink, but this is a deception meant to ensnare them.

a. NO CHANGE
b. land upon
c. arrive on
d. crash on

73. Which of the following would be the best choice for this sentence (reproduced below)?

In order to (73) assure his and the crew's safety, Odysseus must look past her empty courtesy and deceive her in a way that will remedy the situation.

a. NO CHANGE
b. Ensure
c. Prevent
d. Vindicate

74. Which of the following would be the best choice for this sentence (reproduced below)?

Like Agamemnon, Odysseus (74) is returning home to his wife.

a. NO CHANGE
b. returns
c. returned
d. was returned

75. Which of the following would be the best choice for this sentence (reproduced below)?

(75) As the text progresses, Odysseus encounters the Sirens and Calypso, who seem to corroborate the idea that women are bad news.

a. NO CHANGE
b. As the text progresses Odysseus
c. The text progresses with Odysseus
d. As Odysseus progresses in the text

Writing

Please read the prompt below and answer in an essay format.

> Technology has been invading cars for the last several years, but there are some new high tech trends that are pretty amazing. It is now standard in many car models to have a rear-view camera, hands-free phone and text, and a touch screen digital display. Music can be streamed from a paired cell phone, and some displays can even be programmed with a personal photo. Sensors beep to indicate there is something in the driver's path when reversing and changing lanes. Rain-sensing windshield wipers and lights are automatic, leaving the driver with little to do but watch the road and enjoy the ride. The next wave of technology will include cars that automatically parallel park, and a self-driving car is on the horizon. These technological advances make it a good time to be a driver.

1. Analyze and evaluate the passage given.

2. State and develop your own perspective.

3. Explain the relationship between your perspective and the one given.

Answer Explanations #3

Reading Comprehension

1. B: Strong dislike. This vocabulary question can be answered using context clues. Based on the rest of the conversation, the reader can gather that Albert isn't looking forward to his marriage. As the Count notes that "you don't appear to me to be very enthusiastic on the subject of this marriage," and also remarks on Albert's "objection to a young lady who is both rich and beautiful," readers can guess Albert's feelings. The answer choice that most closely matches "objection" and "not . . . very enthusiastic" is *B, strong dislike*.

2. C: Their name is more respected than the Danglars'. This inference question can be answered by eliminating incorrect answers. Choice *A* is tempting, considering that Albert mentions money as a concern in his marriage. However, although he may not be as rich as his fiancée, his father still has a stable income of 50,000 francs a year. Choice *B* isn't mentioned at all in the passage, so it's impossible to make an inference. Finally, Choice *D* is clearly false because Albert's father arranged his marriage, but his mother doesn't approve of it. Evidence for Choice *C* can be found in the Count's comparison of Albert and Eugénie: "she will enrich you, and you will ennoble her." In other words, the Danglars are wealthier but the Morcerf family has a more noble background.

3. D: Apprehensive. There are many clues in the passage that indicate Albert's attitude towards his marriage—far from enthusiastic, he has many reservations. This question requires test takers to understand the vocabulary in the answer choices. *Pragmatic* is closest in meaning to *realistic*, and *indifferent* means *uninterested*. The only word related to feeling worried, uncertain, or unfavorable about the future is *apprehensive*.

4. B: He is like a wise uncle, giving practical advice to Albert. Choice *A* is incorrect because the Count's tone is friendly and conversational. Choice *C* is also incorrect because the Count questions why Albert doesn't want to marry a young, beautiful, and rich girl. While the Count asks many questions, he isn't particularly *probing* or *suspicious*—instead, he's asking to find out more about Albert's situation and then give him advice about marriage.

5. A: She belongs to a noble family. Though Albert's mother doesn't appear in the scene, there's more than enough information to answer this question. More than once is his family's noble background mentioned (not to mention that Albert's mother is the Comtess de Morcerf, a noble title). The other answer choices can be eliminated—she is deeply concerned about her son's future; money isn't her highest priority because otherwise she would favor a marriage with the wealthy Danglars; and Albert describes her "clear and penetrating judgment," meaning she makes good decisions.

6. C: The richest people in society were also the most respected. The Danglars family is wealthier but the r family has a more aristocratic name, which gives them a higher social standing. Evidence for the other answer choices can be found throughout the passage: Albert mentioned receiving money from his father's fortune after his marriage; Albert's father has arranged this marriage for him; and the Count speculates that Albert's mother disapproves of this marriage because Eugénie isn't from a noble background like the Morcerf family, implying that she would prefer a match with a girl from aristocratic society.

7. A: He seems reluctant to marry Eugénie, despite her wealth and beauty. This is a reading comprehension question, and the answer can be found in the following lines: '"I confess," observed Monte Cristo, "that I have some difficulty in comprehending your objection to a young lady who is both rich and beautiful."' Choice *B* is the opposite (Albert's father is the one who insists on the marriage), Choice *C* incorrectly represents Albert's eagerness to marry, and Choice *D* describes a more positive attitude than Albert actually feels (*repugnance*).

8. B: The passage is mostly made up of dialogue. We can see this in the way the two characters communicate with each other, in this case through the use of quotations marks, or dialogue. Narration is when the narrator (not the characters) is explaining things that are happening in the story. Description is when the narrator describes a specific setting and its images. Explanation is when the author is analyzing or defining something for the reader's benefit.

9. D: The meaning of the word *ennoble* in the middle of the paragraph means to give someone a noble rank or title. In the passage, we can infer that Albert is noble but not rich, and Mademoiselle Eugénie is rich but not noble.

10. C: Because he finally understands Albert's point of view but still doesn't agree with it. The other choices aren't mentioned anywhere in the passage. Remember, although this passage is part of a larger text, the test taker should only pay attention to what's in the passage itself in order to find the correct answer.

11. C: In lines 6 and 7, it is stated that avarice can prevent a man from being necessitously poor, but too timorous, or fearful, to achieve real wealth. According to the passage, avarice does not tend to make a person very wealthy. The passage states that oppression, not avarice, is the consequence of wealth. The passage does not state that avarice drives a person's desire to be wealthy.

12. D: Paine believes that the distinction that is beyond a natural or religious reason is between king and subjects. He states that the distinction between good and bad is made in heaven. The distinction between male and female is natural. He does not mention anything about the distinction between humans and animals.

13. A: The passage states that the Heathens were the first to introduce government by kings into the world. The quiet lives of patriarchs came before the Heathens introduced this type of government. It was Christians, not Heathens, who paid divine honors to living kings. Heathens honored deceased kings. Equal rights of nature are mentioned in the paragraph, but not in relation to the Heathens.

14. B: Paine asserts that a monarchy is against the equal rights of nature and cites several parts of scripture that also denounce it. He doesn't say it is against the laws of nature. Because he uses scripture to further his argument, it is not despite scripture that he denounces the monarchy. Paine addresses the law by saying the courts also do not support a monarchical government.

15. A: To be *idolatrous* is to worship idols or heroes, in this case, kings. It is not defined as being deceitful. While idolatry is considered a sin, it is an example of a sin, not a synonym for it. Idolatry may have been considered illegal in some cultures, but it is not a definition for the term.

16. A: The essential meaning of the passage is that the Almighty, God, would disapprove of this type of government. While heaven is mentioned, it is done so to suggest that the monarchical government is irreverent, not that heaven isn't promised. God's disapproval is mentioned, not his punishment. The passage refers to the Jewish monarchy, which required both belief in God and kings.

17. A: The word *timorous* means being full of fear. The author concludes that extreme greed (avarice) makes people too afraid to be prosperous.

18. B: The author's attitude is closest to Choice *B*, *impassioned and critical*. Choice *A* is incorrect; the author is not *indifferent or fatigued*—on the contrary, there is a lot of energy and some underlying passion in the writing. Choice *C* is incorrect; the word *enchanted* means delighted, and the author is more critical and concerned of a monarchial government than enchanted with it. Choice *D* is not the best answer; although the author is passionate and critical of a monarchy, there is more logic than anger coming from the words.

19. B: To explain how monarchs came into existence and how Christians adapted to this way of government. Choice *A* is incorrect; the author does not agree that heathens were more advanced than Christians in this paragraph, it only explains the catalyst of the monarchial systems. Choice *C* is incorrect; the author would in fact disagree with the divination of the English monarchs. Choice *D* is incorrect; the paragraph *does* believe that monarchs cause damage, but the paragraph does not act as a counterargument to the one preceding it.

20. D: The author implies that the recorded history of creation is a collection, collage, or pattern taken from various accounts of cultures. Choice *A* is incorrect; there is no talk of cells or biology in the paragraph. Since "mosaic" modifies the word "account," we know that it is the account of creation that is mosaic, not creation itself, which makes Choice *B* incorrect. Choice *C* is also incorrect; the paragraph does not mention kings developing a system of recording accounts of creation.

21. B: But in fact, there is not much substance to such speculation, and most anti-Stratfordian arguments can be refuted with a little background about Shakespeare's time and upbringing. The thesis is a statement that contains the author's topic and main idea. The main purpose of this article is to use historical evidence to provide counterarguments to anti-Stratfordians. Choice *A* is simply a definition; Choice *C* is a supporting detail, not a main idea; and Choice *D* represents an idea of anti-Stratfordians, not the author's opinion.

22. C: Rhetorical question. This requires readers to be familiar with different types of rhetorical devices. A rhetorical question is a question that is asked not to obtain an answer but to encourage readers to consider an issue more deeply.

23. B: By explaining grade school curriculum in Shakespeare's time. This question asks readers to refer to the organizational structure of the article and demonstrate understanding of how the author provides details to support the argument. This particular detail can be found in the second paragraph: "even though he did not attend university, grade school education in Shakespeare's time was actually quite rigorous."

24. A: Busy. This is a vocabulary question that can be answered using context clues. Other sentences in the paragraph describe London as "the most populous city in England" filled with "crowds of people," giving an image of a busy city full of people. Choice *B* is incorrect because London was in Shakespeare's home country, not a foreign one. Choice *C* is not mentioned in the passage. Choice *D* is not a good answer choice because the passage describes how London was a popular and important city, probably not an underdeveloped one.

25. B: This sentence is an example of a metaphor. Metaphors make a comparison between two things, usually saying that one thing *is* another thing. Here, the author is saying that Shakespeare *is* "the great magician." Choice *A*, *personification*, is when an inanimate object is given human characteristics, so this is incorrect. Choice *C*, *simile*, is making a comparison between two things using *like* or *as*, so this is incorrect. Choice *D*, *allusion*, is an indirect reference to a place, person, or event that happened in the past, so this is also incorrect.

26. D: Remember from the first passage that anti-Stratfordians are those who believe that Shakespeare *did not* write the plays, so Stratfordians are people who believe that Shakespeare *did* write the plays. The author of Passage 2 is disbelieving and critical of the Stratfordian point of view. We see this especially in the second paragraph, where the author states it is a supposition "so wild that it can only be entertained by those who are prepared to accept it as a miracle." All of the other answer choices are incorrect.

27. D: Sentence 2 is a contrast to the idea in Sentence 1. In the first sentence, the author states that they, at one time, believed that Shakespeare was the author of his plays. The second sentence is a contrast to that statement by saying the author no longer believes that the author of the plays is Shakespeare. The other answer choices are incorrect.

28. B: This writing style is best described as persuasive. The author is trying to persuade the audience, with evidence, that Shakespeare actually wrote his own dramas. Choice *A*, expository writing, means to inform or explain. Expository writing usually does not set out to persuade the audience of something, only to inform them, so this choice is incorrect. Choice *C*, narrative writing, is used to tell a story, so this is incorrect. Choice *D*, descriptive writing, uses all five senses to paint a picture for the reader, so this choice is also incorrect.

29. C: Topography is the shape and features of the Earth. The author is implying here that whoever wrote Shakespeare's plays studied the physical features of foreign cities. Choices *A, B,* and *D* are incorrect. Choice *A* is simply known as climate. Choice *B* would just be considered the "agriculture of a particular area." Choice *D*, aspects of humans within society, would be known as *anthropology*.

30. A: The author of Passage 2 believes that Shakespeare the actor did not write the plays. We see this at the end of the first paragraph where the author contends that the "'Stratford rustic' is not the true Shakespeare." The author does believe that Shakespeare was an actor, as the author calls this Shakespeare a "Player" throughout the text, so Choices *B* and *D* are incorrect. Choice *C* is incorrect, as the author does not believe that Shakespeare wrote the plays.

31. C: *Extraneous* most nearly means *superfluous*, or *trivial*. Choice *A*, *indispensable*, is incorrect because it means the opposite of *extraneous*. Choice *B, bewildering*, means *confusing* and is not relevant to the context of the sentence. Finally, Choice *D* is incorrect because although the prefix of the word is the same, *ex-*, the word *exuberant* means *elated* or *enthusiastic*, and is irrelevant to the context of the sentence.

32. A: The author's purpose is to bring to light an alternative view on human perception by examining the role of technology in human understanding. This is a challenging question because the author's purpose is somewhat open-ended. The author concludes by stating that the questions regarding human perception and observation can be approached from many angles. Thus, the author does not seem to be attempting to prove one thing or another. Choice *B* is incorrect because we cannot know for certain whether the electron experiment is the latest discovery in astroparticle physics because no date is given. Choice *C* is a broad generalization that does not reflect accurately on the writer's views. While the author does appear to reflect on opposing views of human understanding (Choice *D*), the best answer is Choice *A*.

33. C: It presents a problem, explains the details of that problem, and then ends with more inquiry. The beginning of this paragraph literally "presents a conundrum," explains the problem of partial understanding, and then ends with more questions, or inquiry. There is no solution offered in this paragraph, making Choices *A* and *B* incorrect. Choice *D* is incorrect because the paragraph does not begin with a definition.

34. D: Looking back in the text, the author describes that classical philosophy holds that understanding can be reached by careful observation. This will not work if they are overly invested or biased in their pursuit. Choices *A*, *B*, and *C* are in no way related and are completely unnecessary. A specific theory is not necessary to understanding, according to classical philosophy mentioned by the author.

35. B: The electrons passed through both holes and then onto the plate. Choices *A* and *C* are incorrect because such movement is not mentioned at all in the text. In the passage, the author says that electrons that were physically observed appeared to pass through one hole or another. Remember, the electrons that were observed doing this were described as acting like particles. Therefore, Choice *D* is incorrect. Recall that the plate actually recorded electrons passing through both holes simultaneously and hitting the plate. This behavior, the electron activity that wasn't seen by humans, was characteristic of waves. Thus, Choice *B* is the correct answer.

36. C: The author mentions "gravity" to demonstrate an example of natural phenomena humans discovered and understood without the use of tools or machines. Choice *A* mirrors the language in the beginning of the paragraph but is incorrect in its intent. Choice *B* is incorrect; the paragraph mentions nothing of "not knowing the true nature of gravity." Choice *D* is incorrect as well. There is no mention of an "alternative solution" in this paragraph.

37. A: The important thing to keep in mind is that we must choose a scenario that best parallels, or is most similar to, the discovery of the experiment mentioned in the passage. The important aspects of the experiment can be summed up like so: humans directly observed one behavior of electrons and then through analyzing a tool (the plate that recorded electron hits), discovered that there was another electron behavior that could not be physically seen by human eyes. This summary best parallels the scenario in Choice *A*. Like Feynman, the colorblind person can observe one aspect of the world but through the special goggles (a tool), he is able to see a natural phenomenon that he could not physically see on his own. While Choice *D* is compelling, the x-ray helps humans see the broken bone, but it does not necessarily reveal that the bone is broken in the first place. The other choices do not parallel the scenario in question. Therefore, Choice *A* is the best choice.

38. B: The author would not agree that technology renders human observation irrelevant. Choice *A* is incorrect because much of the passage discusses how technology helps humans observe what cannot be seen with the naked eye; therefore, the author would agree with this statement. This line of reasoning is also why the author would agree with Choice *D*, making it incorrect as well. As indicated in the second paragraph, the author seems to think that humans create inventions and tools with the goal of studying phenomena more precisely. This indicates increased understanding as people recognize limitations and develop items to help bypass the limitations and learn. Therefore, Choice *C* is incorrect as well. Again, the author doesn't attempt to disprove or dismiss classical philosophy.

39. B: The word *conundrum* most nearly means *enigma*, which is a mystery or riddle. *Platitude* means a banal or overused saying. *Solution* is incorrect here; and *hypothesis* implies a theory or assumption, so this is also incorrect.

40. A: To prove to the audience the thesis of the passage by providing evidence suggesting that electrons behave differently when observed by the human eye. The thesis' best evidence is found in this paragraph because of the experiment depicting how electrons behave in a dual nature. Choice *B* is incorrect; the paragraph mentions nothing about the experiment being unethical. Choice *C* is incorrect; this is characteristic of the first paragraph. Choice *D* is incorrect; this is more characteristic of the second paragraph.

English Language

1. C: The next paragraph states that "These advanced offices oftentimes require a Professional Engineering (PE) license which can be obtained through additional college courses, professional experience, and acceptable scores on the Fundamentals of Engineering (FE) and Professional Engineering (PE) standardized assessments." Since the word *oftentimes* is used instead of *always*, Choice *C* is the best response.

2. C: The best answer is Choice *C*. Items in a list should be separated by a comma. Choice *A* is incorrect because there are no commas within the list to separate the items. Choice *B* is incorrect; a semicolon is used in a series only when a comma is present within the list itself. Choice *D* is incorrect because the conjunction *and* is missing before the word *calculus*.

3. A: The sentence is correct as-is. The words *one* and *bachelor* have apostrophe *-s* at the end because they show possession for the words that come after. The other answer choices do not indicate possession is being shown.

4. D: To begin, *of* is not required here. *Apprenticeship* is also more appropriate in this context than *apprentice opportunities*; *apprentice* describes an individual in an apprenticeship, not an apprenticeship itself. Both of these changes are needed, making Choice *D* the correct answer.

5. D: Choice *D* is correct because it breaks the section into coherent sentences and emphasizes the main point the author is trying to communicate: the PE license is required for some higher positions, it's obtained by scoring well on the two standardized assessments, and college and experience can be used to prepare for the assessments in order to gain the certification. The original sentence is a run-on and contains confusing information, so Choice *A* is incorrect. Choice *B* fixes the run-on aspect, but the sentence is indirect and awkward in construction. Choice *C* is incorrect for the same reason as Choice *B*, and it is a run on.

6. B: *Once the job begins, this line of work* is the best way to phrase this sentence. Choice *A* is incorrect because *lines* does not match up with *this*; it would instead match up with the word *these*. Choice *C* is incorrect; *these line* should say *this line*. Choice *D* is incorrect; *job begin* is faulty subject/verb agreement.

7. A: The word is spelled correctly as it is: *expertise*.

8. C: *Allows* is inappropriate because it does not stress what those in the position of aircraft engineers actually need to be able to do. *Requires* is the only alternative that fits because it actually describes necessary skills of the job.

9. D: The words *equations* and *processes* in this sentence should be plural. Choices *A, B,* and *C* have one or both words as singular, which is incorrect.

10. A: The correct response is Choice *A* because this statement's intent is to give examples as to how aircraft engineers apply mathematical equations and scientific processes towards aeronautical and aerospace issues and/or inventions. The answer is not *Therefore*, Choice *B,* or *Furthermore*, Choice *D,* because no causality is being made between ideas. Two items are neither being compared nor contrasted, so *However*, Choice *C,* is also not the correct answer.

11. A: No change is required. The comma is properly placed after the introductory phrase *In May of 2015*. Choice *B* is missing the word *In*. Choice *C* does not separate the introductory phrase from the rest of the sentence. Choice *D* places an extra comma prior to 2015.

12. A: The word *conversely* best demonstrates the opposite sentiments in this passage. Choice *B* is incorrect because it denotes agreement with the previous statement. Choice *C* is incorrect because the sentiment is not restated but opposed. Choice *D* is incorrect because the previous statement is not a cause for the sentence in question.

13. A: The correct answer is Choice *A*, *are projected*. The present tense *are* matches with the rest of the sentence. The verb *are* also matches with the plural *employment opportunities*. Choice *B* uses *will be projected*, which is incorrect because the statistic is being used as evidence, which demands a present or past tense verb. In this case it is present tense to maintain consistency. Choice *C* is incorrect because the singular verb *is* does not match with the plural subject *employment opportunities*. Choice *D* is incorrect because the past tense verb *were* does not maintain consistency with the present tense in the rest of the passage.

14. C: Choice *C* is the best answer because introductory words like "Nevertheless" are always succeeded by a comma.

15. D: The main subject and verb in this sentence are far apart from each other. The subject is *engineers* and the subject is *are projected*. Although there is a clause which interrupts the subject and the verb, they still must agree with each other.

16. D: The correct phrase should be "War on Terror." The phrase is capitalized because it was part of the campaign phrase that was launched by the U.S. government after September 11. Punctuation should always be used inside double quotes as well, making Choice *D* the best answer.

17. C: Terrorists commonly use fear and violence to achieve political goals. Choice *A* is incorrect because the subject *Terrorists* is plural while the verb *uses* is singular, so the subject and verb do not agree with each other. Choice *B* is incorrect because the word *Terrorist's* with the apostrophe -*s* shows possession, but the terrorists aren't in possession of anything in this sentence. Choice *D* is incorrect because the word *achieves* should be *achieve*.

18. A: No change is needed. Choices *B* and *C* utilize incorrect comma placements. Choice *D* utilizes an incorrect verb tense (*responding*).

19. B: The best answer Choice is *B*, *who live mainly in the South and Southwest Asia*. The directional terms *South Asia* and *Southwest Asia* are integral parts of a proper name and should therefore be capitalized.

20. D: This is the best answer choice because *America's* with the apostrophe -*s* shows possession of the word *support*, and *Israel* should be capitalized because it is a country and therefore a proper noun.

Choice *A* does not show possession in the word *Americas*. Choice *B* does not capitalize the word *Israel*. Choice *C* does not show possession and does not include the necessary comma at the end of the phrase.

21. A: This sentence is correct as-is. The verb tense should be in the past—the other three answer choices either have a present or continuous verb tense, so these are incorrect.

22. C: Choice *C* is the most straightforward version of this independent clause, because it follows the "subject + verb + prepositional phrase" order which usually provides the most clarity.

23. B: Although *diverging* means to separate from the main route and go in a different direction, it is used awkwardly and unconventionally in this sentence. Therefore, Choice *A* is not the answer. Choice *B* is the correct answer because it implies that the passengers distracted the terrorists, which caused a change in the plane's direction. *Converging*, Choice *C,* is incorrect because it implies that the plane met another in a central location. Although the passengers may have distracted the terrorists, they did not distract the plane. Therefore, Choice *D* is incorrect.

24. B: Choice *B* is the best answer because it is straightforward and clear. Choice *A* is incorrect because the phrase *the fact that* is redundant. Choice *C* is inverted and doesn't make much sense because the subject comes after the verb. Choice *D* is incorrect because it does not have the appropriate transition, *but*, which is intended to show a contrast to the *uncertainty* phrase that comes before it.

25. A: Choice *A* is the best choice for this sentence because it is the most straightforward and easiest to understand. Choice *B* is incorrect because it leaves out the hedging language. Choice *C* keeps the hedging language, but the sentence begins with a verb which is not the best decision for clarity. Choice *D* is incorrect because it begins with a preposition which is not the best choice for a straightforward presentation of the facts.

26. A: The word *valiantly* is spelled correctly in the original sentence.

27. D: Airspace and airports must be closed by people; they don't just close themselves, so it is proper to include an action to indicate that they were sealed off. Choice *B* is incorrect because the verb *close* is in the incorrect tense. Choice *C* is also incorrect because *airspace* does not need to become *airspaces* and the issue still remains: while there is action, it is not in the proper form to indicate human action. Choice *D* is correct because it correctly uses the helping verb *were*, which indicates human action.

28. C: This sentence contains improper verb agreement in the fragment *as cancelled flights are rescheduled*. *Are* is a present-tense verb while *rescheduled* is a past-tense verb. Because the attacks occurred in the past, both verbs need to be written in the past tense, as done in Choice *C*.

29. C: *Intended* means planned or meant to. *Intended* is a far better choice than *desired,* because it would communicate goals and strategy more than simply saying that Bush desired to do something. *Desired* communicates wishing or direct motive. Choices *B* and *D* have irrelevant meanings and wouldn't serve the sentence at all.

30. A: The original structure of the two sentences is correct. Choice *B* lacks the direct nature that the original sentence has. By breaking up the sentences, the connection between the Taliban's defeat and the ongoing war is separated by an unnecessary second sentence. Choice *C* corrects this problem, but the fluidity of the sentence is marred because of the awkward construction of the first sentence. Choice *D* begins well but lacks the use of *was* before *overthrown*.

31. C: Choice *C* is the best answer choice here because we have "subject + verb + prepositional phrases" which is usually the most direct sentence combination. Choice *A* is incorrect because the verbs *seeing* and *see* are repetitive. Choice *B* is incorrect because the subject and verb are separated, which is not the best way to divulge information in this particular sentence. Choice *D* is incorrect because the sentence uses a continuous verb form instead of past tense.

32. A: The comma after *result* is necessary for the sentence structure, making it an imperative component. The original sentence is correct, making Choice *A* correct. Choice *B* is incorrect because it lacks the crucial comma that introduces a new idea. Choice *C* is incorrect because a colon is unnecessary, and Choice *D* is incorrect because the addition of the word *of* is unnecessary when applied to the rest of the sentence.

33. B: Hampton was born and raised in Maywood of Chicago, Illinois in 1948. Choice *A* is incorrect because the subject and verb are at the end, and this is not the most straightforward syntax. Choice *C* is incorrect because the rest of the passage is in past tense. Choice *D* is incorrect because there should be a comma between the names of a city and a state.

34. D: Choice *D* is the best answer because it fixes the comma splice in the original sentence by creating a modifying clause at the beginning of the sentence. Choice *A* is incorrect because it contains a comma splice. Choice *B* is too wordy. Choice *C* has an unnecessary comma.

35. A: The sentence is correct as-is. Choice *B* is incorrect because we are missing the chronological signpost *after*. Choice *C* is incorrect because there is no subject represented in this sentence. Choice *D* is incorrect because it also doesn't have a subject.

36. C: Choice *C* is the best sentence because it is a compound sentence with the appropriate syntax. Choice *A* is incorrect because *resulting* is not as clear as the phrase *as a result*. Choice *B* is incorrect because the syntax is clunky—to say something happened to the NAACP rather than the NAACP making the gain is awkward. Choice *D* is incorrect because this is passive voice; active voice would be better to use here as in Choice *C*.

37. D: Choice *D* is the best answer. Choice *A* is incorrect; if the second clause was independent we would need a comma in the middle, but the two clauses have the same single subject, so a comma is unnecessary. Choice *B* is incorrect; semicolons go in between two independent clauses without conjunctions. Choice *C* is incorrect; there needs to be a conjunction before the word *relocated*.

38. B: *enabled him to quickly rise* is the best answer. Although the passage is in past tense, the verb *enabled* is followed by the "to + infinitive." The infinitive is the base form of the verb; that's why *rise* is the best answer choice, because the verb follows *to* and represents the infinitive after the verb *enabled*.

39. A: No change is needed. The list of events should be separated by a comma. Choice *B* is incorrect. Although a colon can be used to introduce a list of items, it is not a conventional choice for separating items within a series. Semicolons are used to separate at least three items in a series that have an internal comma. Therefore, Choice *C* is incorrect. Choice *D* is incorrect because a dash is not a conventional choice for punctuating items in a series.

40. C: *Hampton's greatest achievement as the leader of the BPP* is the best way to phrase this sentence because it is the most straightforward and clear. Choice *A* is incorrect because the sentence starts out with a gerund when it could start out with Hampton, reducing confusion as to who is leading the BPP. Choice *B* is incorrect for the same reason; the sentence starts off with the subject inside the preposition, which is not the best syntax. Choice *D* is incorrect because it doesn't signify that the achievement was Hampton's.

41. D: Choice *D* is the most straightforward answer, "Hampton held a press conference." Choice *A* is incorrect because usually one isn't held "by" a press conference. Choice *B* is incorrect because likewise, a press conference doesn't "hold" someone, but someone would "hold" a press conference. Choice *C* is incorrect because again, someone isn't held "by" a press conference, and the syntax is inverted here.

42. A: The term *neutralize* means to counteract, or render ineffective, which is exactly what the FBI is wanting to do. Accommodate means to be helpful or lend aid, which is the opposite of *neutralize*. Therefore, Choice *B* is incorrect. *Assuage* means to ease, while *praise* means to express warm feeling, so they are in no way close to the needed context. Therefore, *neutralize* is the best option, making Choice *A* the correct answer.

43. C: Choice *C* is the most straightforward answer choice. Choice *A* is incorrect because the sentence is inverted and not very clear. Choice *B* is incorrect because the change in syntax changes the meaning in the sentence. Choice *D* isn't the best way to organize the sentence because it creates wordiness.

44. D: Choice *D* is the best answer choice because it matches with the past tense of the passage. The other answer choices are either in present tense or a present continuous tense.

45. B: Choice *B* is the most straightforward sentence, beginning with the subject and verb, then leading off with two prepositions. Choice *A* is incorrect because the sentence is passive and thus more wordy than the active voice in Choice *B*. Choice *C* is incorrect because the sentence starts out with two prepositions which isn't the best syntax for clarity here. Choice *D* is incorrect because the verb is in present tense instead of past tense.

46. A: Choice *A* is the best answer because *commemorates* means to show respect for something through recognition. Choice *B*, *disparages,* means to discourage, so this is incorrect. Choice *C*, *exculpates*, means to show that someone is not guilty of wrongdoing, and this does not make sense within the context of the sentence. Choice *D*, *brandish*, means to swing or flaunt, and is not the best choice here.

47. D: Choice *D* is the best answer. Choice *A* is incorrect; the comma is not necessary here because both clauses use the same subject, *Floods*. Choice *B* is incorrect because *causing by* is not an appropriate verb phrase. Choice *C* is incorrect because *so to cause by* is also not an appropriate verb phrase.

48. C: The sentence is best written with a comma before the clause *as are low-lying regions*. Choice *A* is incorrect because the comma before the clause is missing. Choice *B* is incorrect; there is a comma splice and this sentence is repetitive. Choice *D* is incorrect because the syntax is not straightforward, and it is also repetitive.

49. D: Choice *D* is the best arrangement of the sentence. Choice *A* is incorrect; *sun* should be possessive of *radiation* and thus have an apostrophe *-s* at the end of the word. Choice *B* is incorrect; the addition of the word *which* adds unnecessary wordiness to the sentence. Choices *C* is incorrect; the word *being* is used twice which creates repetition.

50. B: In this sentence, the word *ocean* does not require an *s* after it to make it plural because *ocean levels* is plural. Therefore, Choices *A* and *C* are incorrect. Because the sentence is referring to multiple—if not all ocean levels—*ocean* does not require an apostrophe (*'s*) because that would indicate that only one ocean is the focus, which is not the case. Choice *D* does not fit well into the sentence and, once again, we see that *ocean* has an *s* after it. This leaves Choice *B,* which correctly completes the sentence and maintains the intended meaning.

51. C: Choice *C* is the best answer. Choice *A* is incorrect because *the water* is doing the overflowing, so it should come before the phrase *to overflow*. Choice *B* is incorrect because *may been causing* isn't an appropriate verb phrase. Choice *D* is incorrect because the word *water* is used repetitively.

52. D: Choice *A* is incorrect; semicolons separate items in a list only when an item in the list contains a comma itself. Choice *B* is incorrect; items in a list should always be separated by commas. Choice *C* is incorrect because the word *beavers* is missing a possessive -*'s* at the end.

53. B: The best conjunction to use in this sentence is the word *or*. The other conjunctions used, *then, so,* and *but*, do not fit in the context of the sentence here.

54. A: Choice *A* is the best answer. Choice *B* is incorrect because it has incorrect subject/verb agreement, *waters begins*. Choice *C* is incorrect because it is missing the word *to* in front of the word *grow*. Choice *D* is incorrect; technically this sentence is grammatically correct, but by using the conjunction *and,* it implies that water begins to drain and mold grows at the same time, which is not what the passage intended.

55. A: Choice *C* can be eliminated because creating a new sentence with *not* is grammatically incorrect, and it throws off the rest of the sentence. Choice *B* is incorrect because a comma is needed after *devastation* in the sentence. Choice *D* is also incorrect because *while* is a poor substitute for *although. Although* in this context is meant to show contradiction with the idea that floods are associated with devastation. Therefore, none of these choices would be suitable revisions because the original was correct.

56. B: Choice *B* is the best answer because it is the most straightforward syntax. Choice *A* is incorrect because *floodplains of rivers* is unnecessarily long. Choice *C* is incorrect because a comma is missing after the prepositional phrase. Choice *D* is incorrect because the word *thousands* is plural and therefore should not have an apostrophe.

57. B: Choice *B* is the best answer here. Choice *A* is incorrect because the text should specify what type of examples are about to be named. Choice *C* is incorrect because items in a list should be separated by commas, not by ellipses. Choice *D* is incorrect because, again, items in a list should be separated by commas.

58. D: Choice *D* is correct because it is in the indefinite present tense and is consistent with the passage. Choice *A* is incorrect because *caused* is inconsistent with the rest of the verb tense in the passage. Choice *B* is incorrect because this does not agree with the subject *the flooding. Causing,* Choice *C,* is in the present continuous tense which does not fit with the subject, *Flooding . . . causing*.

59. A: To *project* means to anticipate or forecast. This goes very well with the sentence because it describes how new technology is trying to estimate flood activity in order to prevent damage and save lives. *Project* in this case needs to be assisted by *to* in order to function in the sentence. Therefore, Choice *A* is correct. Choices *B* and *D* are the incorrect tenses. Choice *C* is incorrect because it lacks *to*.

60. B: The correct conjunction is *then*. The word *then* implies *after that* or *afterward*.

61. C: Choice *C* is the correct answer. Shorter poems should be in quotation marks, but tiles of long, epic poems like *The Odyssey* should be written with italics.

62. A: Choice *A* is the best answer. *However* is an appropriate word to begin this sentence since it illustrates the idea of contrast: some of the females Odysseus encountered were helpful, *however* some were clearly not. Therefore, we can eliminate Choice *D*. Choice *B* is also incorrect because it eliminates the word *several*, which is also useful in distinguishing that, while some female characters were benevolent, several were deceptive and even harmful. Choice *C* is incorrect because it lacks the comma after *However*.

63. D: Choice *D* is the best answer because it uses a comma between an independent clause and a dependent clause and gets rid of the word *himself*, eliminating wordiness. Choice *A* is incorrect because the comma between two independent clauses causes a comma splice. Additionally, the word *himself* is repetitive, making Choice *C* incorrect. Choice *B* is incorrect because the absence of a semicolon or period after *harder* creates a run-on sentence.

64. C: We would say *By the time Odysseus reaches* home to denote that one event occurs before the other. The other answer choices don't make this distinction.

65. A: Choice *A* is correct because it is in active voice rather than passive voice. Choice *B* is incorrect because *he had to be concealed himself* is passive voice and also creates wordiness with *himself*. Choice *C* is grammatically incorrect. Choice *D* is incorrect because *concealing* does not go with the helping verb *had*. *Had concealing* is not a proper verb phrase.

66. B: Choice *B* is the best answer. Choice *A* is incorrect because it is a run-on sentence. Choice *C* is incorrect because the comma between two independent clauses creates a comma splice. Choice *D* is incorrect; semicolons should have independent clauses on either side of them, and the first phrase is not a complete sentence.

67. B: Choice *B, conceals,* is the best option because Odysseus does in fact hide (or conceal) his true identity behind a false name. Choice *A* is incorrect; *relinquishes* means to give up or to voluntarily cease control of something. This is not something Odysseus does because he does not surrender his true name—he just hides it. He does not *withhold* (Choice *C*) his true identity but offers an alternative. Choice *D, surrenders,* is synonymous with *relinquishes*.

68. A: Reading through the sentence, one can see that it flows and uses proper punctuation and grammar, which means that no change is necessary; Choice *A* is the correct answer. Choice *B* lacks the necessary comma after *Clearly*. Choice *C* utilizes an unnecessary semicolon. Choice *D* makes the sentence awkward by placing *clearly* in the middle of the sentence.

69. C: Choice *C* is the best answer choice. Choice *A* is incorrect because the author of the passage uses present tense when speaking about the text in question, so the verb should be *describes*. Choice *B* is incorrect because *passages* should be *passage*, singular. Choice *D* is incorrect because the word *These* should be *This*, describing a singular passage.

70. B: Choice *B* is the best answer because it avoids the wordiness of the original phrase *also like*, which makes Choice *A* incorrect. Choice *C* is compelling, but it lacks the necessary information that the original sentence has: we need to have Polyphemus still in the sentence. Choice *D* is a decent option, but much of it is unnecessary and already addressed in the remainder of the sentence that isn't underlined.

71. B: The issue with this word is that it lacks proper punctuation. *One* is referring to an individual, and it needs to show possession of *identity*. Therefore, *ones* must have an apostrophe to show ownership and to be correct. Thus, Choice *B, one's*, is the correct answer.

72. C: The current phrase repeats itself, so we can eliminate Choice *A*. Choices *B* and *D* are compelling but are somewhat specific. What must be communicated is that all men who reach the island, in whatever fashion, risk being seduced by Circe. Choice *C* is the most practical revision and is more direct, while allowing for other circumstances in which men come to Circe's island.

73. B: The best answer is Choice *B, ensure*, which means to make certain. Odysseus is trying to make certain that he and the crew will be safe by beating Circe at her own game. Choice *A, assure*, means to speak to someone in a way that eliminates doubt. This indirectly relates to what Odysseus wants to do, but to *assure* specifically refers to speaking to someone. Choices *C* and *D* are totally irrelevant. *Vindicate* means to free from blame, while *prevent* means to stop from happening.

74. B: The best verb to use here is *returns*. When talking about text we use present tense verbs.

75. A: Choice *A* is the best answer. Choice *B* is incorrect because it is missing a comma after the introductory clause, *As the text progresses*. Choice *C* is incorrect; Odysseus is the subject of the sentence and must be outside of any phrases—Choice *C* has the subject *Odysseus* inside a prepositional phrase starting with the word *with*, so this is incorrect. Choice *D* is incorrect because again, our subject is inside a clause and therefore does not pair with the verb *encounters*.

Dear High School English Language and Arts Test Taker,

We would like to start by thanking you for purchasing this study guide for your high school exam. We hope that we exceeded your expectations.

Our goal in creating this study guide was to cover all of the topics that you will see on the test. We also strove to make our practice questions as similar as possible to what you will encounter on test day. With that being said, if you found something that you feel was not up to your standards, please send us an email and let us know.

We would also like to let you know about other books in our catalog that may interest you.

GMAT

This can be found on Amazon: amazon.com/dp/1628457929

GRE

amazon.com/dp/162845900X

SAT

amazon.com/dp/1628456868

ACT

amazon.com/dp/1628459468

We have study guides in a wide variety of fields. If the one you are looking for isn't listed above, then try searching for it on Amazon or send us an email.

Thanks Again and Happy Testing!
Product Development Team
info@studyguideteam.com

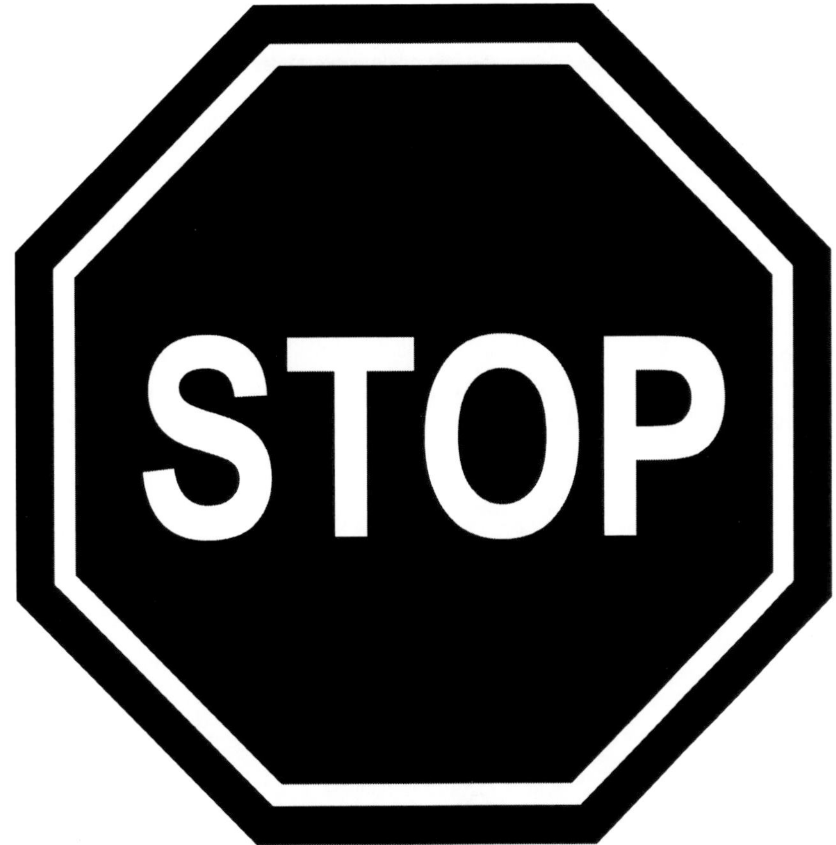

FREE Test Taking Tips DVD Offer

To help us better serve you, we have developed a Test Taking Tips DVD that we would like to give you for FREE. **This DVD covers world-class test taking tips that you can use to be even more successful when you are taking your test.**

All that we ask is that you email us your feedback about your study guide. Please let us know what you thought about it – whether that is good, bad or indifferent.

To get your **FREE Test Taking Tips DVD**, email freedvd@studyguideteam.com with "FREE DVD" in the subject line and the following information in the body of the email:

a. The title of your study guide.

b. Your product rating on a scale of 1-5, with 5 being the highest rating.

c. Your feedback about the study guide. What did you think of it?

d. Your full name and shipping address to send your free DVD.

If you have any questions or concerns, please don't hesitate to contact us at freedvd@studyguideteam.com.

Thanks again!

Made in United States
North Haven, CT
18 May 2024

52668419R00130